UNEARTHING CONFLICT

UNEARTHING CONFLICT

Corporate Mining, Activism, and Expertise in Peru

Fabiana Li

Duke University Press   Durham and London   2015

Unless otherwise indicated, photos are by the author.

© 2015 Duke University Press
All rights reserved
Printed in the United States of America on acid-free
paper ∞
Designed by Heather Hensley
Typeset in Warnock Pro by Tseng Information Systems, Inc.

Library of Congress Cataloging-in-Publication Data
Li, Fabiana, 1976–
Unearthing conflict : corporate mining, activism, and
expertise in Peru / Fabiana Li.
pages cm
Includes bibliographical references and index.
ISBN 978-0-8223-5819-0 (hardcover : alk. paper)
ISBN 978-0-8223-5831-2 (pbk. : alk. paper)
ISBN 978-0-8223-7586-9 (e-book)
1. Mineral industries—Social aspects—Peru.
2. Mineral industries—Political aspects—Peru.
3. Mineral industries—Economic aspects—
Peru. 4. Mineral industries—Environmental
aspects—Peru. 5. Mines and mineral resources—
Peru. 6. Social conflict—Peru. I. Title.
HD9506.P42L54 2015
338.20985—dc23
2014038000

Cover art: (*from left*) View of Cerro Quilish, from
the neighboring community of Tual, photo by author.
Opencast mine, Yanacocha Gold Mine, Cajamarca,
imageBROKER/Alamy.

CONTENTS

ACKNOWLEDGMENTS

This book is the product of journeys between Peru, Canada, and the United States, and the many people who marked the routes traveled.

My work would not have been possible without the generosity of community leaders, activists, engineers, company representatives, researchers, journalists, and NGO workers who took the time to share their views with me and contributed to my understanding of mining controversies. In situations that were often filled with tension and distrust, I am grateful to them for granting me access to archives, documents, meetings, and events. I am especially thankful to the whole team at GRUFIDES, including staff members, volunteers, interns, and friends of the organization who were an integral part of my experience in Cajamarca. In particular, my heartfelt thanks and appreciation go to Marco Arana, Pablo Sanchez, Patricia Rojas, Mirtha Vasquez, Jorge Camacho, Ofelia Vargas, and Ivette Sánchez. From my initial research explorations in La Oroya and Tambogrande to later periods of fieldwork in Cajamarca, Anthony Bebbington, Denise Humphreys Bebbington, Stephanie Boyd, Maribel Chavez, Mariluz Chavez, José de Echave, Hunter Farrell, and Martin Scurrah shared their extensive knowledge and experience and were important sources of insight into extractive industries.

I am profoundly grateful for the kindness and generosity of the families that welcomed me into their homes during my fieldwork. In particular, I thank Dolores, Rosario, José and María, Eriberto, Victor, Bremilda, Samuel, Maritza, Gaby, and Miriam, and their respective families, for their warmth and caring. A number of friends enriched my research and daily life in Cajamarca and Lima: Gina Alvarado, Karin Anchelía, Maria Annala, Florian Aschinger, Victor Bardales, Fanny Briceño, Andrés Caballero, Oswaldo Cepeda, Molly Clinehens, Daniel Cotrina, Ryan Culp, Nilton Deza, Rosa Díaz, Nancy Fuentes, Alfredo Mires, Angélica Motta, Hortensia Muñoz, Brando Palacios, Milagros Salazar, Reinhart Seifert, Chiky Tafur, Yorcka Torres, and Fátima Valdivia. I also thank my relatives in Lima for their hospitality during my stays in the city, and Susan Vincent for providing me with my first opportunity to explore the Central Highlands.

At the University of California, Davis, I was especially lucky to have two exceptional mentors. I am grateful for Suzana Sawyer's valuable feedback, encouragement, and caring guidance throughout my graduate studies and beyond. Marisol de la Cadena provided unwavering support, and her generous engagement with my work never failed to both challenge and inspire. Additionally, Ben Orlove's wide-ranging knowledge and thoughtful advice brought clarity and perspective and expanded my outlook beyond disciplinary boundaries. Joe Dumit joined my dissertation committee when this project had already taken shape, yet his insightful comments were indispensable. Patrick Carroll, Alan Klima, and Tim Choy provided helpful feedback at different points in the development of this project. I would also like to thank the rest of the faculty of the Department of Anthropology and the graduate students who have come through during and after my time there for forming a supportive academic community.

The research for this book was made possible by the University of California's Pacific Rim Research Program and an International Dissertation Research Fellowship from the Social Sciences Research Council. A Newton International Fellowship from the British Academy and the Royal Society allowed me to carry out postdoctoral research on mining conflicts in South America and work toward the completion of this manuscript. I thank Penny Harvey for giving me the opportunity to work with her in Manchester as part of the Centre for Research on Socio-Cultural Change (CRESC), and for her generous reading of previous drafts of this manuscript.

Many others have taken the time to read versions of papers and chapters, and I have benefited from the insights of coparticipants in panels and workshops where I presented my work, including the "Engaging Resources" colloquium organized by Tanya Richardson and Gisa Weszkalnys, the "Nature Inc." conference in The Hague, and sessions of the American Anthropological Association meetings. Special thanks to Mario Blaser, Jessica O'Reilly, and Teresa Velásquez for their constructive feedback, and reviewers for Duke University Press whose suggestions helped me to improve the manuscript. Like any academic work, this book is necessarily an unfinished story. I hope that other scholars of mining will continue to fill in the gaps and omissions of my research.

Through many years, much traveling and numerous relocations, my friends and family have been a constant source of encouragement, advice, inspiration, humor, and companionship. I thank especially Esa Díaz-León, Kregg Hetherington, Serenity Joo, Shawn Jordan, Amy Kung, Stephanie Kwan, Bernardo Li, Claudia Li, Rossio Motta, Erin Nelson, Gowoon Noh, Patricia Pinho, Rima Praspaliauskiene, Astrid Stensrud, and Leslie Wu. Clinton Roberts came into my life as this book was nearing completion, just in time for new beginnings.

The University of Manitoba has given me a supportive environment in which to finish this work. I thank my colleagues in the Anthropology Department and the larger university community, as well as students who have taken an interest in my work and who invigorate my research through the courses I've taught. As I prepared my book manuscript for publication, I received support from the Dean's Office at the Faculty of Arts, the Global Political Economy Research Fund, and the Anthropology Department, as well as research assistance from David Landry, Daniel Leonard, and Laura Hubert. I also wish to thank Valerie Millholland, Miriam Angress, Susan Albury, and Kathleen Kageff from Duke University Press for their help at various stages of the publication process, and Brando Palacios, Elois Eichenlaub, Bill Nelson, Laura Lucio, Clinton Roberts, GRUFIDES, and CooperAcción for the images and maps included in the book.

Finally, I thank my parents, Luis and Graciela, for their patience and support as I undertook what seemed like a never-ending and unusual career path that led me back to the country they chose to leave. Their hard work and constant search for new opportunities opened doors for me to study, travel, and find my way back to Peru to carry out this research.

An earlier version of chapter 5 appeared as "Documenting Accountability: Environmental Impact Assessment in a Peruvian Mining Project" in the *Political and Legal Anthropology Review* (*PoLAR*) 32, no. 2:218–36. An earlier version of chapter 3 was published as "Relating Divergent Worlds: Mines, Aquifers and Sacred Mountains in Peru," *Anthropologica* 55, no. 2:399–411.

Parts of chapter 4 were included in a book chapter in *The Social Life of Water*, Berghahn Books, 2013. Portions of chapter 1 originally appeared in *Corporate Social Responsibility: Discourses, Practices, Perspectives*, Palgrave Macmillan UK, 2010.

INTRODUCTION

A Mining Country

Peru was, is, and will be a mining country. To say otherwise is an illusion.

—ANTONIO BRACK, BIOLOGIST AND PERU'S FIRST MINISTER OF THE ENVIRONMENT

From balconies lining the narrow streets of Cajamarca, onlookers watched with a mixture of curiosity and concern as streams of people headed toward the Plaza de Armas on a late morning in May 2012. Organized into groups representing unions, neighborhood committees, educational institutions, and *rondas campesinas* (peasant patrols), the marchers passed storefronts that had been covered up as store owners braced themselves for another protest. These scenes had become all too familiar for residents of this highland town known for its dairy industry and, more recently, gold production at Yanacocha, South America's largest gold mine. Yanacocha was a joint venture of the U.S.-based Newmont Mining Corporation (which holds 51.35 percent of shares), the Peruvian company Buenaventura (with 43.65 percent of shares), and the World Bank's International Finance Corporation (with the remaining 5 percent of shares). These same actors were involved in the development of the Conga mining project, which would extract copper and gold from a deposit twenty-four kilometers (15 miles) northeast of the Yanacocha mine.

The march was in opposition to the proposed Conga mine; just a few days prior, the company and its allies had organized its own march in support of the project. Residents had grown used to an increasingly polarized climate and the mass mobilizations that periodically took over the city's streets. The marchers approached the plaza chanting *"Agua Sí, Oro No!"* (Water Yes, Gold No!), the ubiquitous slogan repeated on banners and in the chorus of a song screeching from the loudspeakers outside the Church of San Francisco. Nuns in brown habits and peasant women in colorful woolen skirts cooked a communal meal for protestors who had traveled from rural communities and intended to stay in the city for what they were calling an indefinite strike. Sitting in the church courtyard, they shielded their faces from the sun with their straw hats or tabloid newspapers covering the latest developments of the conflict.

Controversies over the proposed mine were being played out on the streets of Cajamarca, at roadblocks, and in clashes with police, but they were also being debated by experts whose reports made the project's Environmental Impact Assessment a major point of contention in the conflict. Actors both for and against the project turned to engineers, hydrologists, and other specialists to evaluate the effects of mining activity on water quality and quantity. Protestors argued that four mountain lakes or lagoons (*lagunas*) would be destroyed if minerals were to be dug for, while the company promised to mitigate these impacts by constructing four reservoirs for local communities. The lagoons had also become a site of protest, where *campesinos* (peasant farmers) branded as their "guardians" were in turn guarded by police officers. The company had tried to make the lagoons commensurable with reservoirs, but protestors rejected the company's claims that natural sources of water could be replaced with chemically treated water and artificial reservoirs. By rejecting the project, they also defied the state's assertion that the country's economic development depended on resource extraction.

Since the late 1990s, marches, protests, and roadblocks had become common occurrences in many parts of the country, from Cajamarca and Piura in the North, to the smelter town of La Oroya in the Central Highlands, to the southern departments of Cuzco and Arequipa. At the time of the Conga protests, mining dominated newspaper headlines, public debate, and the government's political agenda. Given the country's long history of mineral extraction, political activism in mining regions was certainly not unprecedented. In the 1920s and 1930s, mining camps were a focus of union organizing and leftist politics around workers' rights (see DeWind 1987; Flores Galindo 1974; Long and Roberts 1984), while in the early 1970s, campaigns focused on nationalizing the mines controlled by foreign interests. Beginning in the 1990s, however, the protests emerging in various parts of the country seemed to differ from the miners' strikes of the past and efforts to nationalize the industry. Calls for higher pay, better working conditions, and nationalization continued to surface, along with demands for a more equitable distribution of mining revenues and more investment in local communities.[1] However, such claims were accompanied by (and often subordinated to) a series of other issues: the defense of agricultural land, diminished water flows in irrigation canals, polluted rivers, mercury and lead poisoning, and disappearing water springs. The protestors' demands were sometimes expressed in "environmental" terms that resonated with global environmentalist discourses, including concerns about pollution, biodiversity, and water scarcity. At other times, their claims were more generally articulated as the "defense of life"—as with slogans against Conga and other projects proclaiming that "water is life." Gradually, *water*—protection of aquifers, reductions in irrigation water, polluted water resources, and destruction of mountain lakes— emerged as a key concern in protests over mining.[2]

While other Latin American countries, from Ecuador to Guatemala, also saw a rise in mining conflicts in the 1990s and 2000s, the intensity and frequency of conflicts in Peru was unparalleled.[3] Why was it that, in this so-called mining country, extractive activity ended up at the center of controversy and local resistance? How did water and pollution emerge as main points of contention in these conflicts?[4] This book addresses these questions by examining changing technologies and practices of mineral extraction, the deployment of expert and nonexpert knowledges in disputes over nature, and emergent forms of political activism that have accompanied mining activity in Peru.

Over the country's history, mining technologies have had transformative effects on landscapes and ways of life. For Peruvians, the place that epitomizes the country's long engagement with extractive activity is the Central Highland region. One of the main symbols of mining is the department of Cerro de Pasco, which gave its name to the North American company that monopolized extractive activity in the region in the early 1900s. The Cerro de Pasco Corporation built a smelter in the town of La Oroya to process the ores from nearby mines. In the early twentieth century, mining produced runoff and toxic emissions from metal smelting that devastated agricultural production and farming, which in turn spurred migration and urban development. Yet in the smelter town of La Oroya, toxic emissions from the metallurgical complex became an environmental and public health concern only after nearly a century of the smelter's operation. In the late 1990s, local and international campaigns began to call attention to the dangers of lead and the spread of contaminants beyond La Oroya and into neighboring agricultural valleys and watersheds. The language and tools of environmental science and transnational activism turned "pollution" into a new object of national and global concern.

In the province of Cajamarca, to the north of La Oroya (see map I.1), the development of large-scale gold mining led to other kinds of transformations as the government embraced economic reforms and foreign investment in mining in the 1990s. The technologies of modern mining—vast open pits and cyanide leaching processes—*unearthed* new entities. Mining diverted streams and irrigation canals that transformed collective organizing, while sediments and heavy metals changed the properties of water and became a focus of studies, monitoring, and management plans. A sacred mountain galvanized opposition to mining activity, and lagoons emerged as key protagonists in protests to stop mining expansion. The expansive footprint of mining operations has made bodies of water, canals, and pollutants visible and politically relevant. These entities—though not usually recognized analytically as politically generative—mobilized communities and entered into protestors' claims over rights, enabling alliances among various actors (or preventing their collaboration).

In this book, I examine how modern mining technologies have brought "things" (a term I use to include other-than-human elements of the landscape) to the forefront of Peruvian politics.[5] The invasive character of extractive technologies has made these new entities central players in ways that "exceed politics as we know them" (de la Cadena 2010), taking politicians and corporations by surprise. Not knowing how to handle the situation, they have resorted to force to suppress opposition. Protests against Conga and other mining projects in the country have become emblem-

MAP I.1 The Central Highlands, and particularly Cerro de Pasco and La Oroya, have come to symbolize Peru's long mining history. Meanwhile, Cajamarca, home to Peru's largest gold mine, is emblematic of "mega-mining" projects developed in the 1990s.

atic of an "anti-mining" front. However, the participants involved in these forms of organizing do not necessarily share common interests or an ideological stance that defines their position vis-à-vis extractive activity. They cannot be easily categorized into "pro-" or "anti-" mining sides, nor do they fit into clearly defined groups pitted against each other (e.g., peasants vs. capitalists, Left vs. Right, corporations vs. environmentalists, etc.). Mobilizations have been loosely organized around a variety of demands and have involved a diverse group of actors, including peasant farmers, unions, students, environmentalists, urban professionals, church groups, and nongovernmental organizations (NGOs). Significantly, demonstrations have been held in support of mining companies, and not just against them.

Conflicts are sites of antagonisms and collaborations among groups of actors that do not necessarily fit within the usual sociological categories (political parties, classes, ethnicities, or other social groupings) used to analyze political organizing. In such situations, the stakeholder model (which presents a sometimes monolithic view of corporations, states, and communities) has proved inadequate to understand the dynamics of resource conflicts (Ballard and Banks 2003). Moving away from depictions of environmental conflict as a standoff between opposing interest groups, Kim Fortun (2001) writes about "enunciatory communities" that emerge in response to the contradictions of environmental disaster. Enunciatory communities do not preexist, and they are not unchanging or internally coherent; they are not made up of members who share a common identity, but rather, they produce new identities.

In a similar vein, Anna Tsing (2005) examines how collaboration creates new interests and identities through the kinds of local-global encounters that characterize environmental politics. Collaboration does not mean that participants are driven by common goals; indeed, they may not even understand each other's agendas. Collaboration is not about consensus making but rather maintains friction at its heart. Drawing on these insights, I do not treat activist networks and corporate networks as ideologically antagonistic but emphasize the shifting alliances among various actors, and the ways in which they work both with and against corporate interests. I examine how the ambiguous and contradictory relationships between communities and mining companies sometimes produce unintended collaborations, but without negating the tensions, divergent interests, and incommensurable views that lie at their core.

At the turn of the twenty-first century, neoliberal economic reforms, technological innovations in the mining industry, new corporate practices, and changing forms of activism accompanied an aggressive expansion of mining activity. The chapters that follow examine the collectives of people and things that animate particular controversies over resource extraction, and the ways in which the effects of modern mining came to matter politically as mining activity emerged as one of the most hotly debated issues in Peru. I aim to open up the concept of "conflict" in ways that reveal the entangled relationships between people, places, and things that these controversies encompass.

The Proliferation of Conflict

In the opening epigraph, Antonio Brack suggests that Peru's mineral riches are inextricably tied to the country's past, present and future.[6] His statement implies that the country's development inevitably depends on resource extraction, and reflects the will of the government to impose an extractive model of development in spite of growing opposition. To understand the tensions that have arisen in response to mining activity, this book situates the emergence of recent conflicts in the larger context of Peru's mining history. I begin with a chapter on mining and metallurgical activity in the Central Highlands (chapter 1), a region that was central to the development of the mining industry at the turn of the twentieth century. The core of the book (chapters 2, 3, 4 and 5) deal with the Yanacocha mine, illustrating the challenges posed by a project that has become emblematic of "modern" mining technologies and corporate practices. I conclude with a chapter on the Conga conflict (conclusion) to reflect on the nature of grassroots organizing amid continued mining expansion.

My interest in mining and its complicated legacy was sparked when I traveled to the Central Highlands for the first time in 1999, when I returned to Peru to rediscover my country of birth after thirteen years living in Canada. At the time, La Oroya was a familiar name, the place where my maternal grandfather was born and lived until he left for Lima in his late teens. His parents had emigrated from China at the turn of the twentieth century and set up a general store in its main street. Like other migrants, I surmise that they, too, were lured to this highland town by the new commercial opportunities offered by the construction of the railway, the smelter, and the nearby mines.

At the time of this first visit, mining did not make national headlines, and politicians were not yet debating about water or mining royalties. But it was around this time that the problems between communities and mining corporations were starting to intensify. When I returned to La Oroya to conduct fieldwork as a master's student a year later, campaigns around lead poisoning were starting to attract attention at the national and international level. The case of La Oroya showed me that environmental problems—and how people react to them—are not self-evident. The way that mining's toxic legacy would be apprehended by local people, scientists, and activists took shape over the course of a century of extractive activity. Once the pollution was made visible and recognized as a threat, nascent activist campaigns in La Oroya influenced debates around health and the environment just as mining began to generate opposition and conflict elsewhere in the country.

Evolving narratives around mining and the environment in the Central Highlands enabled me to see processes that were just beginning to take shape and foreshadowed the rising tensions in other mining areas. At the time of my subsequent research visits to Peru in the early 2000s, mining was taking a new place in the political scene. One of the proposed mines that generated significant local resistance was the Tambogrande project on Peru's northern coast, in the department of Piura. The Canadian "junior" company Manhattan Minerals sought to extract US$1 billion worth of minerals from beneath the town of Tambogrande, which would require relocating about eight thousand people. To be developed in an agricultural valley producing mangos and lemons for local and international markets, the proposed project inspired protests from townspeople and farmers concerned about the mine's potential impacts on water and agricultural production. In a nonbinding referendum in 2002, 93 percent of voters said "No" to the project (Alvarado Merino 2008), which was ultimately halted when the company withdrew from Tambogrande, a decision allegedly made for financial reasons, but undoubtedly influenced by local opposition. The Tambogrande referendum inspired other communities opposing mining in Latin America, and the conflict was one of the first to receive widespread national and international media attention. It was only the first of a series of conflicts yet to come.

By the early 2000s, the term *mining conflict* (*conflicto minero*) had become ubiquitous in debates related to extractive activity in Peru. The term permeated the media, political debates, academic analyses, and even everyday conversation. When I arrived in Peru in January 2005 to begin doctoral research on "the conflicts," an article in the national newspaper *El Comercio* exemplified the growing public concern over the proliferation of protests against mining activity. The article noted that "the year 2004 was a particularly problematic one for mining companies," with ninety-seven cases of conflict requiring the intervention of the Ministry of Energy and Mines, and warned that 2005 could bring an increase in mining-related social problems (*El Comercio* 2005). The map that accompanied the article was titled "*Campo minado*" (referring to mined territory, but also alluding to a minefield) and classified the numerous conflicts around the country into three groups: "resolved" (marked with a green checkmark), "uncertain" (question marks) and "pending solution" (marked with an "X"). In spite of its pessimistic prognosis, the map's checkmarks implied that a number of conflicts had been definitively resolved.

The map typified the popular image of *conflictos* as having spread throughout the country, with the potential to explode. The accompanying article, meanwhile, noted the absence of mechanisms for local participation and a lack of information, allowing companies to impose their will on the population. What was necessary, the article suggested, was for the Ministry of Energy and Mines and other state institutions to play a stronger role. In the popular discourse on mining activity, the emphasis was on strategies that aimed to resolve the conflicts through dialogue and agreements reached by governments, corporations, and affected communities. During my two years of field research in 2005 and 2006, the conflicts did indeed seem to multiply, but the possibility for "solutions" seemed more and more elusive.

While conflictos mineros appeared regularly in newspaper headlines, they also began to surface in the work of government agencies and nongovernmental organizations. In October 2006, the Council of Ministers created the Comisión Multisectorial de Prevención de Conflictos (Multisectoral Commission for Conflict Prevention) to respond to cases of social unrest in various parts of the country.[7] Having been sworn into office in July of that year, President Alan García needed to show that his government was capable of controlling the problems in mining areas. That same year, the Defensoría del Pueblo (ombudsman's office) created the Unidad de Conflictos Sociales (social conflict unit), which was responsible for conflict monitoring and mediation, and for submitting recommendations to the government. The Defensoría tracked the number of active conflicts per year and classified them according to various types, including "socio-environmental" ones, and those specifically related to mining activity. On the NGO front, the Red Muqui,[8] an umbrella group bringing together NGOs working on mining issues, created the Observatorio de Conflictos Socioambientales (Socio-Environmental Conflict Observatory). The Observatorio produced reports and a monthly electronic bulletin with regional updates on issues relating to resource extraction. These and other organizations contributed to the ongoing work of monitoring, counting, and classifying conflicts.[9]

Discussion about conflictos abounded, but the term seemed to be a sort of shorthand used to talk about problems that defied simple explanations. It could be said that conflictos had become a kind of "black box," a term whose meaning is taken for granted, and whose histories and inner workings need not be known (Latour 1988). In popular analyses, the term "conflict" glossed over the intricacies of what was being described, often obscuring more than it revealed. To explain the cause of popular discontent about mining, analysts (whether representing the government, corporations, NGOs, or the media) tended to cite a similar set of issues: the lack of transparency of mining operations; inadequate processes of consultation; environmental regulations that were too lenient or not enforced; and the scarce economic benefits received by communities affected by mining activity (see, for example, Defensoría del Pueblo 2005; Alayza 2007; CooperAcción 2006). Many of these reports called for public participation in decision making, more stringent environmental regulations, and more investment in local communities. In some cases, these recommendations were framed in terms of increased accountability and a stronger commitment to "Corporate Social Responsibility," another term ubiquitous in discussions around extractive activity.[10]

Over the course of my fieldwork, corporations and state institutions seemed to gradually adopt many of the recommended mechanisms of accountability. They invested unprecedented amounts of money on community relations and local development, implemented participatory environmental monitoring programs, and organized public assemblies and information sessions intended to foster dialogue and public participation. It could be argued that these measures were not sufficient, or were not adequately implemented, but it was evident that companies were responding to public criticism and following at least some of the recommendations made by government bodies and NGOs. Even as these measures were adopted, however, tensions seemed to intensify and the conflicts continued to multiply. That these efforts did not ease the problems between mining companies and people living in the vicinity of the mines was something that puzzled corporations, state officials, and NGOs alike.

To explore the apparent contradiction between the proliferation of protests and an increased emphasis on practices of accountability, I draw on anthropological studies of "audit cultures" (Strathern 2000a; Power 1994; Hetherington 2011). Both terms (audit and accountability) come out of financial accounting but have been introduced into other aspects of modern life and have become so widespread internationally that they are both ubiquitous and taken for granted. According to anthropologist Marilyn Strathern (2000a:2), these practices are characteristic of a period in which governance has been reconfigured by a proliferation of NGOs and environmental liability has emerged as an issue of global concern. She relates audit regimes to the emergence of neoliberalism and the changing role of governments in the management of corporations, public entities, and individuals. An audit seeks to make explicit the norms and procedures necessary to monitor indicators of performance, and transparency is equated with integrity. Ultimately, however, audits not only *monitor* performance, but come to *define* efficiency, quality, and good practice.

I bring these insights to the analysis of mechanisms that corporations and the state use to monitor environmental performance in mining operations, and that have accompanied the expansion of mining activity in Peru. These practices do not simply enforce an economic model and limit the role of governments; they also contribute to new ethical and moral standards that shape understandings of risk and responsibility. In conflicts over mining, practices of accountability often appeal to values such as democratic participation, transparency, and environmental stewardship, making them very difficult to criticize. Those who challenge these practices (or seek to redefine them) face an additional risk: being accused of being against dialogue, democracy, and development.

Instead of taking transparency and participation as the end point of the analysis (the desired outcome that will prevent or reduce the incidence of conflicts), I consider how mechanisms of audit, environmental management, and accountability take shape and become enmeshed in the controversies. What I am proposing is an analysis that gets beyond common-sense understandings of the "conflicts" as a failure of state and corporate accountability. I am not suggesting that companies should forego public consultation, environmental audits, and other ways of demonstrating their accountability to the public and the state. Certainly, these mechanisms are necessary, and calls for more measures of accountability have led to some changes in the mining industry in response to public pressure. Before 2003, for example, Environmental Impact Assessments were publicly presented only in the capital city of Lima, not in the communities closest to a proposed mine site. In 2003, Peru adopted mine closure requirements, which obligate companies to include reclamation measures beyond the productive life of the mine. These are significant changes, and more needs to be done to incorporate environmental safeguards and community participation into the legal framework.

Regardless of the legal exigencies, however, mining companies are not all the same, and they operate with different standards. Some companies have adopted voluntary guidelines of "best practice" and invested in technologies intended to improve environmental performance (as defined by the industry), while others fail to meet even the minimum legal requirements and have received sanctions for their lack of compliance. However, some companies like Newmont have won industry awards even as the wider public criticizes their operations. Newmont has gained notoriety for infractions in other countries where it operates, in addition to its problems in Peru. In Indonesia, a government lawsuit accused Newmont of polluting the fishing village of Buyat Bay and affecting the health of the local people, accusations that the company denied (Perlez 2005). In Ghana, authorities fined Newmont for a cyanide spill in 2009, resulting in water contamination and fish kills (Earthworks 2010).

Evaluating corporate performance on a case-by-case basis can yield contradictory results, and can obviate the larger context of mining expansion and the political, legal, and technical mechanisms that facilitate it. Thus, an analysis of mining conflicts needs to situate the practices of individual companies within a hegemonic economic model that has emphasized resource extraction as a necessary path to "progress" and "development." In Peru, this economic model has been promoted by successive governments but has been met with anger and resistance from an increasingly large segment of the population. The tensions surrounding extractive activity have brought to light the profound inequalities entrenched in Peru's socioeconomic landscape.

The Promise of Extraction

"Peru is a beggar sitting on a bench of gold" (*El Perú es un mendigo sentado en un banco de oro*).[11] This popular saying reflects what some Peruvians see as the contradiction between the country's extensive natural wealth and the conditions of poverty that prevail. While some scholars have written about the "resource curse" to highlight conditions of economic underdevelopment in countries that rely on resource extraction (e.g., Sachs and Warner 2001), these theories have a specific local resonance in current debates over mining in Peru. The multiple meanings of this aphorism capture the tensions, contradictions, and ambiguities that drive controversies over extraction. For some Peruvians, the story of the proverbial "beggar" began with the Spanish conquest, continued with the extraction of mineral wealth during the colonial period (1550–1824), and changed form as colonial interests were replaced by those of foreign corporations during the republican period. As mining activity intensified in the 1990s and a rise in the price of metals brought windfall earnings to transnational companies, the aphorism took on new significance for those who saw this as a new kind of plunder. For others, however, the saying had another meaning: it placed the blame on Peruvians who seemed unwilling or unable to make effective use of the country's bountiful resources. In the case of mining, the aphorism implied that those who protested against mining development were condemning the country to continued poverty in spite of the wealth of mineral resources beneath the ground.

President Alan García expressed this sentiment most explicitly when, in an editorial piece in the newspaper *El Comercio*, he evoked another saying: *"El perro del hortelano, que no come ni deja comer"*; this parable refers to the fable about a dog in the manger, who spitefully prevents others from having what he himself does not need. The moral of the fable is that people often begrudge others and prevent them from having something that they themselves have no use for. Many Peruvians, García argued, are unable to make land productive, or to commercialize the country's vast resources, yet they are also stubbornly unwilling to let others (i.e., private investors) do so. He attributed the country's underdevelopment to "demagoguery and lies which say that these lands cannot be touched because they are sacred," and to unsubstantiated fears about polluting mining technologies, which he characterized as a "topic of the past century" and irrelevant for today's clean modern mining industry. Local people who oppose mining, or who argue that lands cannot be touched because they are sacred, are like the "old communist anticapitalists of the nineteenth century, [who] disguised themselves as nationalists in the twentieth century, and changed shirts again in the twenty-first century to become environmentalists" (García 2007). In other words, protestors cloak their arguments in environmentalist terms to hide their true intentions, and in doing so, they stand in the way of the nation's progress. García's assessment reflects the polarized views that have permeated political and public rhetoric: specifically, the idea that modern mining represents a break from the polluting practices of the past and a new vision for the future that protestors fail to see because they are still caught in another era.

García's comments and much public discussion around mining invoke the country's long history of extractive activity to suggest both rupture and continuity. The legacy of mining in Peru continues to inform popular sentiment and debates over mining. These mining imaginaries and debates often rely on simplified oppositions between "old" and "new" mining, to distinguish the technologies and practices of older mines, such as those in the Central Highlands, from the "mega-projects" that began to operate in the 1990s. Transnational companies have been particularly adept at using this distinction in their public relations campaigns, insisting that "modern" mines like Yanacocha operate in a more socially and environmentally sustainable manner than older mines. A recognition of the environmental "passives" of older mines made this distinction particularly important, since the visible signs of mine runoff, dead rivers, and abandoned tailing ponds was not one that companies wanted to have associated with their operations.

While transnational companies and the government have been eager to play up the benefits of "new" mining over the "old" mines of the past, I do not want to treat these as unproblematic and mutually exclusive categories. Mining projects in Peru include large-scale open-pit mines, smaller underground mines, and informal (also called artisanal) mining. Sometimes these different types of mining can coexist in the same district. The technologies and labor practices of current mining projects do not necessarily correspond to the categories of "old" and "modern"; nevertheless, I want to examine how different actors give these terms meaning and strategically deploy them in current debates. I also make a distinction between "old" and "modern" mining to examine how neoliberal policies and the subsequent expansion of mining activity contributed to the particular dynamics of recent conflicts.

Given Peru's long history of dependence on extractive industries, economic policies encouraging investment in mining activity cannot be solely attributed to the neoliberal shift that took place in the Latin American region in the 1990s.[12] By drawing attention to the turn of the twenty-first century as a significant temporal marker in this long history, I do not mean to suggest a complete break from earlier policies of extraction. Nevertheless, the turn of the century brought with it policies of economic liberalization and deregulation that would significantly influence extractive activity and local reactions to it, including a marked proliferation of protest activity in response to extraction that neoliberalism did not foresee (see Sawyer 2004).

In Peru, neoliberal policies were tied to the controversial government of Alberto Fujimori,[13] who was elected in 1990 and implemented a series of measures intended to bring the country out of an acute political and economic crisis. To curtail hyperinflation and revitalize the economy, Fujimori introduced a radical program of liberalization that focused on removing subsidies, privatizing state-owned companies, and reducing the role of the state in the economy. This restructuring program followed the neoliberal guidelines established by the International Monetary Fund and the World Bank as a precondition for receiving loans and technical assistance.

When criticized for his authoritarian leadership, Fujimori justified these reforms and his discretionary use of power (including an "auto-coup" in 1992 that dissolved Congress and suspended the Constitution) as necessary to defeat the Shining Path guerrilla movement and end the violence that had ravaged the country since 1980.[14] In keeping with this larger goal of overcoming political turmoil and economic instability, reforms in the mining sector were aimed at creating an investor-friendly climate. Legislative reforms resulted in the elimination of restrictions on remittances of profits, royalties, and capital; changes to indigenous land tenure; the lowering of taxes; and the elimination of royalties. Furthermore, tributary stabilization agreements guaranteed fixed tax rates and the application of current statutes on environmental regulations for a period of ten to fifteen years. With these reforms, the role of the state was limited to the regulation of technical issues and newly introduced environmental regulations mandated by the World Bank through its loan incentives and technical assistance programs (Szablowski 2007; de Echave and Torres 2005). For example, the Environmental Impact Assessment was introduced as part of the environmental legislation implemented in the 1990s.

Neoliberal reforms also introduced new labor legislation that reduced the influence of unions, which were already weakened by the Shining Path's armed struggle. On the one hand, the Shining Path intimidated and murdered union leaders and other activists who refused to join their movement, while on the other, the Fujimori government repressed all union activity as part of its efforts to eliminate subversive activity. Caught between the Shining Path and the government's antiterrorism campaigns, the trade-union movement and popular organizations more generally were dealt a severe blow that would have long-lasting repercussions for political organizing and grassroots activism in the country (Boyd 1998).

As economic reforms were implemented in the early 1990s, there was a general slowdown in the global mining industry and a drop in mineral prices, but liberalizing the economy ultimately brought the desired results. The period from 1993 to 1997 was characterized by a global "mining boom," and interest in Peruvian mineral deposits resulted in a six-fold expansion of surface area allocated to mining activity (from 4 million hectares to 24 million hectares) (de Echave and Torres 2005:10). Between 1990 and 1997, investment in mining exploration grew by 90 percent at the global level, by 400 percent in Latin America, and by 2,000 percent in Peru (World Bank 2005, cited in Bebbington 2007). In the 2000s, the high price of metals continued to drive the expansion of mining's frontiers, pushing extractive activity into areas formerly used for agriculture and farming and affecting more than half of Peru's approximately six thousand campesino communities (de Echave and Torres 2005) (see figure I.1). During the mining boom, the single largest venture in Peruvian mining was the Antamina project, a copper and zinc mine in the department of Ancash developed in 1998 with a US$2.3 billion investment by a consortium of Canadian companies. Another significant investment involved the Canadian company

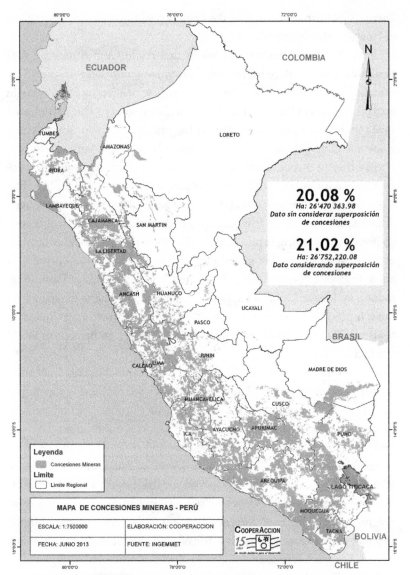

FIGURE I.1 NGOs have called attention to the rapid expansion of mining activity. This map shows that mining concessions made up approximately 20 percent of the country's territory in 2013. Courtesy of CooperAcción.

Barrick Gold, which developed the Pierina gold mine (in the department of Huaraz), also in 1998.

The shift toward neoliberal policies that made Latin America a particularly attractive place for mining investment coincided with the diversification of the global gold mining industry, which led to an increase in gold production in Peru. A look at the world's top gold producers since the 1970s shows the extent of changes in the industry. In 1970, South Africa alone accounted for 67.7 percent of world production, with the former USSR a distant second. Canada, the United States, and Australia were the next largest producers, while the rest of the world accounted for less than 9 percent of total production. By the year 2000, the picture had changed dramatically, with these five countries together accounting for just over 50 percent of total world production. This diversification trend continued as South Africa's share of global production declined to 10.8 percent in 2006; that year, South Africa, the United States, Australia, China, Peru, Indonesia, Russia, Canada, Papua New Guinea, and Ghana ranked as the top ten producers, while a host of other countries (including Chile, Uzbekistan, Tanzania, Mali, and Brazil) accounted for 30 percent of world production (Johnson 2013).

At the turn of the twenty-first century, Peru was the most important gold-producing country in Latin America, in large part due to the output from the Yanacocha mine in Cajamarca. Aside from its economic significance, the symbolic importance of the Yanacocha mine cannot be overlooked: the mine was owned in part by Newmont, one of the largest mining companies in the world, and had the avowal and financial backing of the World Bank. For the Fujimori government, this project was an opportunity to showcase the country's new stability and attractiveness to foreign investors. Highlighting this point, President Fujimori was featured in the national media receiving the first bar of gold produced by the company Minera Yanacocha, in 1993.

Meanwhile, the state embarked on a privatization program that included the enterprises and concessions of Centromin, the state-run mining consortium formed in the mid-1970s from the expropriated holdings of the Cerro de Pasco Corporation. Among the Centromin enterprises that went back to private ownership was the metallurgical complex at La Oroya, which was purchased by the American company Doe Run (see figure I.2). While mining projects like Yanacocha symbolized a new era of

FIGURE I.2 The smelter in La Oroya, constructed in 1922, attests to the consequences of mining activity in the Central Highlands.

"modern" mining practices, the smelter at La Oroya represented the "old" mining of decades past—albeit in a new "green" guise that accompanied Doe Run's efforts to modernize the metallurgical complex and project an image of social and environmental responsibility.

Transnational corporations like the Newmont and Barrick Gold sought to differentiate modern mining from the underground tunnels and pick-axes of traditional mines, and from the legacy of pollution in places like La Oroya and the Central Highlands. In an effort to break free from these images, companies argued that new mining relied on chemical processes, powerful machinery, and sophisticated laboratories that made its operations safer and more efficient. But there were other significant differences from the mines of the past. Unlike underground mines, newer mines required a small labor force and created few opportunities for direct employment relative to the population in the mine's area of influence. And in comparison to earlier mines, modern open-pit mines made a huge imprint on areas that overlapped with peasant communities, pastures, and agricultural land (see figure I.3). Activists used the term *mega-mining* (*mega-minería*) to describe the large-scale, chemical mining that characterized

FIGURE I.3 The Yanacocha gold mine in Cajamarca, an example of an open-pit "mega-mining" project. Photograph by Brando Palacios.

these projects and brought about new challenges, risks, and uncertainties even as it continued a long history of extraction in this "mining country."

Transforming Landscapes

As foreign investment, privatization, and mining expansion intensified in the late 1990s, responses to mining activity reflected a new set of concerns. In La Oroya, air quality (particularly high levels of lead) became an object of study, monitoring, and transnational activism. In Cajamarca and other mining centers, issues around water quality and quantity became the focus of campaigns against the mine *and* of efforts by companies to demonstrate a commitment to social and environmental responsibility. The effects of mining could not always be measured and quantified (as mandated by the new audit culture) and became the focus of contestation. Determining what counted as an "impact" or what constituted "pollution" became points of controversy, as various actors sought to make perceptible (or imperceptible) the indeterminate and often unpredictable threats of mining activity.

As mining technologies transformed, severed, or realigned relationships between people and the landscape, "the environment" emerged as an increasingly contested terrain of political action. By treating the environment as a political terrain, I build on foundational work in political ecology (see, for example, Bunker 1985; Peluso 1992; Peet and Watts 1996; Bryant and Bailey 1997), which seeks to combine political economy with a concern for the environment, including the unequal relations of power that characterize environmental conflicts and shape the emergence of social movements. Extending the field of political ecology, scholars have produced critical studies of landscapes that consider its material and agentive qualities (e.g., Kosek 2006; Cruikshank 2005; Raffles 2002). Others have suggested that resource conflicts are not only conflicts over the production of knowledge, but are also *ontological* conflicts over the making (or destruction) of worlds (Escobar 2008; de la Cadena 2010; Blaser 2009). I draw inspiration from these bodies of literature to examine *how* things like pollution take form and become tangible, *when* they matter, and *for whom* they become politically significant. These questions move us away from the idea of nature as a commodity or fixed external reality by considering the continuous process through which a substance comes into being, and its potential to reconfigure political terrains.

Pollutants and other entities (like a sacred mountain or a threatened lake) are not fixed or constant, but are the effect of practices that create stability and fixity, or that perpetuate the *in*stability of their material form. "The environment" and its constituent elements are not part of an external reality-out-there (Law 2004) but are the effect of relations among a collective of actors. Similarly, an entity like pollution also emerges from historically situated practices and performances, and it is only through its continuous enactment that it stabilizes and congeals (and in some instances, it may fail to congeal). These entities do not exist prior to or independently of the practices that revolve around them but are produced through "processes of history, concrete social and technical arrangements and the effects of power" (Murphy 2006:15). Protest actions, claims for compensation, and corporate public relations campaigns contributed to making pollution materialize as an entity, but maintaining the stability of objects requires continuous effort (Mol 2002). What are usually glossed as "conflicts," I suggest, consist of these ongoing efforts at stabilization, efforts that are fraught with tensions and which do not always produce the intended effects.

My analysis of materialization draws on Bruno Latour's distinction between "matters of fact" and "matters of concern." Latour (2004) questions
the scientific certainty about nature and notes that—as mining makes
clear—ecological crises open up controversies that preclude the establishment of indubitable "matters of fact" that can serve as the base for
political decisions. In the face of this situation, two attitudes are possible:
"We can wait for the sciences to come up with additional proofs that will
put an end to the uncertainties, or we can consider uncertainty as the
inevitable ingredient of crises in the environment and in public health.
The second attitude has the advantage of replacing something that is not
open to discussion with something that can be debated, and of binding
together the two notions of objective science and controversy: the more
realities there are, the more arguments there are. Matters of concern have
replaced matters of fact" (Latour 2004:63). Latour uses the term "controversies" to describe this shift from matters of fact to matters of concern,
through which indisputable, obstinate, and self-evident "facts" become
destabilized, contentious, and connected to an ever-wider range of actors.
A matter of concern is "what happens to a matter of fact when you add to
it its whole scenography, much like you would do by shifting your attention from the stage to the whole machinery of a theater" (Latour 2008:39).
Analyzing the "conflicts" as matters of concern requires shifting our attention to the networks of relations and the making of knowledges that shape
the controversies.

In the case of resource extraction, the long-term effects of mining
activity are indeterminate and uncertain and have become the basis of
heated debate, producing controversies that cannot be settled through
consensus or negotiation. Matters of concern challenge the idea of an in-
contestable, monolithic Nature that scientists must learn to speak for. Instead, Latour's commitment to ontological multiplicity suggests that not
only are there many cultures (multiculturalism) that produce different
representations of a unitary Nature, but a multiplicity of actors and agencies that enact socionatural worlds.

Water, land, and other entities are often thought of as "resources," and
although their value might be contested, nothing seems more solid and
self-evident than these elements of the landscape that are so crucial for
human survival. Yet conflicts over mining reveal the multiple ways of con-
figuring what we usually conceive of as "Nature" and its constituent ele-

ments.[15] The physical properties of the landscape are not natural or uncontested; rather, they are the product of constant negotiation, which
sometimes exceeds human intentionality. People's relationships to the
landscape are not based only on its utilitarian value, nor can these relationships necessarily be understood in terms of an environmentalist ethic.
In the Andes, for example, people engage in practices that "enact the respect and affect necessary to maintain the relational condition between
humans and other-than-human beings" that make life possible (de la
Cadena 2010).[16] The idea that nature is ontologically plural challenges the
conception of "resources" as targets of either extraction or conservation
projects.[17] The multiplicity of nature also enables a different kind of politics
and opens up the possibility that "reality might be otherwise" (Law 2004).

The emergence of new actors and concerns in conflicts over mining
has opened up the space of the political, challenging dominant representations of nature. At the same time, the focus on water and pollution in
recent conflicts has sometimes led to a reliance on technical solutions
and scientific arguments that can exclude other forms of knowledge (and
other socionatural worlds) from view. The technocratic management of
the conflicts includes a focus on mechanisms of accountability aimed at
promoting transparency, environmental management, and participation.
Such initiatives can take the form of community dialogue, participatory
environmental monitoring, and other initiatives under the rubric of "Corporate Social Responsibility."

Efforts to resolve the conflicts through these mechanisms of accountability rely on the knowledge of experts, who are called on to evaluate and
monitor the practices of mining corporations. Increased transparency is
often presented as a solution to the conflicts, but making corporate performance *explicit* can have the effect of making other things invisible (cf.
Strathern 2000a; Barry 2009). What I want to draw attention to is that
which remains outside of the frames of visibility: those elements that are
not overtly part of political discussions about mining but nonetheless
contribute to and perpetuate the controversies around it. To get at these
undercurrents I use the concept of *equivalence* as an analytical tool to examine, on the one hand, how solutions to the conflicts are conceptualized,
and on the other, the underlying tensions that remain beneath the surface.
The term *equivalence* is intended to capture two related processes: First,
equivalence refers to forms of expertise and technical tools used to make

things quantifiable and comparable; second, I take equivalence to be a political relationship that involves constant negotiation over what counts as authoritative knowledge.

Contested Equivalences

My interest in equivalence arose from efforts to understand how engineers and company officials rationalized their environmental management plans even as these were rejected by local people, who presented a different set of arguments to support their claims about the mine's negative effects. More generally, some politicians, industry representatives, and local residents sought to justify the expansion of mining as an activity that would contribute to the greater good, neutralizing any potential harm. Embedded in their respective arguments were calculations of costs and benefits, inputs and outputs, damages and reparations. Although people did not necessarily use the term, a logic of equivalence was implicit in many contexts that I observed in my fieldwork: in agreements that assigned a monetary value to the damages caused by the mine's operations; in environmental management plans that sought to balance water inputs and outputs; and in efforts to measure water quality against national and international legal standards.

My treatment of equivalence overlaps with but also differs from the way this concept has been employed in the literature. Equivalence has been a long-standing concern in anthropology, generally focusing on how things are made comparable and exchangeable. Rhoda Halperin (1994) provides an overview of this literature and traces the concept of equivalencies to the work of Karl Polanyi on the evolution of the market economy and cross-cultural models of economic organization. This and other work in economic anthropology centers on the social and ideological structures that condition equivalencies, and take equivalency-formation processes to be fundamental in all economies and for all facets of production, distribution, and consumption. My own use of equivalence, by contrast, is not restricted to markets and exchange. In my conception, equivalences involve processes of negotiation that can help elucidate the dynamics of contemporary conflicts, precisely because what is being negotiated often falls outside the logic of the market and rational calculation.

Any discussion of equivalence inevitably leads us to questions of value, a concept that refers to the meaning or importance society ascribes to a thing.[18] As Miller (2008) notes, value can allude to both the alienable and inalienable qualities of an object: the work of giving it calculable monetary value (i.e., price), as well as that which makes it impossible to do so. If we look at the classical literature on value, however, value implies a comparison of entities, and commodity exchange is seen as establishing a quantitative equivalence of value between objects. According to Maurer (2006), the usual story told in works spanning from Karl Marx, Max Weber, and Georg Simmel to more recent works in the social sciences is that modern money transforms that which is socially embedded into abstracted economic forms. Money, we are told, commensurates the incommensurable, bringing things into a common metric. Money is often seen as the ultimate objectifier that transforms all aspects of life—from the material to the affective—into numerical cash equivalents. Yet scholars have shown that this is not necessarily the case and have drawn attention to the way people create or assign value to things within various social, political, and economic contexts. In a study of domestic money, for example, Zelizer (1989) shows that money is differentiated through the different meanings and uses we assign to it (for instance, compensation money, lottery winnings, and an ordinary paycheck are not all equal kinds of money).

By emphasizing the cultural and social structural factors that give value to things, these studies point to questions that are also fundamental to the conflicts I address in this book. How do people assign value to things deemed to be incommensurable? How are things made comparable? Zelizer (1989) and Maurer (2006) problematize the argument that money homogenizes all qualitative distinctions into abstract quantity. Contrary to many academic theories and popular assumptions, money (and quantification more generally) does not flatten social relations or erase the cultural dynamics of commensuration. Drawing on these insights, I want to explore how attempts to make and dispute equivalences create *new* social relations of collaboration and antagonism. More specifically, I want to examine what counts as equivalence in the calculation and evaluation of the effects of mining activity. To do so, I focus on the knowledge practices and mechanisms of comparison that make equivalences possible (or lead to their rejection).[19]

The equivalences I analyze include, but are not restricted to, monetary exchange and quantification. I also ask: How do people interpret and negotiate radically incompatible knowledge practices and forms of ethical reasoning (cf. Povinelli 2001)? How do mechanisms of comparison help make some problems or places visible and worthy of attention? How does a logic of equivalence disallow different ways of knowing and inhabiting the landscape that do not correspond to technical language, systems of measurement, or legal frameworks? How do technical devices (for example, legal environmental standards, international guidelines, and corporate codes of conduct) make it possible to assess and compare the quality of different objects and practices (Barry 2001)?

Claims and counterclaims about equivalence lie at the core of controversies over mining and strategies for conflict resolution but remain unexplored in the ways that conflicts get analyzed and "resolved." Some of the chapters that follow examine how this logic of equivalence is promulgated and contested, but I am also interested in what is excluded from equivalences, and what falls outside the legal and scientific frameworks that inform strategies for environmental management and conflict resolution. Perhaps it is useful in such cases to think about the *remainder*, that which cannot be subsumed by the measure of equivalences (Obarrio 2010). The conflicts that I look at in this book are never absolutely resolved, since the dramatic changes to land and livelihoods that are produced by mining activity cannot be fully compensated. The remainder represents what cannot be repaid, and this "leftover" has ramifications that open up a circuit of debt (Obarrio 2010:164). Communities in the vicinity of the Yanacocha mine continue to demand further compensation, employment opportunities, services, and benefits that they consider to be their right, even if they cannot always turn to the law to substantiate their demands. The remainder is outside the guidelines that inform strategies for environmental management and conflict resolution. In some cases, the remainder is also outside of any identifiable political arena, since the tensions that erupt from it do not easily translate into established political interests (e.g., leftist politics, environmentalism, or labor activism).

In my fieldwork, a logic of equivalence was implicit in discussion about extractive activity and embedded in calculations, comparisons, and exchanges that shaped the dynamics of mining conflicts. For instance, compensation agreements can be seen as a form of commensuration, a process of transforming different values or units into a common metric (Espeland 1998). Price, cost-benefit ratios, and other forms of quantification and standardization make different entities comparable. In other words, two values or goods can be said to be commensurable if they are deemed to be equivalent based on a common standard of value (such as money), unit of measurement (e.g., rate of water flow), or system of classification (e.g., chemical composition).

A dispute over the mine's effects on an irrigation canal is one of the cases I use to show how a logic of equivalence was used to bring disparate entities into relation, with the aim of comparing (and ultimately reconciling) different forms of value. Canal users were awarded monetary compensation and received chemically treated water pumped from the mine's treatment plant into their canal in order to compensate for reduced water flows. These negotiations reflected a logic of equivalence that relied on a series of assumptions. First, it implied that water from a natural source was interchangeable with water coming from a treatment plant. Second, the mining company considered water quality acceptable if proven to meet the established legal standards for trace minerals and other substances. Third, the company asserted that the mine's effects on the canal could be reversed by "returning" the same amount of water that was lost and by compensating canal users with monetary payments, employment opportunities, and development projects.

In the canal controversy, equivalences enabled the mining company to turn protestors' demands into compensation packages and programs that aimed to demonstrate a commitment to Corporate Social Responsibility. However, equivalences must be negotiated and are thus always open to contestation. In some instances, canal users worked within the logic of universal equivalence to obtain benefits from the mining company: jobs, community development, compensation packages, and more water in their canals. At other times, however, they employed a different logic of equivalence, one that did not depend on universal currencies and measurements. They argued that legal classifications and water quality standards for canal water did not correspond to the campesinos' daily use of the water for domestic consumption, and that the compensation agreements did not make up for their investment in the construction, maintenance, and administration of the canal. In these cases, canal users argued that some things were incommensurable; the water from the canal was not just a resource to be used, and could not simply be "returned" in the form of chemically treated water pumped into the canal. Rather, the canal encompassed things, people, and experiences that were defined as unique and thus incommensurable with the mine's offer of compensation (cf. Espeland 1998).

While these equivalence-making processes were used to measure and compare water and air quality, or in negotiations between canal users and the mining company, the equivalence of knowledges was also at stake. Underlying the disputes over mining were disagreements about what counts as evidence and whose knowledge (that of mining experts, scientists, NGOs, or peasant farmers) was credible and legitimate. The language and tools of science and expertise lend knowledge legitimacy and make it possible for knowledge to travel. Technical devices and regulatory regimes, from maps and measuring instruments to laws and environmental standards, enable otherwise incommensurable and isolated knowledges to move in space and time from the local site and moment of their production (Turnbull 2000).

Entering into equivalences was crucial for validating arguments for and against mining activity. A logic of equivalence informs assumptions about when toxic substances or alterations in the landscape exceed the threshold at which an "impact" becomes irreversible. This threshold is established through commensuration with legal norms—for example, the established legally permissible limits for trace minerals in water and air. These environmental standards, in turn, serve as a basis of comparison with international guidelines that activists can use to challenge the validity of existing norms. The principle of equivalence provides a powerful tool for environmentalism, which insists on international standards for environmental protection. For example, establishing equivalence between La Oroya and the North American site of a smelter owned by the same company revealed the discrepancies between Peruvian and international environmental standards. In this case, engaging the political through equivalence served as a strategy to create regional and transnational networks of solidarity.

According to anthropologist Tim Choy (2011:11), ecological politics, as well as our own forms of academic analysis, work through comparisons, "acts of relations—of nature, culture, politics and more—through which a given animal, plant, health problem, landscape, or question comes to matter epistemically and politically." In the chapters that follow, I explore how equivalences are made and contested. In doing so, I seek to make visible the relations between people, things, places, and issues unearthed by intensive processes of extraction. The lens of equivalence elucidates the politics of comparison that are central to controversies over extraction, including the possibilities for action that it enables and the conditions that contribute to the perpetuation of conflict.

Unearthing Conflict

This book is based on a long-term engagement with environmental and mining issues in Peru, including two years of ethnographic research from January 2005 to December 2006. During this time, I was based primarily in the city of Cajamarca, in the northern province of the same name. The focus of my analysis was the Yanacocha mine. In Cajamarca, I divided my time between the city and rural communities in the vicinity of the mine. My research sites were varied: a public hearing to present an Environmental Impact Assessment; the inspection of an irrigation canal; protests and roadblocks; NGO offices; participatory water studies; information sessions; and other mining-related events. Working in a context of increasing polarization made it necessary for me to be explicit about my allegiances while being cautious about the information that was shared with me.[20] My initial contacts were made through NGO networks and led me to the offices of GRUFIDES (Grupo de Formación e Intervención para el Desarrollo Sostenible [Training and Intervention Group for Sustainable Development]), a local organization that became a key protagonist in the conflicts. Much of my time was spent among a circle of activists and leaders who took a critical stance on mining. I did not have the same level of access to corporate actors or their allies, but my position as an academic researcher allowed me to interview some Yanacocha representatives and others who supported the company. I also attended the many public events organized by the mining company and other institutions that were held in Cajamarca and traveled to communities where allegiances were far from clear-cut.

My fieldwork was empirically grounded in Cajamarca but followed the reverberations of the conflict beyond its borders. Short trips to the capital city of Lima allowed me to keep sight of the national context while following mining debates as they developed in conferences and NGO circles. Additionally, I traveled to other mining areas, including the Central Highlands. In this book, the case of La Oroya provides some background on the history of mining in the Central Highlands, showing that the conflicts are not isolated from larger national and international debates, or disconnected from global forces and processes of extraction.

I returned to Cajamarca in 2009 for follow-up research, and again in 2012 to examine the development of another conflict, over the Conga mining project, which offers a glimpse of the future of mining controversies and related activism.

The chapters in this book are divided into three parts. Part I, "Mining Past and Present," examines how mining transformed the landscape and forms of livelihood in the Central and Northern Highlands. I focus on mining technologies, political activism, and corporate practices in two time periods: the beginning of the twentieth century, and the turn of the twenty-first century. Chapter 1 traces the story of La Oroya from the early 1900s and the arrival of the Cerro de Pasco Corporation to the early 2000s, when a North American environmental organization named La Oroya one of the world's ten most polluted places. This global notoriety allowed for an expansion of alliances as residents, NGOs, scientists, solidarity activists, and other supporters worked to make pollution visible. At the same time, corporate programs that sought to control pollution shifted the burden of responsibility from the company to the larger community. By exploring the emergence of activism, changes in corporate practices, and the processes through which pollution comes to matter, this chapter situates recent controversies over mining within national debates and historical processes.

In chapter 2, I examine the technologies of mega-mining used at the Yanacocha gold mine. To distance their operations from the problematic legacy of environmental degradation in mining areas such as the Central Highlands, transnational corporations have sought to create a new image of *modern* mining that branded their practices as more socially and environmentally responsible than those of earlier operations. Meanwhile, protestors argued that the mine would reduce the quantity and quality of water available to local communities. I focus on a participatory water monitoring program to show how various actors used the language and tools of science and participation to support their claims.

Part II, "Water and Life," looks at water's capacity to provoke politics, inspiring large-scale protests and international activism against the mine as well as the day-to-day altercations that characterize relationships between the mine and neighboring communities. In chapter 3, I discuss one of the most significant protests against mining activity in recent years: protests against the expansion of the Yanacocha gold mine into Cerro Quilish

(Mount Quilish). In campaigns against the mining project, Cerro Quilish entered the struggles as an aquifer (a store of life-sustaining water) and an Apu (usually translated from Quechua as "sacred mountain"). Crucially, the knowledges that shaped the Quilish campaigns were not part of an already existing "indigenous tradition," nor were they simply a set of meanings that environmentalists, scientists, and protestors assigned to a preexisting thing. Rather, their discursive practices and the mountain's material form (as a mineral deposit, aquifer, and Apu) were mutually articulated as the controversy took shape. Cerro Quilish's changing form illustrates the political consequences of Nature's multiplicity. The many definitions of Cerro Quilish did not need to be reconciled into a single identity, for its multiplicity was precisely what enabled the creation of alliances across difference.

In chapter 4, I describe how an irrigation canal and the fluid relations built around it became the focus of disagreements about the effects of the mine on water quantity and quality. An attention to the material and affective connections between people and landscapes inspired me to think about irrigation canals as sites of entangled social and natural histories. The canals connected people and landscapes through relations that encompassed but were not reducible to economic or utilitarian concerns. Thinking relationally about a canal and those who used it revealed how landscapes are made through constant engagement and interactions between people, land, and other elements of the environment. These various relationships—made through affect and kinship, antagonisms and necessity—were crucial for understanding the disputes with the mining company.

Part III, "Activism and Expertise," examines the role of expertise in the conflicts, focusing on mechanisms of accountability that sometimes reduce conflicts to their technical dimensions. In chapter 5, I examine a key process in the making of social and environmental accountability in mining projects: Environmental Impact Assessment (EIA). I argue that the form of the documents produced for the EIAs (i.e., their required components, as established in legal frameworks) and the process of making them public (participatory meetings and public forums) can take precedence over their content. Two aspects of the EIA make this possible. First, the risks that are identified in the EIA are those that a company deems to be technically manageable based on the solutions and interventions that it has to offer. Second, the participatory process of the EIA creates collaborative relationships among state agents, corporations, NGOs, and communities. These forms of collaboration strengthen the EIA's claims of accountability while circumscribing the spaces for opposition to a proposed project.

The delegitimization of opposition to mining activity (and the criminalization of protest) has contributed to the persistence of conflict in a climate of continued mining expansion. In the conclusion, I examine the continued problems in Cajamarca and their implications for thinking about corporate accountability and political activism. I relate the book's chapters to the 2012 protests over the Conga mining project, which once again brought resource extraction to the national consciousness and produced a marked shift in public opinion. The book's conclusion offers a reflection on Peru's expanding frontiers of extraction, the techno-political and economic regimes that make it possible, and the potential of grassroots movements to reshape national politics.

PART I   MINING PAST AND PRESENT

CHAPTER 1

TOXIC LEGACIES, NASCENT ACTIVISM

In 2006, the smelter town of La Oroya, located in Peru's Central Highlands, was named one of the world's top ten most polluted places by the Blacksmith Institute, a nonprofit environmental group based in New York. This dubious distinction placed La Oroya alongside Chernobyl and other toxic sites around the globe,[1] capturing the attention (and indignation) of Peruvians and people around the world. This increased attention on La Oroya coincided with the emergence of conflicts around mining activity in various parts of the country and contributed to discussions about pollution and health that would shape national debates around mining activity. News stories of La Oroya's "children of lead"[2]—their blood poisoned by the constant exposure to the smelter's toxic emissions—proliferated in the national and international media, yet the problems that these stories captured were not new. The smelter in La Oroya had been operating since the Cerro de Pasco Copper Corporation built it in 1922, and residents had been living with the toxic emissions spewed from its chimneys for nearly a century.

The smelter town of La Oroya, a 174-kilometer (108-mile) ascent into the mountains from the capital city of Lima, is located in a deep gorge where the Mantaro and Yauli Rivers meet. La Oroya is at the junction of the principal highways that connect the coast with the Central Highland and Amazonian regions.

Travelers must pass it on the way to other destinations, but few have reason to linger in this cold industrial town 3,700 meters above sea level. Clearly visible from the main highway (which is also La Oroya's principal street), the metallurgical complex is made up of smelters and refineries that transform polymetallic ores into ten metals (copper, zinc, silver, lead, indium, bismuth, gold, selenium, tellurium, and antimony) and nine by-products.[3] The smelting facilities are a throwback to another era, but when it was constructed, it boasted the most sophisticated technology of any smelter in the world. At the beginning of the twentieth century, the metallurgical complex was a testament to industrial development in the region, employment opportunities, and a growing economy spurred by mining activity—and for some Peruvians, this image of progress did not fade with time.

By the end of the 1990s, however, La Oroya began to carry another set of associations: pollution, lead poisoning, underdevelopment, and a population condemned to life in one of the country's most degraded environments. In 1997, during the presidency of Alberto Fujimori, the smelter was privatized and transferred from the state-owned Centromin to the U.S.-based Doe Run Company.[4] Activism in La Oroya slowly burgeoned as a small group of residents, NGOs, and international supporters denounced the pollution. A series of studies and published reports provided the evidence needed to draw attention to the problems, particularly the impact of lead on children and pregnant women. One of the earliest was a study presented by the Peruvian Ministry of Health's Environmental Health Division (DIGESA 1999), which showed that 99 percent of children had blood lead levels that exceed the limits recommended by the World Health Organization (WHO).

As the problems began to receive increasing attention from the media, many smelter workers and other residents organized marches and rallies in support of Doe Run. Even some of those living directly across from the smelter, who were most exposed to the toxic emissions, opposed the suggestion made by some organizations that they should be relocated to the outskirts of the city. They feared that complaints about the pollution would put their livelihoods and the metallurgical industry at risk. In La Oroya's volatile and contradictory politics, local residents threw stones at visiting scientists conducting a study on lead pollution (Mellado 2005), and local activists faced the harassment and threats of Doe Run supporters.

In this chapter, La Oroya and the Central Highlands serve as a lens through which to analyze past and present practices and discourses related to mining activity and pollution in Peru, as well as the changing dynamics of resource conflicts over the country's long engagement with the extractive industry. Starting with the story of the Oroya smelter and the Cerro de Pasco Corporation, I examine how the smelter's toxic emissions—though present from the moment the smelter began to operate—took different forms at various points in time, and evoked different responses from the companies operating the smelter and from the local population.

Pollution in La Oroya *came to matter* (socially, economically, politically, and materially) through historically specific practices. These practices include corporate programs that monitored the health of workers and focused on controlling risks in the workplace; scientific studies that began to measure toxicity beyond the smelter and its effects on the population at large; and local and international environmental advocacy. These various forms of knowledge made pollution at times perceptible and at others invisible, in ways that both encouraged and restricted political action. In my analysis, pollutants are not indisputable "matters of fact," or objects that exist independently as elements of "nature," to be measured and controlled by scientists and engineers. Instead, I suggest that pollution must be treated not as a single object to be analyzed from different perspectives, but as *multiple* in and of itself (Mol 2002). The existence of pollution is dependent on the particular practices that bring it into being. Rather than something detected through objective study and analysis, it is best seen as an effect of relations, or a set of associations within a collective of people, technologies, and the "things" of nature. Acknowledging the multiplicity of an object like "pollution" allows us to see the changes in the collectives that bring it into being, and the continuous work that is required to stabilize its shifting identity.

The new visibility of pollution enabled alliances that involved a wide range of participants, from lead particles that made their way to the fields of agriculturalists in the valley, to American scientists conducting a health study facilitated by the region's Catholic archbishop. Pollution's uncontainable effects transformed what had generally been considered a problem of La Oroya into an issue that affected an entire watershed, valley, and region. In response, Doe Run collaborated with government institutions and community groups to implement a series of health and environmental programs that invoked a sense of shared responsibility for the problems of La Oroya. The events taking place in La Oroya reverberated beyond the region and are illustrative of the dynamics taking shape in other communities affected by the mining industry. By the late 1990s, the increased visibility of pollution and its effects on air, soil, water, and bodies inspired social activism in other parts of the country, enabled different ways of understanding the impacts of mining activity, and contributed to new forms of organization. Nascent forms of activism that focused on health and the environment, along with corporate strategies emphasizing community participation and environmental stewardship, contributed to a climate of polarization. In this chapter, I examine changes in corporate practices and activism over time in order to elucidate when (and for whom) pollution matters *and when it does not*—in other words, the contingent nature of its local, national, and international significance.

City of Smoke and Chimneys

Valle estrecho en profundas gargantas,
con amor te llamamos así,
ciudad de humos y de chimineas,
el sustento de nuestra nación.

Narrow valley in deep gorges,
With love we call you thus,
City of smoke and chimneys,
The sustenance of our nation.
—VERSE FROM HYMN OF LA OROYA

A sweet aroma. These were the words Alfonso used to talk about the air in La Oroya. They are not the words that come to my mind to describe the smell of sulfur dioxide that (along with lead and other toxic substances) came out of the smelter chimney. The burning sensation that gripped my throat and made me cough as I stepped outside in the mornings is the memory that comes to my mind. But perhaps one needs to have spent a lifetime living in La Oroya and working in the smelter, like Alfonso, to notice the subtle changes in the air's smell and taste.

For Alfonso, the smelter and its towering chimneys were simply part of the landscape, like the brownish waters of the Mantaro River and the glistening white rock of the mountains surrounding the town, the result of years of exposure to the smelter's emissions and acid rain. I had heard from other residents who grew up in La Oroya or had lived there most of their lives that they learned to tolerate the noxious clouds that sometimes hovered above the town, and the smell of minerals that permeated the air. They shut their doors and windows when the smoke was at its worst, got used to the itching in their eyes and throats, and carried a handkerchief to cover their faces when the gases became intolerable. Things were much worse before Doe Run, Alfonso insisted, when the air filled with white flakes that "rained down like dandruff—and nobody said a thing."

We sat in the living room of the small apartment he shared with his wife, Josefina, who was active in the Asociación de Promotoras de Salud, a community health group sponsored by Doe Run that brought together the wives of smelter workers, and whose members had gained a reputation for being some of Doe Run's staunchest supporters. The middle-aged couple lived in Marcavalle, a neighborhood known as the "New Oroya," made up of multicolored apartment blocks that were home to those smelter workers fortunate enough to qualify for company housing based on a point system. Built in the 1970s, the apartments were not luxurious by any means but provided the comforts of an urban life unlike that of a peasant community or the now demolished workers' camps: cement construction, modern furniture and amenities, and a small landscaped garden outside every block. In sharp contrast to Old Oroya, with its dilapidated houses built precariously on the sloping mountain directly across from the metallurgical complex, New Oroya was further removed from the smelter's emissions.

Thinking that I might be a reporter, Alfonso and Josefina were initially hesitant to talk to me because they resented the spate of recent articles in the media painting a negative picture of Doe Run and the situation in La Oroya, but their reticence soon gave way to an eagerness to tell me their side of the story. What they wanted me to see was that all the recent talk about health-threatening pollution in La Oroya was simply hype and misinformation. It was not that the pollution has gotten worse in recent years, Alfonso explained. It was just that the recent switch from petroleum to gas to run the smelter had changed the air, giving it a sweet aroma. Sure, La Oroya is polluted, he conceded; but what place isn't?

Echoing the statements commonly made by company officials and their supporters, Alfonso blamed NGOs, journalists, and other outsiders for instilling fear and distrust in people. He felt they were out of touch with the reality of La Oroya, and that if I wanted to understand that reality, I had to know the history of mining in the region. What Alfonso wanted me to understand was La Oroya's reason for being: the town came into existence alongside the smelter and the Cerro de Pasco Corporation, the mining company that dominated the regional economy at the turn of the twentieth century. For Alfonso, a look at the past would also reveal what he called "new paradigms" that accompanied each stage of the smelter's history, which brought changes in corporate practices and to the lives of workers and their families. Heeding Alfonso's words, I will begin with the smelter's history, which is also the story of the Cerro de Pasco Corporation.

A Century of Mining

Toward the end of the nineteenth century, a group of North American engineers arrived in the Central Highlands to conduct mineral exploration and found silver deposits and immense reserves of copper at Cerro de Pasco. In 1901, a New York mining syndicate formed by investors in the United States bought approximately 80 percent of the mining concessions in Cerro de Pasco and the surrounding region,[5] and in 1915, the investment company incorporated as the Cerro de Pasco Copper Corporation. Although the company changed its name at various times to reflect the changing nature of its production and corporate structure, I will refer to it as the Cerro de Pasco Corporation (CPC), the name by which it was known during most of its years of operation, or simply as "the company" (*la compañia*), as it was called by locals. For decades after it was established, the CPC would be the most influential company in the industry, since it owned the richest mines in Peru and monopolized the smelting and refinery of minerals (it owned all three refineries in the country, and two of the four smelters).[6]

As the CPC began its operations in the difficult terrain of the Andean mountain range, transportation posed the biggest challenge, since moving large quantities of unprocessed ore around the highlands was expensive. Copper, in particular, was more bulky and less valuable than silver and needed to be smelted to reduce its weight and make its extraction profitable. Although the company already operated a smelter in Tinyahuarco, near Cerro de Pasco, the construction of a central smelter would allow for expanded production while minimizing freight and fuel costs. La Oroya provided an ideal site for the project: flattish land, a river for water use and waste disposal, a supply of labor from nearby communities, and room to accommodate the workers.

Before the construction of the smelter, La Oroya was already well integrated into the national and international economy, a consequence of the arrival of the railway in 1893. Building the railway required a large labor force that included many Chinese workers, attesting to the difficulty of recruiting local people into the industrial labor force. Around this time, the community of San Jeronimo de La Oroya was made up of some 150 adults;[7] most of them were peasant farmers and shepherds, and a smaller number were engaged in mining and trading. It was also an area where migrants (many from communities in the Mantaro valley) had settled during the first half of the nineteenth century, drawn by the nearby mines and opportunities for raising sheep and cattle. The expansion of the railway stimulated mining and agriculture and turned La Oroya into an important commercial center from which ores and agricultural products were shipped. The influx of workers also opened up opportunities for those who were able to set up businesses, build houses and shops, or rent and sell land for development. The consequences of these early developments are reflected in modern-day La Oroya: in the chaotic bustle of activity in its markets; in the constant flow of freight trains and the nonstop traffic along the highway that runs through the town; and in a population made up of migrants who, at various points in time, settled here to take advantage of the newest opportunities that the town had to offer.

Construction of the smelter began in 1919, with the labor of two thousand men who were nearly all hired under a system of *enganche*, by which laborers were paid in advance and then worked off their debts in thirty- to ninety-day periods. Some scholars (e.g., Bonilla 1974; DeWind 1987; Laite 1981) have noted the initial reluctance of campesinos to work in the mines. They suggest that their economic independence, based on their integration into a subsistence agricultural economy and communal ties, made wage labor unappealing and made it necessary for the company to initially rely on enganche to draw people to mining work.

According to historian Florencia Mallon (1983), the enganche system became expensive and increasingly less attractive for the company, since it had to advance large amounts of money to the *enganchadores* (who received a commission), and always ran the risk of workers leaving before paying off their debts (the runaway rate was 50 percent). The construction of the Oroya smelter was a key factor in changing this pattern of labor recruitment and seasonal migration; indeed, it was central to the reorganization of the mining industry in the central highlands. The smelter became the "technological hub of the company's entire operation, reorganizing the flow of mineral and metals and imparting a new rhythm and rationale to the extraction process" (Mallon 1983:223). With the centralization and modernization of the company, increased production at the mines, and the full-time operation of the Oroya smelter, the seasonal and unstable nature of the enganche system no longer met the company's labor demands. The company required a more permanent and skilled labor force and began to hire workers directly and offer a higher wage.

In spite of these changes, the workforce in the mining sector continued to be predominantly made up of migrant peasants who would eventually return to agriculture, and whose cash remittances helped sustain a semi–subsistence economy in their home villages. For the first three decades of the company's operations, wage labor constituted a complement to small-scale agriculture, compensating for an inadequate and fragmenting economic base (Long and Roberts 1984). Nevertheless, some workers began to settle on a more permanent basis, often with their families, in workers' camps such as those built in La Oroya.

The company's effort to recruit a more stable workforce was not the only factor that contributed to the increased migration of campesinos and their enrollment into the labor force. Also significant was what Bonilla (1974) called a "curious mechanism of proletarianization": the degradation of land and resources caused by the smelting and mineral extraction process. The smelter's emissions and the toxic runoff from the mines contaminated the water and reduced the soil's productive capacity and the amount of pastureland available for livestock. The incursion of foreign capital, the damages produced by the pollution, changing patterns of migration, and technological advances came together in ways that contributed to the dominance of the Cerro de Pasco Corporation and urban development in La Oroya.

The Smoke Problem

When the metallurgical complex was completed in 1922, the effects of its operations were felt immediately in the surrounding countryside. The chimneys released into the air a mixture of lead, bismuth, sulfur dioxide, arsenic, and other poisonous substances, which spread like "an invisible fire" (Muñiz 1935:46) on once fertile fields. The sulfur dioxide reacted with moisture in the atmosphere to produce sulfuric acid, which was deposited over an extensive area around the smelter, burning up agricultural crops and pasture grasses. Solid particulates like arsenic and antimony were also deposited on the countryside, causing illnesses and death in the livestock. In the area around La Oroya, six haciendas that partnered to create the Sociedad Ganadera de Junín found that their sheep and cattle were dying of diarrhea, lack of edible vegetation, and direct poisoning (Laite 1981). Toxic substances had the power to immediately destroy crops, kill livestock, and alter people's lives. They also played a role as *hacendados* (hacienda owners) whose land was affected used their clout to bring "the smoke" into the political arena.

The hacendados used their political contacts to put pressure on the company, and a government "smoke commission" (the first of five) formed in 1923 to study the problem. At the same time, hacendados initiated legal action against the company. Thirty surrounding communities also brought claims against the company for the effects of the smoke on their land and rivers (Muñiz 1935). The Cerro de Pasco Corporation's general manager in Peru, Harold Kingsmill, argued that the damages were being exaggerated in order to seek compensation and accused the complainers of what he called "smoke farming" (DeWind 1987:55), by which he meant taking advantage of the "smoke" problem to extort compensation money from the company. However, the government commission supported the hacendados' claims, forcing the company to suspend most of its operations until it implemented emission control measures. The unintended alliance between hacendados and campesinos urged the Cerro de Pasco Corporation to respond to their demands, since it had to be seen as doing something to curb the smelter's toxic smoke. The company built a small plant to treat the heavy emissions from the converters, which removed enough lead to noticeably reduce the effects on animals (DeWind 1987). These measures to filter the emissions were taken in response to the public outcry, but they had an economic benefit for the corporation: the filtering process provided a way to reclaim commercially valuable metals, including lead and bismuth (Laite 1981).

In spite of the public pressure and the legal action brought against it, the smelter's emissions created a series of effects that strengthened the company's economic monopoly in the Central Highlands. In order to resolve the lawsuits and avoid future indemnifications, the company purchased twenty-seven affected haciendas covering 1,047 square miles (DeWind 1987). The expectation was that once the smelter's emissions were reduced, the costly acquisition of land could be turned into a profit-making enterprise. The company formed the Cerro de Pasco Farm Division with the purchased land and hired experts to improve the livestock, resulting in the creation of a new breed of sheep (the now popular "Junín" breed, which boasts a high productivity of wool and meat). In time, the Farm Division enabled the company to reap from its investment; the food produced was sold to workers at a low cost, which in turn allowed the company to maintain workers' low wages.

Purchasing hacienda land was a simple way out of its legal problems, but dealing with peasant communities was not as straightforward. In the community of La Oroya, the smoke destroyed barley crops almost overnight, and village representatives claimed that 278 cattle, 3,874 sheep, and 200 mules and horses were lost because of smoke poisoning (Laite 1981:61). The community's land was ruined for agricultural use, but the company could use it to build more installations and a waste dump. Some of the land was communally held, and some was privately owned, so the company valued private landholdings and indemnified its owners (mostly migrants) in cash. Since communal land could not be bought or sold, an alternative form of compensation was to donate a parcel of land—a hacienda that the company purchased close to Tarma, a nearby town—where people could relocate. Those who could claim rights to communal land and wished to continue an agricultural life (predominantly older, larger landholders) accepted the land offers. The rest (younger people, many employed by the company or the railway, or working in construction) were paid in cash for the crops and livestock they had lost and chose to stay in La Oroya (Laite 1981:61).

Even though the land was ruined for agricultural use, people who remained in the area now known as Oroya Antigua soon found themselves on valuable urban property. Many of them retained their rights to land within the old *comunidad campesina* (peasant community) and were able to work in the smelter while pursuing commercial activities. They invested their compensation money in shops, restaurants, and houses and rented out rooms and provided services for the migrants arriving to work in the smelter. The devastating effects of the smelter's emissions established the conditions for the explosive and haphazard growth of a residential and commercial area on this mountain slope, the site most directly exposed to the emissions from the smelter. The company itself built housing for its workers in Oroya Antigua, contributing to commercial growth and a rise in property values that, decades later, would make residents hesitant to relocate in spite of the ongoing exposure to the smoke. The compensation benefited *comuneros* (members of the comunidad campesina), but it also had unintended consequences—it enticed people to stay and confined them to a life-long exposure to toxic substances.

When the smelter was constructed, the effects of its toxic emissions, the political maneuvering and legal actions of the hacendados, the claims of comuneros, and pressure from the government-sponsored "smoke commissions" combined to restructure highland agriculture, making the company owner of one of the largest haciendas in the country. The dramatic changes taking place in the Central Highlands in the early twentieth century were part of processes of capitalist expansion, industrialization, and proletarianization. However, these processes interacted with a variety of forces that were not exclusively human. The company did not anticipate the smoke's far-reaching effects on land and animals, and the smelter's operations ultimately altered the agrarian economy, the system of land tenure, and the mining industry itself (Mallon 1983).

A history of mining that focuses exclusively on human agency ignores other actors, processes, and agencies that also contribute to the making of histories. Mining development in the Central Highlands shows how human and nonhuman actors came together or interacted with one another at specific moments in time to transform historical processes (cf. Mitchell 2002). As pollutants expelled into the atmosphere came into contact with plants, soils, technologies, animals, and people, these actors affected one another, producing a series of chemical, social, and political reactions that would influence the movement of people, the urban development of La Oroya, and the future health of its population. The loyalty that many people feel to the company responsible for polluting their town and their refusal to relocate must be understood within the context of a long history in which pollutants—variously perceived, defined, and dealt with—played a crucial role.

Making Pollution Matter

La Oroya's history is inextricably connected to "smoke"—or *los humos*, the term still used colloquially to refer to the smelter's emissions. Upon the smelter's construction, the Cerro de Pasco Corporation treated the effects of the smoke and the public outcry that followed primarily as an economic problem, which it resolved by purchasing hacienda lands, compensating affected individuals, and using the lands acquired to breed livestock. Inside the smelter, however, toxic substances acquired another role as they became visible through workers' bodies. Within the work environment of the smelter, refineries, and mines, toxic contaminants could not be ignored. Knowledge about these contaminants changed through the years, as mining companies began to monitor the health of their workers and conduct scientific studies.

Some examples of how the Cerro de Pasco Corporation dealt with toxic substances can be seen in its company publications. In 1953, the CPC created the Industrial Hygiene Division to prevent work-related illness, promote good working conditions, establish health and safety standards, and protect the health of workers with the aim of increasing productivity (Cerro de Pasco Corporation 1957). Over the next five years, the Industrial Hygiene Division developed an extensive research program and oversaw working conditions in the company's various facilities. According to the company's newsletter *El Serrano*, the Industrial Hygiene Division comprised the following three sections: The Medical Section sought to control the most common work-related conditions, such as skin diseases or dermatitis "generally caused by an allergic reaction to airborne irritants," lead exposure, silicosis, and eye problems. The Engineering Section was in charge of "research and maintenance of work areas in conditions appropriate for good health, through the study and control of the environment." The Chemical Section was responsible for "determining the quality and quantity of noxious and toxic substances in the environment, such as dusts, gases, vapors, smoke, and fog, to determine their concentration and composition in the air breathed by workers, in relation to their health effects" (Cerro de Pasco Corporation 1957:5–8).

The division's efforts focused primarily on pollutants *in the workplace*, and not as a more general concern related to environmental conditions outside the work areas. Industrial hygiene brought together a concern for health and "the environment," but it reflected a particular understanding of pollutants as something that could interfere with workers' well-being and productivity, yet could be controlled through scientific management. Workers, meanwhile, incorporated some of these concerns into their own struggles for better working conditions. In a pamphlet outlining a complaint against the company in 1946, for example, the Metallurgical Workers' Union demanded a pay increase, a reduction in the workday (six hours instead of eight), and vacation time for workers who worked in the "toxic zones" within the complex. Working in areas that were recognized as "toxic and insalubrious" was something for which workers felt they should receive extra compensation, but it was also reluctantly accepted as an unavoidable aspect of work in this industry.

If pollutants materialized through the company's and workers' concerns about health and safety, they took on a different role upon the smelter's nationalization by the leftist military government of Juan Velasco Alvarado in 1973. In a decree passed to expropriate the mining-metallurgical operations of the Cerro de Pasco Corporation, Velasco's revolutionary military government considered that the company polluted the waters of the Huascacocha lagoon and the Rimac, Mantaro, and San Juan Rivers and had not executed investment projects aimed at reducing the environmental contamination produced for years by the smelter and other metallurgical facilities in La Oroya.[8] The corporation's lack of attention to the pollution was among the justifications given for expropriation, though the state-run company, Centromin, was never able to satisfactorily address the problem.

During the period of state ownership following the nationalization of the metallurgical complex, workers' health continued to be a focus of research and monitoring. Although Centromin continued the work already begun by the Cerro de Pasco Corporation, demonstrating technological efficiency in emissions control and a concern for workers became part of the military government's nationalist agenda. An editorial in the company newsletter praised recent investments to reduce pollution by relating these improvements to the "humanistic politics of the Revolutionary Government of the Armed Forces" (Centromin 1975). As a state-run company, Centromin had to show not only that it could be a leader in the industry, but also that its commitment to the ideals of the military government—translated as the well-being of workers—would contribute to the progress and development of the company *and* the nation.

Since the smelter's early history, polluting substances were a concern of both science (through company-sponsored studies) and politics (as part of a nationalist discourse on workers' well-being). Toxic gases and other non-human elements were already active in the making of La Oroya's socio-natural landscape, but they needed scientists, doctors, industrial hygienists, mining engineers, and workers to make them perceptible. What the corporate practices of the CPC and Centromin reveal, though, is that toxic substances were a concern primarily related to workers' bodies. It was only later that their designation as *environmental* pollutants would contribute to their national and international significance as a public health and environmental threat. I want to now examine how this shift took place, bringing "pollution" into being both scientifically and in the sociopolitical imagination.

Expanding Alliances

The smoke surfaces again in La Oroya's sociopolitical scene. . . .
History repeats itself. But this time it is no longer about land. It is the surrounding population that assumes an irreparable cost.
—CARLOS CHIRINOS, FROM AN ARTICLE ON LA OROYA PUBLISHED IN
THE NATIONAL NEWSPAPER *LA REPÚBLICA*, OCTOBER 18, 2005

"*Life* is what's at stake," said Carmen resolutely. The issue for her was clear: Doe Run could not be allowed to continue operating with impunity. Carmen was a member of CooperAcción, which was founded in 1997 as one of the first Peruvian organizations to specifically target the issue of mining as it related to the environment and human rights. As a national NGO, CooperAcción was headed by Lima-based professionals but opened a small office in La Oroya and formed an umbrella organization called Consorcio UNES with two other local organizations, Filomena Tomaira Pacsi and Grupo de Investigaciones Económicas ECO. Together, they conducted studies to evaluate air, soil, and water quality and organized education and training workshops to raise environmental awareness and promote grassroots leadership. While only in her early twenties, Carmen applied for a position as a "health promoter" (*promotora*), and her knowledge of the area and field experience she had gained while studying to be a practical nurse helped land her the job. Born and raised in La Oroya, she waged a battle with the company that was impassioned and personal, which also meant bearing the criticisms of townspeople and family members who did not share her stance. Her father had worked at the smelter until he injured his leg in a workplace accident and retired. Two of her brothers worked for subcontractors that provided transportation for smelter workers. Lunchtime conversations often led to heated debate, until she found an argument that made them reconsider their views. She asked her brothers: Would they sacrifice their children's future for their own jobs? After much effort, she managed to get her family on her side.

Carmen's views had not always been so clear. She recounted that before taking the job with CooperAcción, she never thought about pollution or its effects on health. Growing up in Oroya Antigua, los humos were ever present, but not something she knew much about: "We felt the burning in our throats, but we didn't know why, or that it could be harming us. Sometimes mom would tell us to stay inside the house [when air quality was at its worst], but we didn't think about the reasons. A teacher would tell us: it's good to get out [of La Oroya] once in a while, to clean our lungs." These experiences made Carmen recognize the challenges of working in a company town, where many people were convinced that if they still felt healthy after a lifetime in La Oroya, pollution was nothing to worry about.

When I first met Carmen in 2000, NGOs locally and at the national level were starting to tackle issues related to mining, health, and the environment, and residents of La Oroya were beginning to organize at the grassroots level. When I went back five years later, the same NGOs were still active. Through CooperAcción, Carmen provided support for grassroots groups like the Association of Environmental Delegates and the MOSAO (Movimiento por la Salud de La Oroya, or Movement for the Health of La Oroya) and coordinated activities with other organizations like the local Catholic parish (through an environment and human rights committee). These smaller groups were often weakened by internal conflicts, but their biggest challenge was Doe Run's concerted effort to delegitimize the opposition and turn local residents against the NGOs.

In December 2004, Doe Run workers and other supporters blocked the Central Highway as part of a two-day strike. The town mayor, a key player in the protest, declared that the measure was intended to safeguard the jobs of thousands of people who indirectly depend on the company's activities. About thirty-five hundred of La Oroya's approximately thirty three thousand residents are on Doe Run's payroll, and two thousand are hired by subcontractors, but those who defend the company argue that many more people benefit indirectly from the economic activity generated by the smelter. Through the protest measures, groups supporting Doe Run (including workers' unions) were demanding that the government approve the company's request to extend the deadline by which it was supposed to complete key environmental upgrades.

When Doe Run acquired the metallurgical complex in 1997 for US$247.9 million—what critics say was a bargain price—it committed itself to investing US$107 million in environmental projects that aimed to put the smelter's emissions within the Maximum Permissible Limits allowable by law. These commitments were outlined in the PAMA (*Programa de Adecuación y Mitigación Ambiental*, or Environmental Remediation and Management Program, a program introduced into Peruvian legislation in 1991) that had been developed by Centromin (the smelter's previous owner) and approved by the Peruvian government. According to the PAMA, the company had to complete these upgrades within a ten-year period, or by the deadline of January 2007. In 2004, the company began lobbying the government for an extension and courting public opinion. The company tried to convince people in La Oroya that the smelter would shut down if the PAMA extension was not granted, people would lose their jobs, and the company would relocate to another part of the world. In response, the government proposed a decree that critics said was made-to-measure: it would allow companies to extend their PAMAs if the local population and local authorities were in agreement.

Doe Run's advantage was the outspoken support of its key allies, including some local authorities, smelter workers and unions, and merchant associations.[9] But at the same time, the company faced a different reality than the smelter's previous owners: the health and environmental problems had gained significant attention outside of La Oroya. Pollution in La Oroya was no longer treated as a local problem, but as an issue that affected the surrounding valley, the Mantaro River watershed, and the surrounding region. For the first time since it bought the smelter in 1997, Doe Run set up an office in Huancayo, the regional capital and closest major city (approximately 125 km [78 miles] from La Oroya), to provide information about its operations and its work to curtail pollution. The company's public relations efforts had to include a wider public, not only because its PAMA extension made it into a national issue, but because the pollution was now seen as traveling far beyond the town's borders.

The new visibility of La Oroya's pollution was enabled in part by an expansive advocacy network that provided support and resources to carry out scientific studies and disseminate information. At the national level, a technical working group based in Lima brought together different NGOs to support efforts in La Oroya. International connections were made through organizations such as Oxfam American and Uniendo Manos contra la Pobreza (Joining Hands against Poverty), an ecumenical network bringing together Peruvian NGOs and partner churches in the United States. Visits to La Oroya by parishioners from the evangelical community in St. Louis, Missouri, acting out of concern for social and environmental justice inspired by Christian teachings, forged important solidarity links. Through these contacts, residents from La Oroya were put in touch with health advocates from Herculaneum, Missouri, the site of another Doe Run Company metal smelter (Farrell 2007). The Herculaneum smelter provided an important point of comparison, and linking these two "sister sites" made evident the company's neglect of citizens' health in both cases, as well as the double standards (for example, in Herculaneum, the company offered to buy 160 houses contaminated by the smelter and cleaned up contaminated soil, something that seemed improbable in La Oroya).

Establishing equivalence between the two sites—and arguing that pollution was unacceptable regardless of the countries where the smelters were found—was a strategy that contributed to the campaigns against Doe Run and the transnational relevance of the problems in Peru. News reports featured stories of the two smelters and their connection to the Renco Group (Doe Run's parent company in the United States), as well as the consequences of having companies relocate to countries with lower environmental and labor standards (e.g., Shipley and Walker 2006). In a 2003 *Vanity Fair* article, La Oroya was depicted not only as a polluted town in the Andes, but as part of a network connecting it to some of the most toxic sites in the United States, which were linked to Ira Rennert, owner of the Renco Group and ostensibly America's "biggest private polluter" (Shnayerson 2003).[10]

NGOS and the international press played a crucial role in making lead pollution in La Oroya known to Peruvians and the international community, but the expansion of alliances involved more than simply expanding activist networks. Lead and other pollutants—made perceptible and quantifiable through scientific studies and advocacy campaigns—were as critical to these new alliances as their human counterparts. Making pollution politically significant did not require having a unified position, for those who contributed to its visibility did not share the same "environmentalist" or health advocacy stance. For example, Doe Run reluctantly acknowledged the lead problem in its own studies (Doe Run 2002), even if it delayed implementing technological improvements that would have compromised the company's economic interests. The alliances that I am concerned with were made through cooperation as well as adversarialism and were possible even though the interests of opposing groups differed greatly. Environmentalists, NGOs, church groups, agriculturalists, corporate executives, and Doe Run employees all worked to make pollution matter in spite of their different aims and shifting allegiances.

In order to make the smelter into a public health and environmental issue, some actors articulated the problems of La Oroya with global discussions around community rights and mining activity in other parts of the world. These strategies appealed to "universals" in an attempt to mobilize people and open up possibilities for political change. As Anna Tsing (2005) points out, environmental politics appeal to universal ideals of science and modernity in an effort to forge transnational connections (as with transboundary issues like acid rain). However, the success of such efforts may obscure the limits and exclusions of universals, as well as the specific conditions in which knowledge travels—as Tsing notes, universals do not travel everywhere at any time. By appealing to universals, efforts to control pollution can produce unintended consequences and unlikely collaborations: "Universalism inspires expansion—for both the powerful and the powerless. Indeed, when those excluded from universal rights protest their exclusion, their protest itself has a twofold effect: It extends the reach of the forms of power they protest, even as it gives voice to their anger and hope" (Tsing 2005:9). Universals like science and environmentalism also appeal to mining companies and mobilize their supporters, potentially extending the forms of power activists are trying to counter. In what follows, I examine both activist and corporate actions that worked together to make pollution matter.

Detecting Pollution

Following the December 2004 blockade in support of Doe Run's PAMA extension, Huancayo's Catholic archbishop, Pedro Barreto, took it on himself to make La Oroya a priority for the archdiocese. Having just arrived at the archdiocese in September of that year, the Jesuit priest was already aware of the conflicts around mining brewing in different parts of the country and was particularly moved by the situation in La Oroya and surrounding mining towns. He issued public communiqués, spoke about the Catholic Church's role in the defense of life and the environment, and built alliances with NGOs and advocates for mining communities nationwide (including other Catholic priests who also took a leadership role in other mining conflicts, such as Marco Arana in Cajamarca).

The archdiocese proposed a new approach to the problems of La Oroya, which it labeled an "integral and sustainable solution to the environmental health and labor problem in La Oroya and the Mantaro River watershed." The initiative brought together over fifty government institutions, corporate representatives, and civil society. Through the advocacy work of the archdiocese and contacts made through the Uniendo Manos network, a group of researchers from St. Louis University's School of Public Health became interested in collaborating on a health study in La Oroya. The Archdiocese of Huancayo formally invited the group and assisted with the logistics of carrying out the study and informing the population of the results.

Several characteristics of the St. Louis University study made it different from previous health studies carried out in La Oroya. First, it was a more comprehensive study than those conducted earlier by NGOs and government bodies (in part because of funding considerations). Significantly, the study promised to examine not only traces of lead, but also other contaminants, including mercury, cadmium, arsenic, antimony, cobalt, and uranium. The St. Louis study confirmed that lead levels in La Oroya were indeed many times higher than those recommended by the World Health Organization, but it also made visible other contaminants that up to this point had not been given serious consideration. The study also called attention to the effects that a combination of various heavy metals and toxic elements could have on a population.

Second, the study focused on residents of La Oroya but used the town of Concepción as a control population. Concepción, a town of 11,400 residents in the Mantaro River valley, located 100 kilometers (62 miles) from La Oroya, was chosen because it had similar characteristics to La Oroya but did not have a smelter as a source of contamination (Arzobispado de Huancayo and St. Louis University 2005). In both cases, participants in the study volunteered to give blood samples, allowed scientists to collect dust, soil, and water samples from their homes, and answered questions about their health. The results of the study showed levels of each toxic substance in La Oroya and Concepción, compared to the average for the U.S. population as a frame of reference. As was expected, La Oroya had high concentrations of most toxic substances analyzed. What was noteworthy for researchers and the local population, however, were the results for Concepción: "Although it was expected that minor levels of pollution (revealed in lead, cadmium, and arsenic biomarkers) would be found in Concepción, it is nevertheless surprising that there exist levels of concern for these three metals in the population of Concepción, the "ecological city" of the Mantaro valley. This suggests that environmental pollution and its effects on health are not circumscribed only to La Oroya, but extend themselves throughout the Mantaro River valley" (Arzobispado de Huancayo and St. Louis University 2005:41). By including Concepción and finding elevated levels of pollution, researchers created a new population sample. Concepción—and by extension, the whole Mantaro valley—was no longer simply a control population for the purpose of the study, but became a population at risk. Through the act of detecting pollution and following its reach, researchers redefined it, making it into a wide-reaching environmental health threat that could affect anyone exposed to it.

From the outset, the St. Louis health study took pollution outside of La Oroya. The Huancayo Archdioceses took a leading role, volunteers from outside La Oroya helped out with the study, and the results were presented to communities in the Mantaro valley as well as La Oroya. And of course, the media coverage of the study took the story to other parts of the country and the world. According to Hunter Farrell (2007), a Presbyterian missionary involved with the Joining Hands Network in Peru, more than five hundred U.S. and Peruvian newspapers and magazines reported on the story, putting pressure on the Peruvian government.

Informed by new environmental knowledges, NGOs and activists began to identify pollution as a public health and environmental threat in which the affected and those responsible were found in and outside La Oroya. A formerly local problem became a *global* responsibility. This globalization of responsibility goes hand in hand with economic globalization; as local markets are liberalized, local problems, too, become global concerns. Local and global forces thus worked together to mobilize different actors: scientists and NGOs looked for evidence of pollution in La Oroya and surrounding communities, the World Health Organization standards set the acceptable limits of contamination, U.S. data served to reveal a double standard between Peruvian and North American communities, and blood samples were analyzed in U.S. laboratories. Monitoring technologies (GIS instruments, pH readers, air pollution detectors, etc.) also gave experts and nonexperts different ways to see and measure pollution and make different sites comparable.

When scientists and NGOs began to trace contaminants in rivers, soils, air, and human bodies, they reframed what had been considered the units of analysis. The smelter's area of influence expanded from the town of La Oroya (and more specifically, Oroya Antigua) to the whole Mantaro valley. In 2006, Peru's National Environmental Council (CONAM) presented a plan to "clean the air in La Oroya's atmospheric basin." Compelled to recognize pollution's expansive reach, the CONAM chose the term *basin*— generally used to describe the drainage area of a river and its tributaries— to refer to the smelter's *atmospheric* area of influence. By identifying the problem as "air pollution," contaminants were no longer situated in the human body (as with previous efforts to protect workers' health) but in the earth's atmosphere.

Pollutants reconfigured the scale of the problems and reframed them as concerns for a region, a valley, the country, and even the planet. Workplace contaminants affecting individual bodies became "air pollution" that put at risk all the communities within its expansive reach. These changing notions of pollution rested on a series of equivalences that led to new approaches to the problems in La Oroya: Instead of focusing on lead, scientific studies brought into view other contaminants, whose effects were deemed to be of equivalent concern, even if these had not been discussed in previous studies. Equivalences also allowed for the standardization of environmental indicators; the recognition of these standards as *universal* indicators deemed Peruvian and North American populations to be equivalent. Finally, the St. Louis University study made La Oroya and Concepción into comparable population samples, emphasizing the need to take the issues outside the confines of La Oroya.

Once experts and local residents began to see that pollutants posed a threat to an entire region, pollution came to be seen as a responsibility that had to be borne by governments, corporations, and citizens. The new visibility of pollution in La Oroya did not result from an organized environmental movement, but from a convergence of interests that was enabled not only by the rhetoric of environmentalism, but by environmental actors themselves—traveling pollutants, a river, and its atmosphere basin worked in collaboration with human actors as they enrolled each other into their networks.

As Doe Run began to publicly acknowledge the effects of pollution on human health, it created a network of a different sort than those of NGOs and solidarity activists. The company, along with workers, workers' wives, medical experts, Ministry of Health officials, local politicians, and other allies, enrolled lead and other toxic elements in an effort to contain pollution and the social imaginary built around it. In the section that follows, I examine the knowledge practices—from the treatment of lead-poisoned children to participatory health and environmental programs—used by Doe Run to recapture pollutants, bringing them back from globalized discourses around the environment and locating them within individual bodies.

From Corporate Accountability to Shared Responsibility

While La Oroya helped ignite a national debate about environmental health and pollution, at the local level, the situation grew increasingly divisive and conflictive. The backlash against NGOs became particularly fierce following the dissemination of the results of the St. Louis University health study, the Blacksmith Institute's inclusion of La Oroya in its annual "Most Polluted" list, and the advocacy work of the Archdiocese of Huancayo. Carmen felt that many environmental activists got discouraged or scared away by this hostile environment, and their work was made more difficult by the fact that Doe Run had been creating its own organizations of environmental and health delegates.

The Association of Health Promoters was one of these groups. Carmen told me that Doe Run's promotoras participated in rallies in defense of the company, openly criticized NGOs, and even intimidated NGO workers and ostracized local residents critical of Doe Run. If this was indeed the case, I wanted to understand how these women became some of Doe Run's most loyal allies. While many critics attributed their actions to some personal economic benefit that they received from the company, these women and other supporters of Doe Run seemed driven by a more complex set of interests. The promotoras' volunteer work exemplified the new knowledge practices that accompanied the expansion and intensification of transnational investment in the Peruvian mining sector. In La Oroya, these practices emphasized public participation and empowerment, institutional transparency, information sharing, and environmental education. These efforts were led by Doe Run, but their effectiveness rested in their collaborative nature, as they brought together state institutions, scientific experts, NGOs, and local communities regardless of their respective interests (whether a company's campaigns to create a "green" image or an NGO's activism to denounce pollution).

When I asked Josefina about the work of the promotoras, she emphasized the voluntary nature of the organization, which was made up of twenty-three presidents (one for each neighborhood or community) and involved more than 250 women in total. Some of their recent projects included neighborhood clean-up campaigns, education on family violence, home visits to provide prenatal care for pregnant women, and assistance with a tuberculosis prevention and control campaign run by the Ministry of Health. The women also participated in leadership training, workshops, and social gatherings organized by the company.

Although I did not want to immediately ask questions about pollution and the environment, it was Josefina herself who quickly shifted the conversation in this direction, as she accused NGOs and "environmentalists" of manipulating local residents for their own economic gain. In Peru, "environmentalist" or *ecologista* had become a term commonly used to refer to people linked to NGOs and grassroots organizations with a critical position toward mining activity—even if they did not necessarily identify themselves as such.

She told me that NGOs may present themselves as having good intentions, but in fact they were the ones generating the conflicts by dividing the population and creating distrust, and benefiting from funding from international organizations. It was an argument that I had gotten used to hearing, and which appeared in sensationalist tabloids and leaflets distributed in La Oroya as part of inflammatory campaigns aimed at discrediting the position of NGOs and grassroots activists. These negative representations of NGOs are not limited to the Peruvian context but are part of a corporate strategy that has become widespread, particularly in the mining industry. By discrediting the actions of NGOs, raising suspicion about their activities, and insisting that NGOs (rather than private companies) are the ones that lack transparency and accountability, mining corporations "seek to actively shape how the genuine environmental problems are defined and who can legitimately claim competence in resolving them" (Welker 2009:156).

Negative representations of NGOs have been adopted by the mining lobby, politicians, and the mainstream media and formed part of a broader national debate spurred by conflicts over mining activity. In 2006, the Peruvian congress passed a law that modified the functions of the Peruvian Agency for International Cooperation (APCI), the government agency that oversaw the use of donations from international funders. Under the guise of increased transparency and fiscal monitoring, the law allowed the APCI to intervene and determine which NGO projects would be approved. Critics argued that the law signified increased vigilance of NGO activities, particularly those seen as going against the interests of the state. Implicit in all these discussions was the role of NGOs in mining conflicts and the threat that mobilizations against mining activity represented to the country.

Josefina and Alfonso wanted me to get a different perspective from the ones presented in the NGO campaigns. They wanted me to realize that the geography of the region—its hostile climate and poor soils—made mining one of the only productive activities possible. Outsiders didn't understand this, Alfonso insisted, or the hardships that they had lived through in times of scarcity, unemployment, and the violence of the Shining Path years. "What do they know about the suffering of La Oroya? We prefer to die from the pollution than from hunger," he said. Josefina added: "What does it matter, if we are being contaminated, as long as we can offer our children a better future?"

I do not claim that the views expressed by Josefina and Alfonso were shared by a majority of La Oroya's residents. What I am interested in, rather, are the questions that their comments raise, and how they reflect the tragic contradictions of life in a toxic place. Fortun (2001) suggests that focusing on fields of contradiction, or double binds, can elucidate the way environmental crises produce new subject positions. In double-bind situations, individuals do not simply opt for the lesser of two evils but are forced to choose between incomparable options. People like Josefina and Alfonso felt condemned to a polluted environment, but their way of coping with this fate was to become advocates of the company that pollutes. To make sense of pollution and its effects on their lives, they interpreted, appropriated, and reconfigured the knowledge they received from different sources: NGOs, the company, and the media. Caught between resignation and resistance, they had to find new ways of understanding and engaging in everyday life, and a new language to justify their decisions. The result was not a predictable or clearly defined position, but the constant oscillation between denying the threats of pollution and defending the company's efforts to control it.

Corporate-community relations cannot be explained solely in terms of coercion or manipulation. When I talked to Alfonso, to Josefina, and to other women in her organization, their adamant support of Doe Run suggested a desire to be seen as agential subjects who were making a conscious compromise, choosing to accept the pollution in their surroundings while supporting the company responsible for causing it.

In his account of La Oroya's history, Alfonso recalled the time when he began to work at the smelter. "Oroya Antigua was [engulfed in] a blue cloud, we would cover our mouths with a wet cloth, we smelled of smoke, of mineral . . . and nobody said a thing. But not anymore. Now in Lima, everyone is talking about La Oroya." Alfonso denied that pollution in La Oroya had led to higher rates of asthma, cancer, and other diseases, as some people claimed. He acknowledged that there was some pollution but felt Doe Run was doing more than had ever been done by its predecessors and was adequately dealing with the problem. Alfonso told me that when Doe Run bought the smelter, it "imported concepts and brought new paradigms." He was referring to new corporate practices that differentiated Doe Run from its predecessor, the state-run Centromin. These "new norms" were part of what he saw as the company's interest in building *human* resources, rather than just focusing on infrastructural improvements. More generally, he was referring to Doe Run's emphasis on Corporate Social Responsibility (CSR),[11] to which he attributed many of the recent changes.

FIGURE 1.1 A billboard across from the smelter promotes Doe Run's work in "Foresting the Peruvian Andes."

Like Doe Run, the Cerro de Pasco Corporation and Centromin had a variety of programs intended to promote the well-being of workers and their families. These programs were usually run by female social workers and had elements of both discipline and surveillance: regular home visits to check on workers' living conditions and household habits, counseling for family problems ranging from alcoholism to family violence, educational seminars on health, literacy programs, and workshops for house-wives.

There was some continuity between these programs and the CSR programs put in place by Doe Run, but there were also some important differences. One was the expansion of social programs to include a larger segment of the population in the smelter's "area of influence," which did not just include people who were economically dependent on the company, but was determined in part by the reach of the pollutants. Second, the amount of money invested in community and environmental programs (and in publicizing them) was unprecedented (see figure 1.1). Finally, Doe Run's social programs had an explicit emphasis on *environmental* health and hygiene, the result of growing public concern around toxic pollution in La Oroya. Alfonso's and Josefina's comments provided a glimpse of how the changes that accompanied the introduction of "imported concepts and new paradigms" were understood and experienced locally.

For Alfonso, Doe Run's new approach prioritized education, skill development, and behavioral changes in the individual. For example, he mentioned that lead levels in workers had gone down in part because of a growing awareness of the workers themselves, who contributed to prevention and control measures. (According to Doe Run's *La Oroya: Report to Our Communities* [2006], the average level was 33.59 micrograms per deciliter [µg/dL], still well above the recommended limit of 10 µg/dL set by the World Health Organization.) Among its many community initiatives, a program called Human and Social Ecology provided low-income children with nutritious meals, tutoring, and weekly "body hygiene sessions," where children learned about hygiene habits and showered in the public bathrooms constructed by Doe Run. "Doe Run trains [*capacita*] the entire family. Even the role of women has changed," Alfonso told me, referring to the role of promotoras in the company's social programs. Josefina noted that if we want to stop pollution, we must first change the individual. She explained how the company's new strategies had changed people's habits: "Now we no longer . . . drink, we know how to manage our budgets. . . . The company has taught us to wash our hands, to dress, to shower, it has brought changes into the household." She implied that the old habits reflected a life of irresponsibility and immorality (excessive drinking and spending, for example). By contrast, she believed the company's programs were commendable precisely because they introduced changes in personal habits at the level of the family (not simply in the workplace).

Josefina's accounts about her volunteer work and Doe Run's environmental and social initiatives pointed to a key aspect of corporate community relations programs in La Oroya: an emphasis of public participation. In company initiatives ranging from participatory air monitoring programs to environmental and health campaigns, participation produced a double bind. Residents were compelled to participate in order to derive some benefit from the programs and to improve their living conditions, but doing so contributed to an appearance of public support for the company while limiting people's ability to speak out against it.[12] These avenues for participation created a grassroots movement that helped to legitimize Doe Run's corporate practices while discrediting the work of NGOs and community groups that protested against the company.[13]

Day Care for Lead-Poisoned Children

Doe Run's programs urged local residents to work on improving their own health and hygiene habits, discouraging them from focusing on the smelter's emissions as the primary source of pollution. Lifestyle changes such as improved nutrition, frequent hand washing, and preventing children from playing in the dirt were promoted as ways of reducing lead exposure and its effects. Neighborhood cleanups and tree planting were other ways in which the company sought to show that since *everyone* pollutes, all were responsible for finding solutions to La Oroya's environmental problems. Doe Run and the Ministry of Health (MINSA) consolidated these efforts into a comprehensive health and hygiene program. The agreement was signed in 2003, and in 2005 the Regional Government of Junín joined the initiative. As part of the program, all parts agreed to "establish general guidelines of cooperation to gradually diminish lead levels in the blood of the population at highest risk of exposure and those most vulnerable in the city of La Oroya with whom Doe Run does not have an employment relationship" (MINSA–Doe Run 2006).

The agreement or *Convenio* (as it came to be known by locals) included a number of programs aimed at reducing the effects of pollution and focused specifically on the most vulnerable group: children less than six years of age. Children are considered to be most susceptible to lead poisoning because their bodies are still developing, and they absorb a higher concentration of lead than adults. The Convenio's work was divided into two areas: First, an *epidemiological vigilance* program monitored lead levels in the population. Around eight hundred children and pregnant women participated in the yearly blood-testing drives. Second, *intervention programs* focused on healthy living and disease prevention. For example, schoolchildren and parents participated in the cleaning of educational institutions, streets, and play areas. Assisted by Convenio personnel, women armed with brooms and buckets swept the ground with water and detergent, with the aim of reducing the amount of lead-containing dust carried by the wind. As an extension of these cleaning campaigns, health promoters made house calls to evaluate household hygiene and cleaning habits. They gave advice to family members on personal hygiene and grooming (hand washing, nail cutting, bathing) and instructed them to clean the house with water and damp cloths to prevent the build-up of dust containing lead.[14]

Finally, in conjunction with these initiatives, the Convenio ran a program of "temporary distancing" (*alejamiento temporal*) for children living in Oroya Antigua. Each day, special buses transported up to eighty children identified as having high lead levels to a facility ten kilometers (six miles) from La Oroya. The children spent eight hours a day from Monday to Friday in the Casaracra Day Care (*Cuna Jardín Casaracra*). Part of the rationale for the program was that the most critical period of lead exposure was the early morning, when the toxic emissions from the smelter became trapped close to the ground, a climate phenomenon called thermal inversion. Thermal inversion occurs when the air close to the ground is colder than the layers of air above it, which reduces air circulation and prevents pollutants from dispersing (under normal conditions, the temperature is higher closer to the surface of the Earth and decreases with altitude). The coldest mornings in La Oroya produce this thermal inversion, which is broken once the sun warms the Earth's surface.

Promotional material described the Casaracra Day Care as a comprehensive educational, nutritional, pediatric, psychological, and hygiene program for children under six years of age. The staff consisted of ten teachers, a pediatrician, two psychologists, nurses, and a nutritionist. Although the teaching curriculum was the same as that of any other educational institution, Casaracra was unlike any day care or kindergarten in the country. On a tour of the facility, Roberto, the nurse in charge, took me around to the various classrooms and introduced me to the teachers. The children were divided by age groups, with names like "little angels," "bunny rabbits," and "bear cubs." Aside from the regular classrooms, there was also an "early stimulation room" for toddlers to develop their fine and gross motor skills (studies show that lead affects early childhood development), and a nap-time room for the youngest children. Modern bathrooms were fully equipped with showers, specially designed sinks, and child-size toilets.

In one of the classrooms, Roberto enthusiastically greeted one of the boys. Johny had the highest blood lead level of all the children: 91 μg/dL. In 1991, the U.S. Centers for Disease Control and Prevention (CDC) established that intervention is needed when a child is found to have a blood lead level above 10 μg/dL but also noted that this should not be seen as defining a threshold level for harmful effects, since children's mental and physical development can be affected even at levels below 10 μg/dL (CDC et al. 2005).[15] Toxicology studies suggest that more than 70 μg/dL presents a medical emergency and can produce health effects such as brain and kidney damage in children (UNEP-UNICEF 1997). Yet Roberto wanted me to see that Johny, based on his outward appearance and behavior, was a "normal" boy: "You can see it for yourself. He has problems like short stature, which is the reality here [in the highlands] . . . but it's not like some people might say, that these are kids who are sick, who cannot do anything . . . they make a series of comments." Roberto was referring to NGO campaigns and newspaper articles that cited developmental problems in children as a way to highlight the urgency of La Oroya's environmental problems. His remark implied that if I hadn't been told his lead level, I would never have guessed that Johny was one of La Oroya's "children of lead."

Lead toxicity levels can be assessed with a numerical equivalent, but the significance of this technical measurement is often malleable. Many people in La Oroya knew their blood lead levels or those of their children, and when the Convenio went into effect, the results of blood-testing drives acquired increased public visibility. For some, elevated blood lead levels signified a life condemned to illness, the cause of a death in the family, or an explanation for ongoing health symptoms with no apparent cure. These realizations motivated some people to denounce Doe Run and become involved in NGO and grassroots activism. Or, blood test results were turned into a resource, a way to acquire benefits such as medical attention and nutritional assistance for one's children. For others still, elevated blood lead levels were not a cause for concern and represented a necessary trade-off for the economic opportunities provided by the smelter. It is in these instances that exposure to risk becomes socially acceptable and normalized as it comes to be seen as an avenue of economic survival (cf. Petryna 2002).

These different ways of experiencing lead exposure in La Oroya led to disagreements about the effects of pollution on children's well-being. Although information on the long-term effects of toxic contaminants is often indeterminate, the health effects of lead poisoning have been long recognized and well studied. According to the U.S. Environmental Protection Agency, "the effects of lead exposure on fetuses and young children can be severe. They include delays in physical and mental development, lower IQ levels, shortened attention spans, and increased behavioral problems" (EPA 2013). Yet, much of the anger harbored by La Oroya residents against NGOs stemmed from reports stating that lead impairs children's development. Many people that I spoke to felt the need to assure me that their children were as intelligent as those anywhere else. They feared that La Oroya had been labeled as a sick town, where children were sickly and mentally challenged. Doe Run took advantage of this fear to fuel a counter-campaign against NGOs. Meanwhile, company officials and other experts attempted to shift the focus of the debate toward factors such as inadequate nutrition and hygiene habits, which were the primary targets of the Casaracra day-care program.

Critics of the Casaracra program pointed out that this was only a temporary solution, and what was needed was the overhaul of the smelter's technology to effectively reduce toxic emissions. In a study commissioned by USAID, scientists from the U.S. Centers for Disease Control and Prevention came to a similar conclusion after they visited La Oroya to provide technical assistance to the Peruvian Ministry of Health in formulating an environmental plan. Based on a ten-day technical visit to La Oroya in March 2004, the CDC report concluded that without the reduction of lead emissions from the smelter and the remediation of soil contamination accumulated over a long history of metallurgical activity, home hygiene and neighborhood cleaning campaigns would be of little value in decreasing elevated blood lead levels in La Oroya (CDC et al. 2005).

In an interview, the director of the Convenio defended their programs. He argued that immediate measures had to be taken before the CDC's recommendations could be met. With reference to the CDC's conclusions, he said: "We are not as drastic as they are. Peru is in a process of adaptation when it comes to mining and environmental management programs. . . . This has been the immediate answer. We cannot wait to intervene when it comes to matters of health." Both the Convenio's proponents and its critics evoked *time* and the immediacy of intervention to justify the strategies they proposed to reduce pollution. In the case of the former, urgent action meant dealing with the already existent pollution through health education and the temporary removal of children from the areas of critical exposure. For some NGOs and environmental advocates, however, urgent action would require the immediate relocation of Oroya Antigua and a radical improvement in the smelter's technology. In both cases, proponents of each type of intervention used the language of health to defend their position. However, while the CDC and NGOs working in La Oroya proposed a comprehensive treatment of air and soil pollution as a public health measure, the Convenio located pollution primarily in the bodies of individuals.

Each of these approaches is implicitly based on particular time frames and ways of measuring pollution that determine what kinds of equivalences are possible. The programs that were part of the Convenio posited that temporary distancing was equivalent to a reduction of risk, as defined by the number of hours that children were exposed to the smelter's emissions (sixteen hours instead of twenty-four hours a day). Recognizing the historical pollution of La Oroya and the continued effects of the smelter's emissions, some individuals and institutions proposed the permanent relocation of Oroya Antigua (e.g., CONAM 2007). These actors rejected Doe Run's claims that fewer hours of exposure signified a reduced health risk. From this perspective, the improvements that could result from health and hygiene campaigns (as defined by average blood lead levels) were not sufficient to counteract the present and future risks of toxic exposure.

On the other hand, some types of equivalence were necessary for advocacy campaigns. Different ways of measuring pollution—blood tests, or the monitoring of sulfur dioxide levels, suspended particulate matter, and other pollutants—allowed for comparisons with international standards, which helped activists make a case for the severity of the situation in La Oroya. International standards set by the WHO led to assertions that the smelter's emissions exceeded the acceptable limits for sulfur dioxide, cadmium, arsenic, and other pollutants (Cederstav and Barandiarán 2002), and that more than 99 percent of children had lead levels above the CDC's recommended limit of 10 µg/dL. International comparisons made a powerful impact, catapulting La Oroya into the international spotlight.

While NGOs and environmental advocates relied on these international indexes of comparison, the comment made by the Convenio's director ("We are not as drastic as they are") suggested that Peru and countries such as the United States were not equivalent. From his point of view, they could not be expected to meet the same environmental standards (at least, not given the same time frame). Programs such as the Casaracra Day Care were intended to resolve the smelter's problems in the present—but in so doing, critics affirmed, they deferred the costs of environmental remediation into the future and avoided dealing with the past (for which neither the corporation nor the government could be held accountable).

The Convenio's day-care and health and hygiene programs could be seen as initiatives designed to produce new, environmental subjects (cf. Agrawal 2005; Murray Li 2007). It was not only children who were the focus of such efforts, but also their parents, caretakers, and the general population of La Oroya. By focusing on the body, and on ways of controlling pollution through the body, these initiatives brought people together in a common project, even if they did not necessarily have faith in the outcomes of the program or in the benevolence of Doe Run. This may well have been the case for parents of the Casaracra children, whose acceptance of the free meals, education, medical care, and other benefits for their children did not necessarily translate into loyalty to the company or a new environmental consciousness.

Doe Run's critics often accused the company (and allies such as the Ministry of Health, in the case of the Convenio) of manipulating people through economic incentives to support their programs. While accusations of corruption abound when it comes to government officials and community leaders, this explanation does not account for the hundreds of local residents who willingly participated in the "grassroots volunteerism" fostered by the company. Certainly, the material rewards played a part in motivating the women to participate. However, perhaps stronger—and much more important in terms of the program's goals—was the shared sense of responsibility that gave meaning to the women's participation, and prompted them to get involved regardless of their stance toward the company. Participation did not necessarily mean compliance; the women's involvement rested on the acceptance of responsibility, rather than the acceptance of Doe Run's corporate agenda or the company's definition of pollution.

Indeed, even NGOs and local residents who were critical of the company and of the Convenio proposed their own campaigns and programs that used many of the same strategies, and that also relied on the same language of empowerment, participation, and health and hygiene promotion. For example, some NGO initiatives involved training "environmental delegates" and providing nutritional assistance (food and vitamin supplements) to children and pregnant and lactating mothers in Oroya Antigua. These programs, too, seemed guided by a sense of shared responsibility and short-term goals that addressed the health crisis.

La Oroya and Mining Conflicts

The controversies over pollution in La Oroya illustrate how, through a span of generations, people in La Oroya have lived their lives *with* and *against* pollution. Following Doe Run's acquisition of the smelter, lead and other contaminants emerged as public health threats. Many factors contributed to this new visibility of pollution, including NGO campaigns and international activism, health studies on lead exposure, and media attention on the environmental problems in La Oroya. However, the company's own actions also played a part. Corporate public relations campaigns, as well as programs in conjunction with government institutions, contributed to making lead and other contaminants into newly significant environmental actors. But corporate discourses and practices constituted these nonhuman actors in very particular ways. Lead was to be found in dust, on children's hands, in households, and in people's bodies—and in all these cases, the company argued that it could be contained and fought through the promotion of hygiene and preventive health measures. This way of conceiving lead pollution ran counter to the knowledges produced by environmentalists and NGOs, who located pollution in the air, water, and soil in La Oroya and the surrounding area—uncontainable, unruly, and potentially threatening to an entire population. It was this definition of pollution—and the political effects that it generated—that Doe Run attempted to control.

It could be said that programs such as the Convenio's day care aimed to fulfill the long-standing promise of "modernity" that the smelter represented. At the turn of the twentieth century, this promise was to be fulfilled by the smelter's technological sophistication; at the turn of the twenty-first century, the promise of modernity rested on new practices of accountability that were to give La Oroya a "green" image consistent with the "modern" mining being heralded by transnational companies elsewhere in the country. Programs that focused on personal transformation through a change of habits related to hygiene, nutrition, health, and the environment were aimed at producing informed subjects responsible for their own well-being. These efforts relied on the rhetoric of public participation, environmental management, and scientific expertise, which served to shift the focus from corporate accountability to the *sharing of responsibility*.

La Oroya was born from the conjuncture of socionatural forces that not only influenced the development of capitalist expansion and industrial development, but created a particular sense of place. People's sense of belonging and attachment to this place emerged from the paradox that defines La Oroya's reason for being: the smelter's promise of modernity, and its capacity to destroy forms of life. In the early 1900s, the convergence of capital, technology, and pollution transformed the Central Highlands and the Peruvian mining industry. The effects of the "smoke" could not be ignored, yet it would take almost one century for chemical reactions and contested knowledges about pollution to come together and make La Oroya into a national and international symbol of pollution. Though present since the construction of the smelter, the emissions *came to matter* as scientific studies, lawsuits, corporate programs, and environmentalist campaigns identified its components, measured them, and monitored their effects. Various forms of expertise—from mining engineering to environmental and health sciences—fostered the emergence of new matters of concern that introduced uncertainties around toxicity and risk.

The new visibility of pollution in La Oroya came at a time when issues related to "the environment" were gaining more public attention in Peru, a trend that also coincided with the intensification of mining activity brought about by neoliberal reforms in the 1990s. These reforms introduced a series of new projects in areas that did not have the same long history of mining as the Central Highlands. As I will explore in the chapters that follow, the exploration and extractive activities of transnational companies were provoking tensions with local communities and, in some cases, organized opposition to mining activity. Activism in other parts of the country also focused on concerns about health and the environment and generated local and international solidarity links that helped raise awareness about the consequences of extractive activity. As in La Oroya, watersheds, rivers, and the spread of pollutants would help mobilize people in opposition to mining companies.

As talk of "mining conflicts" began to take hold, the smelter in La Oroya and the century-old mines that surrounded it came to represent the legacy of "old" mining practices. Meanwhile, transnational corporations sought to remake the industry's image by portraying their operations as a new kind of "environmentally responsible" or "sustainable mining" (cf. Kirsch 2010). These strategies often mirrored Doe Run's emphasis on public participation and the environment and involved communities through an ethic of shared responsibility.

For communities confronted with modern mining projects that promised to operate with zero pollution and jump-start the economy, La Oroya provided dramatic visual evidence—clouds of toxic emissions, lifeless rivers, and lead-poisoned children—of the consequences of mining activity. In protests against mining in different parts of the country, the Central Highlands were often depicted as an impoverished, underdeveloped region where mining has only brought social ills and environmental devastation. "We don't want to be another La Oroya," people declared in rallies and written manifestos opposing mining activity in other regions. NGO networks enabled activists from places like Tambogrande, in the coastal department of Piura, to visit La Oroya as a warning to what could come with mining development. In pamphlets and communiqués put out by grassroots groups, a mention of La Oroya or the town of Cerro de Pasco served as a kind of shorthand to convey the social and environmental costs of mining activity. "Mining that pollutes the health and life of the people in La Oroya and Cerro de Pasco is unsustainable," proclaimed a booklet published in 2004 by CONACAMI (National Confederation of Communities Affected by Mining), countering the "myth" that mining is compatible with sustainable development. La Oroya was to serve as a warning for activists organizing against mining activity elsewhere in the country.

In chapter 2, I turn to another site of controversy: the Yanacocha mine, in the Cajamarca region. For both its supporters and critics, Yanacocha has come to epitomize "modern" mining, with the presumed advantages or threats that come with new mining projects. This chapter showed how efforts to make pollution visible (or invisible) through science, political organizing, and corporate strategies are at the root of controversies over mining. In the next chapter, I focus on controversies over water in Cajamarca as I continue to explore corporate practices, activism, and the ways in which pollution comes to matter in the context of mining activity.

CHAPTER 2

MEGA-MINING AND EMERGENT CONFLICTS

Cajamarca's past and present are linked by gold. It was in Cajamarca's town square that, in 1532, the Spaniard Francisco Pizarro captured Atahualpa, the last Inca emperor. Atahualpa may have underestimated the threat posed by the Europeans and was unprepared for the outcome of his fateful encounter with Pizarro, which led to the massacre of thousands of Atahualpa's soldiers in the town square. In an attempt to gain his freedom upon being captured, Atahualpa promised the Spanish a ransom of gold and silver—enough treasures to fill a room, once with gold, and twice with silver. Atahualpa kept his promise, but after the treasures were melted down and distributed among the Spaniards, he was killed.

Today, the "ransom room" where Atahualpa was purportedly held captive is a popular tourist attraction near the modern-day Plaza de Armas, and the encounter between Atahualpa and Pizarro figures prominently in the popular memory. Not surprisingly, Minera Yanacocha's arrival in Cajamarca in 1992 gave rise to talk about a "second conquest." For the mine's critics, the analogy was meant to evoke the treachery and deceit of the Spaniards, the complicity of the natives who helped them, and the plunder of resources for the benefit of people in foreign lands.

While the story of the conquest was particularly poignant for people in Cajamarca, the arrival of Minera Yanacocha also brought to mind a more recent history of exploitation during the colonial and republican periods. For many Peruvians, the Cerro de Pasco mines and the smelter town of La Oroya in the Central Highlands were a well-known testament to the country's mining history. In the Cajamarca region, the legacy of mining activity could also be seen in the province of Hualgayoc, an important silver mining center since the colonial period. In communities around the Yanacocha mine, many people had worked in Hualgayoc and knew firsthand about the dangers and hardships of the miners' lives. Popular narratives about the conquest, colonial exploitation, and imperialism associated with mining provided a lens for reinterpreting the past with relation to Peru's emergence as one of the world's most important gold-producing countries at the turn of the twenty-first century.

Images of plunder, dangerous underground mines, and exploitative working conditions were precisely the images that the mining industry wanted to dispel as transnational companies began to establish themselves in the Peruvian countryside in the 1990s. An influx of foreign investment brought with it the neoliberal promise of economic growth and development. Yanacocha was not simply another mine—it was to signify the country's political stability after the turbulent decade of the 1980s, a favorable climate for investment, and the ability to compete in the global economy. It also represented a revolution in mining: state-of-the-art technology, economic efficiency, and what seemed like an unlimited potential for expansion. The Yanacocha mine was not only a symbol of the mining bonanza in Peru but single-handedly accounted for more than 40 percent of gold production in the country.[1]

To counter popular narratives of plunder and create a more positive view of mining, companies crafted a rhetoric of "modern mining," which promised to both contribute to local communities (based on a "good neighbor" policy) and safeguard the environment. Although the industry's rhetoric sometimes seems to suggest a complete rupture between "old" and "new" forms of mining, the country's history of extraction presents a picture of both difference and continuity. For example, both "old" and "new" mining have involved transnational actors (except for a period of nationalization during the government of Juan Velasco Alvarado, in office from 1968 to 1975). Thus, foreign investment and corporate practices have played a key role in the development of the extractive sector and the country's political and economic policies since the turn of the twentieth century. It is also true that both "old" and "new" mines make indelible traces on the landscape, release pollutants into the environment, and create risks for workers and neighboring communities. However, in spite of these similarities between mines like Yanacocha and earlier mines in places like Hualgayoc and Cerro de Pasco, there are also differences that have shaped the dynamics of recent conflicts in response to mining activity.

In thinking about these differences, it may be helpful to draw on anthropologist James Ferguson's (2006) distinction between "socially thick" and "socially thin" practices of extraction in Africa. In the case of socially thick projects (such as Zambia's state-owned copper mines, as described by Ferguson), mines employ workers from local communities, providing a source of livelihood for a large segment of the population. In company towns typical of the mining industry, companies might also provide hospitals, schools, a company store, and social services for workers and their families. Some of these characteristics could be observed during the time of the Cerro de Pasco Corporation, as well as during the Centromin period of state ownership. While this model might still be based on relationships of exploitation and paternalism, a business could be deemed to be socially thick if it has a broader engagement with communities in the vicinity of its operations.

By contrast, socially thin operations create enclaves that generate few benefits for people affected by extractive activity. Jobs are specialized, and companies often rely on professionals and skilled workers brought in from other parts of the country and the world. These enclaves are isolated from the larger community not only socially and economically, but sometimes also physically through the use of security firms hired to guard the area and restrict access to the mine's property.

It could be argued that some aspects of "socially thin" extraction projects apply to the case of Peruvian mining. For example, the technologies of modern mines require a small, specialized labor force that cannot absorb the employment needs of campesino communities in the immediate vicinity. In the 1990s, neoliberal reforms introduced labor laws that allowed transnational mining companies to rely on short-term, subcontracted labor. While mine workers' unions were once some of the most powerful in the country, these reforms have weakened organized labor and have created a new dynamic where unionized workers are sometimes allied with mining companies (in part, to protect their jobs). Furthermore, it has also become evident in recent conflicts that companies are relying on private security (with the backing of state forces) and laws that criminalize protest to protect their operations and control local resistance.

The characteristics of new mining projects not only are a result of corporate and state policies but relate to changes in the process of extraction, the technologies used in mining operations, and the location of the mines. In Peru, as in other Latin American countries, the term *megaminería* (mega-mining) refers to open-pit mining projects established in the past couple of decades. The term puts emphasis on the sheer scale of the mines and the technologies necessary to process low-grade ore and implies that these projects have a larger ecological footprint and more profound social consequences than older mines. While modern mining promises to control toxic substances like cyanide from being released into the environment, its technologies have produced significant changes in local communities and people's livelihoods.

As was the case in the Central Highlands, the expansion of mining activity into the Cajamarca region transformed the landscape, albeit with different consequences for local communities. In the Andean world, miners gave offerings (of food, coca leaves, etc.) to earth-beings that they had to appease in exchange for the removal of the mineral wealth and to guarantee their own safety in the mineshafts. By contrast, mega-mining razes mountains, unearthing the beings that inhabit the landscape (de la Cadena 2010). By destroying the mountains, mega-mining also annihilates relationships between people and an agentive landscape.

Open-pit mining is often located at the headwaters of the river basin and takes with it sources of water and pasturelands on which people depend. Thus, these projects not only remake territories but also contribute to the destruction of forms of life and ways of living. In the Central Highlands, mining and metallurgical activity often provided employment while allowing people to continue to live in peasant communities and engage in agriculture. In Cajamarca, on the other hand, the arrival of Minera Yanacocha disrupted existing forms of livelihood, including agriculture and dairy farming, and many campesinos came to see mining as a threat to their survival. In the Peruvian countryside, the laws of the market do not make small-scale highland agriculture economically profitable. For state and corporate actors, the ways of living that campesinos are trying to defend are not a cause worth fighting for, but something that will soon disappear (or that must be made to disappear). How, then, does one argue with an evolutionist logic in which mining is portrayed as the inevitable road to progress?

To counter the dominant narrative that presents mining as a driver of economic growth and national prosperity, people organizing against mining expansion have described their struggle as being over the "defense of life." What linked different sites of mining conflict, from Cajamarca to La Oroya and beyond, were counternarratives focused on the negative consequences of mining activity. In La Oroya, air pollution and a focus on the impacts of lead poisoning on children's health provided a rallying point. In Cajamarca, changes in water quality and quantity became the central point of contention. Minera Yanacocha tried to downplay these concerns and accused protestors of using water issues as a political strategy to gain public support while concealing other motives for the protests. However, examining the technologies of modern mining highlights why water became a relevant player in the conflicts. The Yanacocha mine encompasses bodies of water that were used by local communities. At the same time, Minera Yanacocha has made water into a focal point of its environmental and community relations programs, and the company claims that its operations do not affect water quality or quantity. That water issues have become the basis of contestation shows the indeterminacy of environmental assessment, and the use of corporate strategies to disqualify arguments that challenge its operations.

As one of the first transnational large-scale mining operations in Peru, Yanacocha promised to bring with it a new model for environmental management and community relations. In spite of accidents, spills, and other setbacks, the company put great effort into presenting the mining process as a tightly controlled system that did not produce pollution or harm the environment. The challenge for local people was to counter these claims by calling attention to the negative effects of mining activity on communities and the environment. However, as the previous chapter on La Oroya's toxic emissions demonstrates, making pollution visible is not a straightforward task.

In Cajamarca and other mining regions, controversies over mining have put the language and tools of science at the forefront of debates. In her study of transgenic crops, Abby Kinchy (2012) has observed a tendency toward scientization in contemporary environmental controversies, meaning the transformation of political conflict into debates among scientific experts. In debates over genetically modified foods, as in mining conflicts, discourse around scientific risk puts the focus on the calculation of environmental impacts and the implementation of rational technocratic solutions, overshadowing questions around social and ethical concerns. At the same time, activists and local people have a greater stake in the way science is made, and their struggles are also struggles over whose knowledge counts as legitimate. These are also conflicts over what counts as equivalent in the calculation and evaluation of environmental impacts. Some actors use equivalences to justify mining activity while dismissing nonscientific forms of knowing, including knowledge that is based on experiential and sensory information.[2]

In this chapter I describe Yanacocha's technologies of water and mining to show the intricate connections between the mine and the people whose lives and livelihoods are affected by the water, sediments, and pollutants coming from the mine's property. I then examine how both activism and corporate practices have focused on controversies over water and efforts to monitor water quality, putting science and expertise at the center of recent conflicts. Through environmental studies and water monitoring programs, canal users, NGOs, company spokespeople, and local and international institutions negotiate what counts as valid knowledge.

Visiting the Mine

I arrived at the Yanacocha bus stop, on the edge of the city, shortly before 8 AM in preparation for my visit to the mine. A few weeks earlier, I had submitted a written request to participate in one of the tours of the mine, and once my request was approved I was scheduled to join a group that was convened by the regional Pharmacists' Association. The visits were conducted almost daily as part of Yanacocha's public relations efforts. More than twenty thousand visitors participated in the program each year, about half of them workers of Yanacocha and its subcontractors who must take part in these visits annually (Minera Yanacocha 2006:49). The rest of the visitors were students, workers' family members, campesinos from neighboring communities, professional associations, journalists, and any other groups or individuals that wished to participate.

Once all the participants had arrived, we boarded a large bus that would take us up to the mine. After taking our seats, our guide, Alfredo, warmly welcomed us on behalf of the company and its employees. He passed around consent forms for us to sign, along with a survey containing seven multiple-choice questions about our opinions of the company prior to the visit. For example, we were asked if the water released by Yanacocha from its treatment plant is of good, regular, or bad quality. We were also asked to rate the company with respect to the environment, social responsibility, safety, and mining processes. We received the same questionnaire after our tour of the mine. The practice of handing out the same survey at the beginning and end of the visit suggests that the company wanted to establish whether, once they were *informed* about the operations and environmental programs, people would have a more positive impression of the mine. Indeed, the surveys allowed the company to assert in its 2006 annual report that "70 percent of visitors had a favorable opinion" of Yanacocha after the visit, a 10 percent increase from the previous year (Minera Yanacocha 2006:49).

Alfredo told us about safety requirements, and the need to wear vests, goggles, and hard hats at all times while outside the bus. These details were fundamental to the performance of safety and responsibility throughout our visit. As we got on the highway and the bus began its slow ascent into the mountains, Alfredo began recounting the history of the mine. In the 1960s, prospectors were interested in copper, since it was more profitable and more coveted than gold—a situation that changed dramatically with fluctuations in the price of metals. Peru is a mining country, said Alfredo, noting that mining has been an important activity since pre-Colombian times. Mines from the colonial period, such as those in Hualgayoc, left mine wastes and environmental damages, and even in the republican period, there were no laws that obligated companies to care for the environment. Alfredo's message was that modern mining does what this long history of extraction never did, since regulations now demand environmental assessment, mitigation, and remediation. In his view, Minera Yanacocha represented the new paradigm of Corporate Social Responsibility promoted in the discourse of the mining industry and its supporters.

The Yanacocha mine is located an hour's drive (30 kilometers [19 miles], or 14 kilometers [9 miles] straight line) from the city of Cajamarca (see figure 2.1 and map 2.1). The close proximity of the mine to a major city makes Yanacocha different from mining outposts in highland regions, which are usually located far from major cities. The city of Cajamarca and

FIGURE 2.1 The city of Cajamarca, located south of the Yanacocha mine.

the campesino communities around the mine are essentially Yanacocha's "mining camps." Although workers on a "four by four" schedule stay at the mine facilities (working four consecutive days, twelve hours a day, followed by four days off), there is a constant movement of workers traveling to and from the mine. Engineers and mine executives, too, travel back and forth in their 4x4s from the mine to their homes in the nearby suburb of Baños del Inca. This highway is also used by convoys of vehicles carrying various products that are used or produced at the mine: petroleum, mercury, dynamite, and the bars of "doré" (a mixture of gold and silver) that are transported at night in armored vehicles.

Along the side of the highway were houses of contrasting styles: ones made of adobe and others of *material noble* (cement or brick rather than adobe, often finished with a tile façade). In May, just before the dry season, the hills were still green and the fields looked like a patchwork of small squares and rectangles, filled with corn stalks or rye grass. Eucalyptus and pine trees also covered the rolling mountains. As we traveled along the winding highway, the presence of Minera Yanacocha was evident before

MAP 2.1 The property of the Yanacocha mine with relation to the city of Cajamarca, major rivers, and key field sites. Cartography by Bill Nelson, based on a map elaborated by Laura Lucio.

any of the mine's installations became visible. Latrine doors were painted with the Yanacocha logo, and signs by the side of the road indicated the amounts of money spent by the company on infrastructure and development projects in each of the communities along the way.

The campesino communities in Cajamarca are known as *caseríos*, or hamlets. Around thirty thousand people live in the caseríos around the mine (CAO 2005). Most households are primarily involved in dairy farming, small-scale agricultural production (growing tuber crops, maize, and grains primarily for consumption), sheep herding, and raising small animals like pigs, chickens, ducks, and guinea pigs. A small number of people supplement these activities with weaving, stone carving, and other artisanal crafts. Campesinos have also long relied on seasonal or semipermanent migration to the coast, Lima, or other regions for supplementary incomes (Bury 2005). Before the arrival of the mine, the area had already undergone a series of transformations: the concentration of land into haciendas as a legacy of the colonial period; the growing economic importance of cattle and dairy farming in the early 1900s; and the eventual break-up of the hacienda system beginning in the 1960s.

When Minera Yanacocha arrived in Cajamarca in the early 1990s, the area that was to become the world's second-largest gold mine was a *jalca* ecosystem of tributary basins,[3] lagoons, water springs, bunchgrasses, and cushion plants that characterize the landscape at more than 3,500 meters above sea level. Mining engineers making their first forays into the area to conduct exploratory studies would have found dispersed adobe houses, grazing animals, and irrigation canals carrying water from the springs that feed them to fields downstream, compensating for what can be a treacherously dry climate in the months from May to September. They would also have encountered a campesino economy that both depended on and defied the extreme conditions of the jalca environment: the heavy rains in the wet season, and the arid soils, cold winds, and frosts of the dry season.

In the initial phase of development, Minera Yanacocha purchased land from forty-one families living in the concession area (Obispado de Cajamarca 1998, cited in Leyva Valera and Jahncke Benavente 2002). Small-scale peasant agriculture, sheep grazing, and dairy farming were the main sources of livelihood in communities in the area encompassed by the mining concession; 87 percent of the land sold to Minera Yanacocha had been used for grazing cattle, while around 12 percent was used for barley and potato crops (Leyva Valera and Jahncke Benavente 2002). A growing population, the gradual intensification of dairy farming, and the subdivision of plots of land by parents to be passed on as inheritance to their children had already put a strain on the land and resources necessary to maintain an agricultural way of life. Perhaps it was the hardships of life in the countryside and the precariousness of a peasant livelihood that made some campesinos receptive to the offers made by a group of engineers wanting to buy their land.

For those who agreed to sell, the sum of one hundred soles per hectare (around US$50 at the time) signified unimagined wealth and the promise of a better life in the city. Others were more hesitant but felt obligated to sell their land after being told that it would be expropriated by the government if they refused to sell it voluntarily. None of these *"exproprietarios"* (ex-landowners), as they are now referred to by the mining company, had any inkling that their property would one day form part of one of the largest mines in the world. Indeed, the rapid expansion of the Yanacocha mine and the revenue generated from it surpassed even the company's most optimistic projections. Cyanide leaching technologies, combined with minimal environmental regulations, low labor costs, and low tributary payments, would make the Yanacocha gold mine one of the most profitable in the world.

During the administration of Alberto Fujimori, companies such as Minera Yanacocha signed legal stability agreements that locked in each firm's tax status. The agreements, which were aimed at promoting foreign investment, allowed companies to reinvest profits tax-free, while others were exempt from paying royalties. While Yanacocha's production costs were a record low, the price of gold steadily increased since the time the company began operating. When Minera Yanacocha produced the first bar of gold, the gold price was around US$330 per ounce. By 2006, the price of gold had doubled; and it surpassed the US$1,000 mark for the first time in March 2008. These windfall earnings added to the sense of injustice felt by people who did not feel they had reaped any benefit from the mine's presence, and especially by campesinos who had given up their land.

Between 1992 and 1999, Minera Yanacocha purchased a total of 10,200 hectares of land from 126 families for a sum that the company insists exceeded the market price at the time. But for campesinos and the mine's critics, these initial land sales represent the first of many injustices that would follow. Some ex-proprietarios, with the mediation of the NGO GRUFIDES, demanded compensation for what they saw as deceitful transactions; instead of demanding a cash settlement, however, they pushed for a land-for-land agreement that would give campesinos a piece of property on the coast as compensation for the land they lost. Many of the campesinos who sold their properties simply resigned themselves to the short-lived profits of the land sales and the only privilege that comes with being an ex-proprietario: having priority in the company's hiring of temporary unskilled laborers. For those who continued to live in the surrounding area, having the mine as an increasingly intrusive neighbor brought challenges as well as growing expectations.

For many, the arrival of the mining company signified opportunities for employment. Employment is often the primary reason why people support mining activity, and mining companies have used the motto that "mining creates jobs" as a way to garner public support. Yet one of the characteristics of modern mining is its relatively small labor force. In 2006, Minera Yanacocha had 2,946 workers on its payroll and 9,595 workers hired on a temporary basis by subcontractors.[4] The result then is a situation in which few job opportunities arise, and of these, even fewer are available for unskilled workers or campesinos from the local area. For those who are not on the company payroll, contract work is usually low paying, short-term, unstable, and without benefits. In Cajamarca, the discrepancy between the "messianic expectations" of employment (in the words of local priest Marco Arana) and the reality of a small labor force in modern mines is central to current debates over resource extraction. Along with expectations of employment, mining brought with it a new narrative of progress and promises that, from the outset, were impossible to fulfill.

Large-scale mining cannot meet the demand for jobs in local communities, a situation that shows a marked contrast with mining in the early twentieth century. In the Central Highlands, peasants continued to depend on subsistence agriculture and combined this form of livelihood with wage labor at the mines. Agricultural activity and mining were complementary, and mining work was based on temporary migration, since campesinos had little incentive to move permanently to an urban center. In Cajamarca, too, campesinos worked at the Hualgayoc mines or on the coast as a supplement to their rural economies. This work did not interfere with their agricultural activities or alter their way of life, as did the presence of Minera Yanacocha. With these newer projects, local people were made to compete with the mining company for the same resources: land and water.

Of course, the arrival of the mine is not the only event that has transformed the landscape. As our bus continued to wind up the mountains approaching the mine, it was possible to see some of the elements that, through the years, were introduced into this landscape. Cattle dotting the hillsides represented an important source of livelihood, as dairy farming intensified with an increased demand for milk products and their commercialization by two transnational dairy companies, Nestlé and Gloria. Closer to the mine, an extensive forest of pine trees, planted as part of an internationally funded forestation project and used for the paper and lumber industries, marked the property of the evangelical cooperative known as the Granja Porcón (Porcón Farm). The farm was a popular sightseeing destination that attracted visitors with a small zoo, a restaurant, and programs that had begun to be marketed as "agro-tourism." These and other activities have shaped relationships between people and the land and have created linkages among local, national, and international actors. The Yanacocha mine inserted itself into these rapidly changing relations and contributed to an even more dramatic transformation.

Around 3,500 meters above sea level, as the air cools and the vegetation changes to the high-elevation grassland known as the *puna*, the mine's installations start to become visible. Beyond a row of pines, manufactured mountains punctuate the scenery. These neatly piled mountains of crushed ore, which resemble truncated pyramids, are watered with a cyanide solution to recover the valuable metals contained in the ore. As the mine expanded, Yanacocha became the largest mine in the world using cyanide leaching technology. The Yanacocha mine is made up of a network of open pits at various stages of operation or closure, leach pads, waste dumps, and processing facilities. The mine property covers a total land area in excess of 20,000 hectares (MWH 2009) and lies within four major basins (the Porcón, Honda, Chonta, and Rejo basins) spanning the continental divide. Given its expansive reach, the mine cannot be envisioned as a single entity separate from the surrounding landscape. The mine property encompasses irrigation infrastructure and sources of water used by local farmers and overlaps with grazing areas still used by campesinos who have received permission from the company to do so.

FIGURE 2.2 Lake Yanacocha, 1992. Activists used this image in public presentations and publications to show how the mine made lakes in the region disappear. Photograph by Alois Eichenlaub.

Anthropologist Julie Cruikshank (2005) reminds us that landscape features act as points of reference anchoring memories, values, and tacit knowledge. The effects of modern mining on the landscape are so trans-formative that some people living in the vicinity of the Yanacocha mine say mining swallows up mountains and makes lakes disappear, leaving behind only their names (see figure 2.2). Yanacocha ("Black Lake" in Quechua, Peru's most widely spoken indigenous language) was the name of a lake that was drained in 1999 to mine a mountain of the same name. The mine's other open pits each bear the local names of mountains, lakes, and canyons: Cerro Negro, La Quinua, Carachugo, Maqui Maqui, San José. As Keith Basso writes (1996:13), "place-names can offer evidence of changes in the landscape, showing clearly that certain localities do not present the appearance they did in former times." Named locations make the landscape legible and attest to its radical transformation. After years of uneasy coexistence with the mine, people in the surrounding area are keenly aware not only of the mine's new additions to the landscape, but more importantly, of that which is no longer there. The mine's installa-tions are a visible sign of absence, and their names are an ironic reminder of once familiar landmarks.

Cyanide, Water, and Gold

Our first stop on our mine tour was the Rejo River dike. We got out of the bus and walked on the pedestrian bridge atop the 35-meter dike, giving us a view of the water on both sides. The function of the dike was to control the increased sediment loads generated by operations at the mine, especially during the rainy season. Alfredo pointed out that the water from the dike flowed directly to the fish farm at Granja Porcón just downstream from us, and that the trout served as a kind of bio-indicator of water quality. Alfredo did not mention that the dike was constructed after several incidents that led to the death of thousands of trout at Granja Porcón in 2002. Three events are mentioned in Yanacocha's annual report for that year: On May 28, eight thousand trout died by suffocation when a storm provoked an increased sediment load from the mine's area of operation. On August 3, construction work killed twenty-two hundred trout, while another event between October 26 and November 7 resulted in the "disappearance" of 26,500 trout (Minera Yanacocha 2002:66). Following these events, Minera Yanacocha implemented some sediment control measures at the fish farm. The company signed cooperation agreements with the directive of the Granja, and the fish farm became a kind of showcase used to demonstrate that mining and other economic activities could coexist. For Minera Yanacocha's critics, however, the trout deaths offered a clear indication that there were problems with the quality of the water coming from the mine.

Continuing with the visit, the bus took us from the Rejo River dike farther into the property of the mine. Unlike extractive methods that require tunneling into the earth to follow the mineral veins, open pit mining involves the removal of surface layers of soil to expose low-grade ore deposits beneath it. On average, the ore mined at Yanacocha contains between 0.8 to 1 gram (0.03 ounces) of microscopic gold (also called "invisible gold") in each ton of ore. The first step in the mining process involves drilling holes in the pit and filling them with explosives, which are detonated to break up large blocks of earth. More than 500,000 tons of earth are moved each day as haul trucks remove layer after layer of soil, barren rock, and mineral ore. A mining pit can measure more than 150 hectares in diameter, and more than 500 meters in depth. If the open pit is to extend below the groundwater table, it must be dewatered before being

FIGURE 2.3 Heap leach pad (*background*) and pond. Photograph by Brando Palacios.

mined. In this process, water must be pumped continuously from wells around the mine to lower the water table. Mine dewatering is necessary to ensure the stability of mine walls and prevent flooding. Critics argue that open-pit mining depletes the water table and alters ground and surface water flows, but the company denies that its operations have an effect on water availability.

The ore extracted from the pit is crushed into smaller loose rock and piled in heaps that can reach 120 meters·in height (see figure 2.3). The heap leach pad is watered with a cyanide solution with a concentration of 50 parts per million (or 50 grams of cyanide per 1,000 liters of water). Cyanide has the quality of binding to gold, so as it seeps through the heap leach pad, it picks up and leaches (or lixiviates) the microscopic gold particles. The cyanide solution passes through the mineral to produce the "rich solution" (also called "pregnant solution") containing gold and silver. To construct the pad, the area where the ore will be deposited is cleared of large rocks and covered with a soil liner (compacted clay) 30 centimeters thick. Then, the geomembrane (a polyethylene liner) is installed to create imperme-ability and prevent leaks, and it is covered by another layer of fine soil 30 centimeters thick. Pipes are installed beneath the pad to collect the rich solution and direct it to the heap leach pond, from which it is pumped to the processing plant. The leaching cycle can last from several days to several months, depending on the quantity and quality of the ore.

The gold in the pregnant solution is recovered using one of two processes: the Merrill-Crowe zinc precipitation method (using zinc powder, which reacts with cyanide, to solidify the gold) or carbon adsorption (carbon adsorbs, or attracts, gold particles to its surface). The gold is melted onsite in a smelter and poured to create doré bars, which are about 90 percent pure gold. The doré bars are shipped offsite to a refinery where they undergo further processing.

Once the gold has been recovered, the "barren" solution that remains (and still contains cyanide) is enriched with more cyanide and reutilized in the heap leach process. Since the cyanide solution is recycled, rather than treated and released into the environment, Minera Yanacocha calls its heap leach process a "closed" system. As we gathered by the heap leach pond during our tour of the mine, Alfredo described a seemingly flawless process. Yet environmental activists argue that cyanide spills and accidents pose significant risks for humans and wildlife (Mineral Policy Center 2000). In a spill at the Aural Gold Plant in Romania in 2000, a cyanide-laden tailings spill contaminated the Tisza River, killing aquatic wildlife and poisoning water supplies. The spill led to 1,240 tons of dead fish, and the contamination was found four weeks later 2,000 kilometers from the spill source (Moran 2001b). Because of the highly toxic nature of cyanide, its use in mining is controversial. Cyanide was first used on a large scale in the 1970s,[5] and it is now widely used in the gold industry throughout the world (more than 90 percent of gold is mined using the cyanide leaching process). In the United States, some states (such as Montana) have banned its use, prohibiting the development of new cyanide-leach mines.

In Minera Yanacocha's narrative of the mining process, all toxic substances are carefully controlled with sensors to detect leaks of cyanide solution from the pads and ponds. A system of underdrains, pipes, and storm water ponds collects all excess water from the mining process and overflow produced during the rainy season and directs it to the Excess Water Treatment Plant (EWTP) before being released into the Honda basin. In a different process, acidic water (produced when minerals enter into contact with water and oxygen) is routed to the mine's Acid Water

FIGURE 2.4 Acid Water Treatment Plant, Yanacocha mine. Photograph by Brando Palacios.

Treatment Plant (AWTP) before being released into the environment (see figure 2.4). Our final stop on our tour (before a hearty lunch at the mine cafeteria) was the AWTP, which treats groundwater from mine dewatering and water seeping from waste rock deposits. This water is mixed with lime to neutralize the acidity and passes through a clarifier that precipitates metals, separating liquids from solids. The metal-containing sludge collected after the clarifying process is returned to the leach pad. The company's Environmental Impact Assessments state that acid water from the mining pits will be treated for as long as it is necessary to do so (e.g., MWH 2006b). However, whether this permanent and costly commitment is feasible, and whether it can be enforced by Peruvian authorities, are questions that raise doubts for environmentalists and local people concerned about the future impacts of these operations.

Once the water meets the legally acceptable standards for suspended solids and pH levels, it is released into the San José reservoir, made out of an old mining pit and used to store water for use by local communities. Some water is also released directly into the Rio Grande (see figure 2.5), which supplies water to the El Milagro municipal water treatment plant

FIGURE 2.5 Water from Yanacocha's treatment facilities is released into the Rio Grande. Courtesy of GRUFIDES.

for consumption by residents of the city of Cajamarca. Minera Yanacocha also releases treated water to irrigation canals whose sources of water were contaminated or diverted by the mine's operations. On our tour, some of these irrigation canals were visible amid the mine's installations, showing the uneasy coexistence of the mine and local irrigation systems disrupted by the mine's operations.

Modern mining practices at the Yanacocha mine ruptured, reconfigured, and mobilized connections among campesinos, land, irrigation water, livestock, pastures, and other elements of the landscape. As in the Central Highlands, mining expansion in the Cajamarca region brought about changes that influenced migration, urban development, and economic livelihoods, but the invasive technologies of modern large-scale mining have brought about new concerns for communities living in the vicinity of the Yanacocha mine. One of the significant differences between mega-mining and underground mining is the effect that each kind of mining operation has on water resources. The disappearance of water springs, changes in water flows and water quality in irrigation canals, and the tensions arising from disputes over water and land have triggered intense opposition to mining expansion. At the same time, the mining companies' promise of jobs and economic opportunities has left people with frustrated expectations. The Cerro de Pasco Corporation's difficulty in meeting its labor needs and campesinos' ability to initially maintain an agricultural livelihood along with work in the mining industry contrast sharply with the experience of communities in Cajamarca. In Cajamarca, Minera Yanacocha faced a very different set of conditions—a densely populated area, a surplus of unskilled laborers, and communities whose agricultural and farming activities were compromised by the mine.

Large-scale modern mining also brings with it new risks that are not always evident in the rhetoric of clean, responsible mining. The first major setback for Peru's modern mining industry came with a mercury spill in 2000. By that time, problems in communities surrounding the Yanacocha mine—from lands usurped from campesinos, to trout deaths and diminished water flows in irrigation canals—had already been reported. But it was the mercury spill in Choropampa, considered the largest mercury spill in the world, that made it clear that modern mining was not as safe as it claimed to be. In June 2000, a canister of mercury fell from a truck (owned and operated by RANSA, a Peruvian contractor hired by Minera Yanacocha) traveling from the Yanacocha mine to the coastal capital of Lima. Until the spill, local people had not been aware that mercury is a by-product of the gold mining process, since the company had not made this information public. When 330 pounds of mercury spilled along a stretch of the highway some eighty kilometers (fifty miles) from the mine, the potential threats of modern mining were made all too evident. The company was faulted for its slow response to the spill and the inadequacy of its cleanup efforts. Children and adults handled the mercury before the town was alerted of the dangers, and an estimated 130 people were hospitalized with mercury poisoning. The consequences of the spill, added to Minera Yanacocha's failure to disclose the presence of mercury in its operations, generated public distrust of the company and irrevocably changed people's perceptions of the mine.

In spite of accidents such as the Choropampa spill, mining companies insist that their everyday operations are carefully monitored and do not create pollution or negatively impact the environment. Minera Yanacocha assures local people that it is committed to monitoring environmental conditions and safeguarding water resources, but many people respond to the company's claims with skepticism. Yet gathering scientific evidence to show that a mining company is polluting or reducing water flows in irrigation canals is often difficult, since the effects of cyanide, mercury, and other toxic substances are not always visible or easy to prove definitively.

As I showed in the previous chapter, the visibility of the environmental problems in La Oroya came about through the interaction of various actors and knowledges over the course of the smelter's long history. Similarly in communities around the Yanacocha mine, making the effects of mining visible would also require concerted effort. Mining companies rely on scientific studies and technical tools to support their claims, and protestors are also appropriating the language and tools of science to demonstrate that mining has caused changes in the water, soil, and pastures. In the rest of this chapter, I focus on contested definitions of "pollution" and debates over water quality and quantity. I examine controversies over a participatory water monitoring program, and the depolitization of local conflict through the use of technical studies and practices of transparency, participation, and dialogue.

Conflicts over Water and Pollution

Since the start of Minera Yanacocha's operations, people living in the vicinity of the mine have complained about the effects of mining on water quality and quantity. Some of these complaints were picked up by the Compliance Advisor Ombudsman, or CAO (as in other countries where it operated, it was known locally by its English acronym). The CAO was created in 1999 to investigate complaints by communities affected by projects in which the International Finance Corporation (IFC) and the Multilateral Investment Guarantee Agency (MIGA) (both part of the World Bank Group) were involved. Based in Washington, D.C., the CAO works on "improving social and environmental outcomes on the ground" and "fostering greater public accountability" (CAO 2013) by responding to complaints and requests for audits relating to IFC and MIGA projects.

In Cajamarca, the CAO initially responded to two complaints: one from the Northern Federation of Women's Peasant Patrols about the impacts of the mine, and another from people affected by the mercury spill in Choropampa. In order to address the concerns of local groups, the CAO formed a Mesa de Diálogo y Consenso (Dialogue and Consensus Roundtable) and organized forums for discussion. The CAO's initiatives were plagued with controversy from the start. Many of the groups that were invited to participate in the Mesa argued that, since the CAO was funded by one of the mining project shareholders (the IFC), its work could not be considered impartial. The CAO's work in Cajamarca never gained the trust of local actors, particularly those most critical of the mine. Nevertheless, the work of the Mesa exemplifies the complex politics of water that seemed to dominate Cajamarca's mining conflicts. Questions about the mine's effects on water resources were a constant preoccupation for local people. Was the water safe for human consumption? Had the water level of irrigation canals decreased? Was Yanacocha doing enough to prevent pollution? In a meeting in October 2001, participants in the Mesa collectively determined that concerns over water quality and quantity were the highest priority issues for rural and urban residents (CAO 2006). The Mesa commissioned an independent water study to evaluate the impact of mining activity on water resources and hired a company called Stratus Consulting (based in Colorado, U.S.A.) to carry out the study, which was completed in 2003.

The study concluded that the mine "altered water quality and water quantity in some locations and at some times" (Stratus Consulting 2003). The mine discharges water that has been treated in ways that can raise the acidity and change concentrations of metals, sulfate, and calcium, which can lead to improvements or degradation of water quality. With regard to water quantity, waste rock dumps intercept rainfall and delay the flow of water to streams and the infiltration of water into the ground. Rain also leaches metals and acid from the rock, and even once it is treated, acid seepage and the lime used to treat it can change the quality of water downstream. Other impacts are created with the removal of vegetation and soils for mining, road building, and mine-related construction, all of which increase the amount of water that reaches streams as runoff and reduces the amount of rainfall that soaks into the ground to replenish the groundwater. Finally, mining activity causes increased erosion and transports sediments into streams, particularly during the rainy season (Stratus Consulting 2003). While these impacts were discussed, the study ascertained that water quality changes were not serious enough to pose imminent short-term danger of illness or death to people, livestock, or crops. Further, it concluded that the mine had not affected drinking water quality in the city of Cajamarca.

Nevertheless, acceptable limits of heavy metals and other toxic substances were occasionally exceeded in some locations close to the mine property, prompting the consultants to recommend continued water monitoring. This recommendation was taken on by the Mesa, which established a participatory monitoring program. The goals of the monitoring program were to "increase confidence in and ensure credibility of environmental information being generated on an ongoing basis in Cajamarca; to continue the collaborative, participatory and transparent nature of the Mesa water study; and to stimulate the participation of the community in the vigilant stewardship of water resources" (CAO 2005:2).

The CAO water study brought together Minera Yanacocha, SEDACAJ (the municipal water supply company for the city of Cajamarca), and CO-MOCA, the organization charged with monitoring irrigation canals. Members of the Porcón Farm and the communities of Yanacancha and Llaucán also participated in the study to monitor canals and surface waters in their respective areas. After the Stratus Consulting study, a number of monitoring programs were established, but these organizations were already involved in monitoring water quality with the support and funding of Minera Yanacocha. Thus, the role of the Mesa technical team was not to introduce a new monitoring program, but to accompany the participating organizations while sampling and to collect double samples at a subset of locations in order to compare the results and evaluate the validity and quality of the data (CAO 2005). The study was based on over one hundred monitoring points in streams, canals, and other waters downstream from the mine and was conducted between July 2004 and August 2005.

The monitoring team was made up of a technical coordinator and a technical assistant from the CAO, and *veedores* (observers) from participating organizations. The team went out into the field four days a week in order to cover all the monitoring points identified in the study. I observed the monitoring process during an outing in July 2005, just as the study was coming to a close. The day began at a meeting point in downtown Cajamarca, where I met up with the CAO technicians. Fernando and Emilio were Cajamarca locals who had worked during the Stratus Consulting study and were hired again for this monitoring job. Two representatives from Minera Yanacocha provided vans for transportation and picked up three other people representing the institutions involved. Together we headed up to the mine, since the monitoring points for the day were within the mine's property, although they included canals used by neighboring communities (Quishuar, Encajón Collatán, and Llagamarca). We divided up into two groups, prepared the water bottles and supplies, and walked to the farthest monitoring point.

We were joined by three canal users who would act as veedores on behalf of their communities. The campesinos wore Yanacocha hard hats and safety vests, which gave the impression that they worked for the mining company, but in fact they were obligated to wear protective gear while inspecting their canal because they were within the mine's property. The veedores were given basic training in water sampling procedures, so one of them put on some latex gloves, rinsed the bottles, and filled them with water from the canal. Some of the samples required pumping the water through a filter and into a bottle, a task that was done by the veedores. Fernando, the CAO technical coordinator, measured the pH levels and conductivity and also read the temperature, water level, and Global Positioning System coordinates. The CAO's role was to take double samples in approximately 10 percent of the total number of monitoring points as a form of quality control. It was a fairly quick and simple process, though Fernando said some of their outings required longer and more strenuous walks, and all of this took twice as long in the rainy season.

We repeated these tasks at two more monitoring points. When we finished we met up with the other group, had lunch at the Yanacocha cafeteria, and drove back into town. The names of all people present were recorded in a registry (*Libro de Actas*), which we signed along with the record sheets included in the box of samples that we took to the bus terminal. Once the samples had been delivered to the bus company that would be shipping them to the lab in Lima, we went our separate ways.

Fernando, the technical coordinator for the CAO study, was convinced that this independent monitoring process was as objective and rigorous as possible. He stressed throughout our outing that the results were impartial, and that he was confident this was the case because he himself could verify it; he knew, for example, that the lab results coming back from Lima had not been manipulated. Yet when he explained the monitoring process that morning, he said that the data that they collected and the results derived from it have to go through the Mesa before they were made public. He recounted that people from Minera Yanacocha had been furious with the tests showing that lead has been found in some water sources, and the Mesa decided that it would be irresponsible to "alarm" the public by making this known. Company officials argued that the results were below the legal permissible levels, and therefore it was not a problem. As Fernando explained, however, permissible levels for Peru are sometimes less stringent than the international ones set by the U.S. Environmental Protection Agency (EPA). The CAO water study used both national and international standards for the evaluation of water quality.

Peruvian water quality standards are established by the General Water Law, which distinguishes between three types of water: Class I, water for domestic water use with only simple disinfection; Class II, raw water for domestic consumption; and Class III, raw water for irrigation and livestock consumption. Results were also compared to international guidelines, including those established by the World Health Organization (WHO); the U.S. Environmental Protection Agency (EPA); the State of Nevada Division of Environmental Protection; Environment Canada; and the Food and Agriculture Organization (FAO). These international guidelines were used when Peruvian legal standards were not established, or as a point of reference.

In October, a few months after our outing, the CAO released a summary of the results of monitoring between April and July 2005. A communiqué was published in a local newspaper and further disseminated in other media, by NGOS, and in information sessions organized by the Mesa. The CAO study found that some canals and streams exceeded the maximum permissible limits established by the General Water Law for Class III water in some months. For example, lead exceeded the established Class III limits for irrigation water in the Encajón Collatan and Quishuar canals, and in the San José Creek. When standards from the state of Nevada were applied, the Tual canal and the San José Creek surpassed the limits for total dissolved solids. Applying WHO standards for potable water, the study found that some substances like arsenic, lead, cadmium, and selenium exceeded limits in seven canals. In addition, the study found high levels of total and fecal coliform bacteria in most monitoring points.

In light of these findings, the CAO made the following recommendations: (1) that communities boil water before consuming it (because of the presence of total and fecal coliform bacteria); (2) that the population take precautions in consuming water from the points identified as having high levels of metals that are considered a health risk according to the WHO; and (3) that Minera Yanacocha conduct an evaluation of the monitoring points that exceed permissible limits established by the General Water Law, adopt corrective measures necessary, and monitor those points that exceed international guidelines.

In a communiqué, Minera Yanacocha acknowledged that permissible limits had been exceeded in some cases but argued that these were isolated incidents that had been "detected, corrected, and communicated" to the respective canal users. The CAO study also pointed out instances where samples exceeded international standards for *treated* drinking water (for example, lead concentrations in the Rejo and Chonta basins). The CAO results noted that the sampled water was not treated, but that the guidelines were given for reference, recognizing that some rural people use the canals for domestic consumption because they do not have adequate access to potable water sources. Minera Yanacocha soundly rejected the use of international potable water standards, arguing that these should be used only for drinking water coming from a water treatment plant and could not be used to evaluate the water quality of irrigation canals and streams. The different environmental standards used in the study were a major point of disagreement, and fundamental in the company's efforts to destabilize the validity of the CAO's results.

The CAO communiqué generated a mixed response among the general public in Cajamarca. The Mesa already faced challenges, since many people did not feel they could trust a study funded in part by the mining company and that included Minera Yanacocha's full participation as a member of the Mesa's Technical Committee. Additionally, some people faulted the Mesa for its lack of transparency and representation, and for its inefficiency in dealing with the problems generated by the mine. Why, for example, were the results of monitoring from April to July being announced only in October, and how were people supposed to deal with poor water quality? Since the monitoring was not legally binding, the CAO was in a position only to make recommendations. But the CAO's recommendations to boil water seemed laughable to many people who saw this as absolving the company of blame and putting the emphasis on bacterial coliforms instead of contamination by heavy metals. And what "precautions" could campesinos take, when faced with contamination by toxic substances in their canals?

Yet in spite of the problems, some people were also surprised that such damning results would reach publication. The reaction of Father Marco Arana, one of the mine's staunchest critics, was that "Yanacocha must have fallen asleep one day"; he couldn't understand how the company could have allowed for the communiqué to be published as it was. Though many of the mine's critics felt the CAO did not go far enough, they felt the monitoring results confirmed what they had long been trying to show, and the company could no longer hide what for them was the evident truth of polluted waters. The NGOs, led by Father Arana, GRUFIDES, and ECOVIDA, distributed pamphlets disseminating the CAO results. Activists supported the decision to include parameters for drinking water, arguing that campesinos do in fact drink this water when other sources are not available. Thus, even organizations critical of Minera Yanacocha collaborated indirectly in a process that they had remained peripheral to, strengthening the validity of the study and the reliance on technical data.

In Cajamarca, water helped unite actors with diverse and often contradictory interests into a common struggle. However, water did not just bring together people who are critical of mining activity—the mining company and their allies also framed their arguments in terms of water issues. In thinking about the role of water in Cajamarca's mining controversies, I find it useful to turn to Latour's (1988) discussion of "obligatory points of passage" as an element of translation (see also Callon 1999). In the context of war, Latour writes, an army must concentrate its forces only on certain points where it can penetrate the enemy lines, thus turning its weaknesses into strengths (1988:44). Creating an obligatory point of passage is contingent on the ability of some actors to convince others of its value. The establishment of obligatory points of passage produces a stronghold in which "whatever people do and wherever they go, they have to pass through the contender's position to help him further his own interests" (Latour 1988:253). In conflicts over mining, water was an obligatory passage point, obliging all sides to make their respective arguments with reference to water quality and quantity.

Regardless of their goals and antagonistic positions, Minera Yanacocha, NGOs, public officials, and other actors had to frame their arguments with relation to water. Campesinos recognized the need to translate experience into visual, quantifiable evidence and sometimes turned to NGOs and government agencies to make their claims heard. Local and international institutions like the CAO played a crucial role in this translation work, providing the technological expertise, resources, and equipment to strengthen their arguments against mining companies.

The intervention of the CAO brought along with it the involvement of international institutions and experts. It also enabled comparisons that brought Yanacocha out of the local context and put it alongside other projects funded by the International Finance Corporation. This change of scale not only increased the visibility of Yanacocha's problems but sought to demonstrate the accountability of the mine's stakeholders. The water studies also introduced other standards of measurement, including water quality standards set by the WHO and the U.S. and Canadian governments. These attempts to standardize environmental indices exemplify the translation work necessary to substantiate the changes experienced by local communities. National and international environmental standards, along with the copious amounts of data produced in monitoring and environmental studies, are necessary to make visible risks that are difficult to articulate (Choy 2011). However, the outcomes of the CAO's initiatives demonstrate that these ways of substantiating impacts did not have the intended effect of producing trust, inclusion, or accountability.

Politics and Science

Given the mixed responses to the publication of the monitoring results and other challenges facing the Mesa, the future of the CAO in Cajamarca seemed uncertain. Mr. Ramos, a CAO staff member, told me that Minera Yanacocha preferred bilateral agreements in which it could negotiate directly with affected parties. For the company the Mesa was a necessary evil; it participated reluctantly and sidestepped it whenever possible. Because of all the political wrangling and divisions, the roundtables tended to self-destruct or become weak on their own, which ultimately benefited the company. Mr. Ramos worried that the CAO would cut funding for the Mesa since they were not meeting the institution's requirements, including broad representation and participation. The CAO had recommended that they change the directive of the Mesa, in order to increase participation from other sectors (for example, to include NGOs) and improve public acceptance. But the current members of the directive refused. Part of their concern was that they did not want to "politicize" the Mesa. Mr. Ramos opined that one of the main problems for the CAO was that "the issues are easily manipulated politically." He said every Mesa was "invaded" by individuals with political interests, which meant, for example, people campaigning for office, but the CAO had tried to prevent this from the start. He also talked about "el Curita" (referring to Father Arana by using the diminutive form of the Spanish word for "priest") and his ability to slowly win people over because of his role as a religious authority, since priests have a lot of influence in the countryside. He repeated a comment that I had heard many times before: "Campesinos are very easy to manipulate."

The company's position was that the CAO should be careful to present the results of the monitoring (i.e., those showing the presence of contaminants) in a way that would not alarm or instill fear in people. Furthermore, company officials assumed that NGOs and individuals wanted to make the results public as a way to further their political interests. They believed that the scientific and technical (and thus the "environmental") could be kept separate from the social and the political.

Minera Yanacocha officials and mining industry supporters frequently argued that those who were "radically" opposed to mining had political interests, and therefore their claims were not legitimate. Many of these people were thought to have personal aspirations (for example, courting voters for an upcoming election), to belong to radical leftist groups that were against private investment, or worse, to have links to terrorist organizations. On the other hand, individuals who were critical of the mine's operations felt that their exclusion from these spaces meant that their concerns were not being heard. It was precisely for these reasons that they organized politically, and many felt that involvement in electoral politics was the only way to make concrete changes. Efforts to eliminate "political interests" as a way to ease existing tensions in fact contributed to the conflicts by excluding certain segments of the population, delegitimizing particular arguments (for example, about nationalization or economic restructuring), and denying people the opportunity to participate in established spaces for dialogue.

In spite of their criticisms of the CAO and other industry-sponsored studies, many people still believed that more transparent, participatory monitoring systems could help to prevent conflicts and reveal the truth about pollution and water levels. The language of participatory monitoring had become part of both NGO and corporate discourse, bridging their various interests by providing a common goal. For example, in 2008, a national gathering of "participatory environmental monitoring and vigilance committees in mining areas" was attended by 270 participants, including representatives from twenty-three participatory monitoring committees, sixteen mining companies, nine state institutions, and more than thirty NGOs and international institutions. The event, called "Water Brings Us Together," was funded jointly by NGOs and the mining sector (Asociación Civil Labor 2008). During my fieldwork, I saw many examples of participatory monitoring carried out by Minera Yanacocha and grassroots organizations. In one case, Minera Yanacocha worked with a local collective in San Cirilo, a contentious site of mining expansion, to test water quality and measure flows. This kind of participatory monitoring provided several benefits to the company. First, these activities (which were photographed, videotaped, and widely disseminated in the company's public relations materials) helped to create an image of community consent (even in places which, like San Cirilo, were deeply divided about the company's actions). Second, the monitoring provided baseline data before a mining project began, which might enable the company to ascertain that poor water quality existed *prior* to mining activity. If it can be shown that water is already undrinkable, and that the community has learned to live with these conditions, the company is absolved of further responsibility (Gold-man 2005:117).

In another case, I accompanied members of the Association for Environmental Education and Defense (ADEA), a small and short-lived NGO, to one of the communities closest to the mine. They organized a workshop in which residents were taught to do a simple reading of water acidity levels using pH test strips. It could be argued that the value of such initiatives goes beyond the test results, since these workshops have the indirect effect of educating and empowering local communities (Kinchy 2012). But there are also potential dangers, since corporations can too easily discredit attempts by nonexperts to monitor and document changes in water quality. Furthermore, these initiatives are always contingent on inconsistent and limited NGO funding. The ADEA lost its primary source of funding, which came from a Canadian NGO, when the Canadian government (through its embassy in Lima) pressured NGOs to stop supporting Peruvian organizations that protested against mining companies and threatened to cut off their public funding (Peru Support Group 2007). The targeting of NGOs (by the media, government agents, and international funders) made them increasingly cautious about their involvement with mining issues, lest they be accused of fomenting violence.

The exigencies and priorities of funding agencies may in part contribute to the appeal of activities that emphasize environmental monitoring and environmental education. The rising tensions and controversies around mining also pressured NGOs to focus on activities that they deemed to be less confrontational. Like the mining industry, NGOs also relied on technical mechanisms and scientific data but felt that existing studies and information lacked objectivity. The solution, therefore, rested on their ability to secure funding and expertise that would not depend on the mining industry, financial institutions, or the government.

At the same time that the CAO water monitoring was being carried out, GRUFIDES was working to develop a new "Independent Participatory Monitoring Program" that they would manage, with the technical and financial support of their international allies and partners. The study was intended to be more holistic, incorporating social and health indicators as part of the study. By contrast, GRUFIDES members saw the CAO monitoring as being too limited in scope and compromised by the CAO's association with the IFC and the mining company. Through independent monitoring projects and other initiatives, grassroots organizations and local communities were calling attention to the way that science is made. Their arguments pointed to the social context in which knowledge is produced, and not just the results obtained through scientific studies. It was an implicit recognition that science is never value-free, for how a study is funded and the process through which the data is obtained will determine the validity of the results. This is something that corporations, by insisting on the separation of science and politics, were not willing to recognize.

Following the publication of the CAO communiqué, the preoccupations of canal users remained unresolved. In February 2006, canal users submitted a petition to the CAO for assistance in acquiring information about water quantity in canals, rivers, and streams (CAO 2006). They requested an independent water quantity study and solicited the support of the CAO. In response to their request, the CAO sponsored a two-day information-sharing workshop in July 2006.

The meeting was attended by two of Yanacocha's water experts, who responded to the questions posed by canal users. Twenty-three canal users attended the meeting on the first day, and sixteen on the second day. After the meeting workshop, the CAO reported on the proceedings as follows:

> Canal users asked specific questions about whether the quantity of water has been reduced, where, and by how much. MY [Minera Yanacocha] responded that the company's impact on the quantity of water in the streams and canals is minimal. From the company perspective, MY has very little impact on quantity. In response, canal users listed a number of lakes and springs that existed previously but have now dried out (in the case of the San José area) or disappeared (in the case of Laguna Yanacocha).
>
> Canal users argued that although some water flows in those canals, flows have changed dramatically and sediment content has increased. In some instances, lime has been added, and the flows appear significantly reduced. They believe the overall character of the canals has changed. (CAO 2006)

In response to the canal users' concerns about disappearing water springs, Yanacocha's engineers insisted on a difference between permanent and seasonal springs to argue that a decrease in water flows is normal in the dry season. Canal users responded that they understood this difference, but that the permanent springs had much lower flows than they used to. The canal users' concerns also illustrate differences in the way they and the company were evaluating water quality. Though Yanacocha sought to replace natural spring water with treated water, and relied on legal standards to determine its quality, canal users pointed to other characteristics that they deemed significant: increased sedimentation (which made the water murky), the addition of lime, reduced water flows, and other changes in the characteristics of the canals. However, the CAO's notes on the canal users' comments ("they *believe* that the *general character* of the canal has changed") imply that their complaints are based on perception (not knowledge) of unspecified changes that could not be quantified or scientifically proven.

This interaction between campesinos and company representatives, and the CAO's implicit dismissal of the canal users' concerns, illustrate the impasse that is typical of debates around mining impacts. Water users have ways of evaluating water quality that do not coincide with technical parameters. While campesinos depend on, and even request, further monitoring and scientific studies, their concerns cannot be verified scientifically.

The changes that they experience are a consequence of the transformations produced by the technologies of large-scale mining, which are as dramatic as they are difficult to capture and document in studies conducted by organizations like the CAO and NGOs, and by campesinos themselves. The effects of mega-mining technologies on water have brought the technical aspects of mining to the forefront of debates. At the same time, the indeterminacy of science—its inconclusiveness—compels an expansive network of people to involve themselves in the process, and to have stakes in the making of evidence. The rules of engagement become even more complicated as debates over pollution come to focus on human health and disease, since the long-term effects of mining on bodies and environments are difficult to ascertain. Furthermore, the social and economic costs borne by campesinos become embedded in their concerns over water. These concerns are as likely to be expressed in terms of a demand for jobs and assistance in local development, or as requests for the construction of reservoirs and water studies. The calculation of harm and the negotiation for compensation become deeply contested, especially as people's claims and actions are circumscribed by a technical discourse.

The CAO's studies and monitoring show how science and risk assess-ment often come to replace larger concerns around mining expansion. This process shifts the focus from social, political, and ethical concerns to scientific studies of environmental impacts and technological solutions. In Cajamarca, the many studies commissioned by the company and other institutions provided data about water quality but never fully addressed the concerns of activists and local communities. The participatory nature of endeavors such as water monitoring could not conceal the evident ten-sions and divisions that plagued the Mesa since its inception. Nevertheless, the CAO's efforts produced collaborations, involving multiple actors and producing results that different constituencies would ultimately interpret and use in different ways. On one hand, the study played into the interests of the company, but at the same time, Cajamarca activists used aspects of the study to further their campaigns against the mine, while campesi-nos incorporated the CAO's arguments into their own claims against the company. These and other struggles to make "pollution" visible would help reconfigure political alliances and forms of activism as mining activity unearthed new risks, expectations, and possibilities for political action.

CHAPTER 3

THE HYDROLOGY OF A SACRED MOUNTAIN

Sitting on the grass near Herlinda's two grazing cows, we had a perfect view of Cerro Quilish, the mountain that had become an icon of mining conflict (see figure 3.1). As we watched the clouds moving above Cerro Quilish, she wondered out loud whether Minera Yanacocha might go ahead with plans to mine the mountain. Like many people living in the vicinity of Quilish, Herlinda had participated in the protests in 2004 against the mining project. She pointed to the area where she found herself running as the police went after the protestors with tear gas. At some point, someone set fire to the grass, they started throwing rocks, and the police pushed back. The fear she felt and the intensity of the confrontations were still fresh in her mind. For days, people from Tual and other communities gathered just outside the city of Cajamarca and blocked the highway leading to the mine. They said they were there to protect their water, which had its source at Cerro Quilish.

People wouldn't allow Quilish to be turned into a mine, said Herlinda; they would do anything to defend their source of water. Then she added: "The mountain has to give its consent in order for it to be mined" ("*el cerro tiene que dar su consentimiento para que lo exploten*"). Herlinda went on to tell me that before the mine began operating, Brant Hinze (Yanacocha's general man-

FIGURE 3.1 View of Cerro Quilish, from the neighboring community of Tual.

ager at the time) and other engineers made an offering to the mountain that they were going to mine.[1] A truckload of sugar was given as payment in exchange for the gold: this is what the mountain had requested, Herlinda explained. But this was not all that it wanted, for the mountain was fierce (*bravo*). In the first years of operations, many mine workers lost their lives, "eaten" by the mountain. The company hired workers only from far-away places instead of locals, so that their families would not know their fate. Herlinda had heard from other campesinos that at midnight, the devil (in the form of a blonde female, whom they called "La Gringa") appeared driving a mining truck. The workers were like sacrificial lambs in a pact that the company made with the devil. What would Cerro Quilish demand, Herlinda wondered, if it allowed the company to mine it?

This chapter explores the relationships forged between Cerro Quilish, Minera Yanacocha, and people living in the vicinity of the mine. What does it mean to say that a mountain must give its consent to be mined? How do city dwellers, mining companies, and campesinos relate to an agentive landscape transformed by the continued expansion of mining activity? What compelled thousands of people to protest against the mining project? On the surface, the Quilish protests shared many characteristics with other mobilizations in response to mining expansion. Like other mining-related conflicts, the controversy over the Quilish project centered on the costs and benefits involved in converting mountains into open-pit mines. But what made this case different was that Cerro Quilish emerged in the conflict as a particular kind of mountain: one that holds water and has special significance for the local population. In anti-mining campaign materials and news reports, Cerro Quilish was presented as an aquifer—the source of the main rivers and tributaries that supply water to the city and rural communities. Activists argued that mining activity would compromise the quality of that water (with increased sedimentation and the potential leaching of heavy metals and toxic substances into rivers and streams) and reduce the quantity of water available in what is already a drought-prone region. Protestors also argued that the mine should not be built because campesinos living in the area considered Cerro Quilish to be an Apu, a Quechua term that is commonly translated as "mountain spirit" or "sacred mountain."

The anti-mining campaigns brought together these various concerns in ways that challenged the representation of Cerro Quilish as a valuable mineral deposit. They shifted the debate away from the question of *who* should benefit from the project (the state, foreign corporations, or local communities) or *how* the project should be carried out (i.e., what measures would be taken to ensure social and environmental responsibility). Cerro Quilish, as depicted in the anti-mining campaigns, was not just a mountain rich in mineral deposits; it was that, but it was also an aquifer (a store of life-sustaining water) and an Apu (an animate being). By multiplying the identity of Cerro Quilish, the protests challenged how conflicts over mining had come to be understood: as conflicts of interest that measure the benefits to be derived from a particular project against the social and environmental costs associated with it.

Framed around the protection of an aquifer and an Apu, the aims and strategies of the anti-mining protests did not always fit within the discourses of existing political movements focused on economic justice or the nationalization of resources (for example, local unions or left-leaning political parties). While arguments calling for nationalizing the mines or better pay and working conditions did surface in conflicts emerging throughout the country, activism against mining at once incorporated and exceeded established political discourses and practices. The Quilish protests became part of a movement "in defense of life" that encompassed water and livelihood, landscapes and cultural identity—but it was also more than this.

The mountain was not just an economic resource to be defended, but the embodiment of life itself. By calling Cerro Quilish an Apu, the protestors suggested that it was a living entity, and furthermore, that other lives (both human and nonhuman) depended on its existence. Arguments against mining at Cerro Quilish were entangled with discussions about "water" as a life-sustaining substance—life in a general biological sense, but also with relation to particular (and by some accounts, disappearing) ways of life. Additionally, the mining industry's new ventures in Cajamarca and other parts of the country were coming up against unexpected forms of life: not only the animal and plant species deemed valuable by local people and environmentalists, but also entities like Apus and other earth-beings that animate the Andean landscape. The invasive technologies of open-pit mining were disrupting landscapes and, along with them, the conditions necessary to sustain ways of living and interacting with those landscapes.

As anthropologists Mario Blaser (2009) and Marisol de la Cadena (2010) have noted, many contemporary environmental conflicts are conflicts over different realities or worlds. The conflicts do not simply concern competing interpretations of Nature (which assumes the existence of many cultures but a single reality) but should be understood as struggles over the enactment, stabilization, and protection of multiple socionatural worlds. In the conflict I examine, Cerro Quilish was not only a mountain or a resource, nor was it simply *perceived* in different ways by the various constituencies involved in the controversy. Rather, it emerged as radically different entities—a valuable mineral deposit, a mountain that holds water, a sacred mountain, and a sentient being—through the practices of the actors involved.

This chapter explores the actors and processes that put Cerro Quilish's complex identity as aquifer-water-Apu at the center of the anti-mining campaign and national debates over resource extraction. I suggest that by presenting Cerro Quilish as something more than a contested territory with valuable resources, protestors mobilized elements that are usually absent from public debate: Apus, spirits, and sacred mountains existed only in the sphere of "myth," perhaps accepted as remnants of quickly disappearing Andean worldview, but they were not to be taken seriously in political terms (de la Cadena 2010). Yet Cerro Quilish, as mountain, animate being, water, and livelihood, entered into the sphere of politics and became a powerful force with which corporations and the state had to contend.

Cerro Quilish posed a challenge not only for the mining industry, but also for political and social movements long defined by their identification with parties on the "Left" or "Right"; by nationalist, socialist, or neoliberal ideologies; or by religious affiliation. Amid the diversity of actors that joined in the protests, Cerro Quilish emerged as a kind of "boundary object" (Star and Griesemer 1989) that multiplied as it entered into relationships with different actors. A boundary object is able to travel across borders and inhabit various communities of practice while maintaining a constant identity. In this particular case, the capacity of Cerro Quilish to accommodate diverse viewpoints and interpretations enabled alliances across geographical and political divides. The multiplicity of Cerro Quilish proliferated the relations and material connections that were crucial to the success of the campaign. Water springs, canals, and rivers that have their origins at Cerro Quilish gave people from various communities a direct connection to the struggle; and the mountain itself—not merely its economic potential, but the force of its physical presence (cf. Orlove et al. 2008)—renewed people's sense of connection to a landscape that mining would permanently transform.

Political responses to mining activity involve a diverse group of actors, and mobilizations are often loosely organized around multiple demands. Participants involved in various kinds of mobilizations do not necessarily share common interests or an ideological stance that defines their position vis-à-vis extractive activity. My analysis of the Quilish conflict seeks to show how various actors sometimes came together in ways that strengthened the movement. At other times, their different interests had unpredictable effects. For example, the importance of Quilish as an aquifer helped make water into a focal point of debates over mining. Indeed, it could be argued that the Quilish campaigns' explicit focus on water set the tone of future protests and debates around mining activity at a regional and national level. While these arguments helped draw supporters to the movement against the mine, they also led the mining company to focus its public relations campaigns on technical arguments and water management programs.

In the years immediately following the protests, the situation in Cajamarca changed dramatically; NGOs and mining activism weakened, and Minera Yanacocha mounted a concerted campaign that emphasized the mine's responsible water management practices. I argue that focusing on a single aspect of Cerro Quilish (water) reduced the complexity of the mountain and the challenge that it posed for the company. The shift from multiplicity to singularity helped neutralize opposition to the project. But as I have already noted, the stabilization of facts requires constant effort. Thus, the potential for multiplicity remains, and conflicts that might seem to have been resolved are likely to reemerge.

In Defense of Water and Life

On the morning of September 2, 2004, protestors marched to Cerro Quilish to demand an end to mining exploration activity. Over the course of fifteen days of protesting, thousands filled the town square in the city of Cajamarca (see figure 3.2). The massive protests put a stop to the extraction of an estimated 3.7 million ounces of gold from Cerro Quilish. As activists involved in the protests would later remark, the mobilization of both city and countryside was crucial for halting the mining project.

The protests brought together a diverse mix of people, from urban professionals and irrigation canal users, to unions and religious organizations. As in many social protests, the teachers' union (SUTEP) mobilized its bases, contributing strength in numbers. Although there was a long-standing association between the SUTEP and leftist parties (including communist party Patria Roja), the protests were not organized along party lines. At the time of the conflict, the political scene was characterized by fragmentation. Political parties were severely weakened following Alberto Fujimori's presidency, leaving an eclectic mix of independent parties. Certainly, established and aspiring politicians would have brought their own political ambitions to the Quilish campaigns, but political parties did not play a leadership role in the protests. At least in the memory of those who later recounted the events, the movement was marked not by the protagonism of a few individuals or by political opportunism, but by the massive support of people from all walks of life. What they recalled was the involvement of people like the city's market vendors and *transportistas* (operators of public transit vans and taxis), which essentially gave protestors the power to shut down the city by closing businesses and paralyzing

FIGURE 3.2 Protest against mining at Cerro Quilish in Cajamarca. Courtesy of GRUFIDES.

traffic. Students from the local university, artists, religious organizations, and NGOS joined in the marches and roadblocks.

While the support of the city was essential, the strength of the movement also came from rural communities that would be affected by the mining project. At least four campesino communities were considered to be within the area of the proposed project, but many more were compelled to participate in the protests because their sources of water originated at Cerro Quilish. Irrigation canals became an important link that enabled peasant leaders to mobilize members of the canal users' associations (*juntas de usuarios*). In addition to canal users, the rondas campesinas played an important role in the protests. The region of Cajamarca is the birthplace of the rondas, which began as a means to counter cattle theft (see Starn 1999). Though focused on night patrols and delivering community justice, the rondas are a backbone of peasant political organizing and a source of authority in most communities. The ronderos (members of the rondas) came not only from the province of Cajamarca, but also from Bambamarca. They were drawn into the struggle because the river and other waterways that extended into the province would be affected by the mine's operations. The canal users' associations and the rondas provided the organizational structure (at both the local and regional level) to mobilize people quickly and effectively. Members agreed to support the Quilish protests in communal assemblies, in some cases imposing a penalty or fine for those who did not participate. This ensured high turnouts and the constant presence of people who took turns to sustain the roadblocks.

The protests against the Quilish project did not erupt spontaneously but were the result of tenacious education and advocacy campaigns that spanned almost a decade. Spearheading these efforts was the NGO GRUFIDES—and in particular, Father Marco Arana, one of its founding members. GRUFIDES is a small development organization that was formed in 2001 by former members of the Universidad Nacional de Cajamarca (Cajamarca National University) parish youth group under the guidance of Father Arana, who was the university parish priest. The students, with university training in diverse disciplines such as law, engineering, sociology, and economics, were united by a common interest in social justice from a Catholic faith perspective. Upon graduating from university, the group formed GRUFIDES with Father Arana as executive director, and solicited funding from European and North American institutions for development and education projects in Cajamarca's rural areas. However, the NGO's efforts were gradually consumed by problems brought on by Minera Yanacocha's mining operations.

GRUFIDES became the primary contact and source of information for foreign journalists, researchers, and solidarity activists. These international connections were crucial for much of their work on mining issues, providing not only funding for their work but also expertise and support networks to disseminate information internationally. The GRUFIDES office was a lively and sometimes chaotic environment filled with the energy of its young staff, volunteers, and international interns. The waiting area near the reception was often occupied by campesinos who had come to seek legal counsel or advice for dealing with their latest problems with the company. The NGO's close identification with the defense of communities affected by mining earned them a reputation as *"ecologistas"* ("environmentalists"). In Cajamarca, the label "ecologista" (in the context of mining conflicts) had become a pejorative term to identify any individual or organization with a critical stance on mining.

GRUFIDES came to be seen as the leading "anti-mining" organization, along with other local groups. Most notably, Cajamarca's Frente de Defensa (Defense Front) became known for its uncompromising opposition to mining expansion. The Frente was a diverse group of urban residents, people with experience in political activism, and campesino leaders. One of its key members was Reinhard Seifert, a German national but longtime Cajamarca resident with a background in engineering. Mr. Seifert arrived in Cajamarca to work in rural development and carried out a study of the dairy industry in the region. He brought his field experience, knowledge of the rural economy, and concern for the plight of campesinos to his work with the Frente. Among those who were involved in the Quilish campaigns, even his detractors credited Mr. Seifert for building ties with the rondas and going out to rural communities to give talks on the effects of mining activity.

While recounting his involvement in the campaigns against Minera Yanacocha, Mr. Seifert distinguished between the different strategies used to defend Cerro Quilish. It was Father Arana, he told me, who embraced and helped disseminate the imagery of the sacred Apu; by contrast he, as a scientist, was more interested in the technical arguments against mining. Their joint efforts—even if part of a sometimes conflictive relationship—are indicative of a network of collaboration that contributed to the effectiveness of the Quilish campaign. Their different interests made an alliance possible, even if they did not always converge. While the image of Cerro Quilish as an Apu held romantic appeal and added a new dimension to the anti-mining struggle, the language of aquifers gave it scientific validity.

Looking through papers he had collected over many years campaigning against Minera Yanacocha, Mr. Seifert pulled out an old article from a local paper. He told me this was where the first reference to Cerro Quilish as a mountain that "holds water" appeared. The article published in 1996 in a local weekly publication read: "Mayor Guerrero indicated that these mountains are the water 'sponges' or 'cushions' of the city of Cajamarca, and showed concern over the possible activities of the mining company" (*Clarín* 1996). Having the city's mayor refer to Cerro Quilish as a water source was a major step in a campaign that gradually gained supporters.

For both the city and the countryside, water became a mobilizing force. Flyers and other campaign materials communicated that Cerro Quilish is only 14.5 kilometers (nine miles) from the city of Cajamarca as the crow flies, and a mere eight kilometers from the city's water treatment plant, "El Milagro." Activists stressed that Cerro Quilish was the source of the Porcón and Grande Rivers, which together provided 70 percent of the water consumed in the city. This message struck a chord with city dwellers, who might previously have felt disconnected from the mine and the problems of the countryside.

Alongside the educational campaigns carried out by several organizations, key figures in the movement published books and articles about why Quilish should not be mined. Reinhart Seifert focused his arguments against the mine on evidence of water contamination from mining operations already underway (Seifert 2003). Nilton Deza, a biologist at the University of Cajamarca, wrote about the risks of cyanide leaching (Deza 2002). But it was Father Arana who, in numerous newspaper editorials, e-mail missives, and published reports, imbued the technical arguments against mining with what he saw as a cultural and moral dimension to the struggle against the mine. He based his arguments on the defense of a way of life rooted in Porcón, an area made up of campesino communities that begins just beyond the city of Cajamarca and extends into the property of the mine. His experiences as a rural priest made him attuned to the hardships of campesinos and their particular ways of expressing their identity as "Porconeros" (as the area's locals are called).

Undoubtedly, the effectiveness of narratives that centered on Cerro Quilish's role as aquifer and Apu rested on their seemingly timeless qualities. The mineral deposit that Minera Yanacocha hoped to exploit was located in Porcón, a place that had become emblematic of a precolonial past. These narratives sometimes presumed that locals had always considered Cerro Quilish to be the primary source of water for the city and surrounding region, and implied that it was an Apu according to "Andean tradition." On the other hand, counterclaims to disprove the validity of these arguments dismissed them as "inventions" with the intent to manipulate. Yet both of these views ignore the dynamic and creative connections among people, technologies, and landscapes that brought Cerro Quilish to the center of a complex controversy.

This is the irony of Cerro Quilish: that its protagonism as an Apu took shape in a region where a majority of people have turned to evangelism, and where a Catholic priest became one of its most important spokespersons. It took a proposed mining project—with the threat of open pits, toxic chemicals, and altered water courses—to make the latent "indigeneity" of Porcón and people's relationships to a sentient landscape politically visible and significant in the present. I use the term *indigeneity* recognizing the complex politics of class, language, ethnicity, and race in Peru. First of all, the term is not used by people in rural Cajamarca (who tend to refer to themselves as "campesinos" rather than as "indigenous" or "Indian"). Also, I do not mean to suggest that people are more or less indigenous based on a set of prescribed characteristics (for example, language or dress). As scholars have pointed out, we need to "move beyond thinking of indigeneity in the all-or-nothing terms of authenticity and invention, cultural survival and extinction" (see M. García 2005:6). Recognizing the complex ways in which identities are made and negotiated, I want to explore how indigeneity came to be articulated through the engagement of various actors.

"Quilish Is More Than Quilish"

Three years after the 2004 protests, Father Arana wrote an article reflecting on the significance of the campaigns against mining at Cerro Quilish and asserting his unwavering commitment to protect it: "If the ecological matter put forth by the avarice of gold that has laid eyes on Cerro Quilish is to be understood as merely a technical-scientific problem, then I'll always say no. And I'll do the same if these questions are reduced to problems of a cultural, social, or religious-symbolic character. It is not with these half-truths that life will be protected and defended, but rather with the understanding and practice of ecology as an integral matter: scientific, cultural, social, political, historical, and ethical" (Arana 2007). For Father Arana, the Quilish conflict could not simply be addressed with technical solutions. If the controversy was to be considered from an "ecological" point of view, in his definition of the term, it would be necessary to take a holistic approach that incorporates the scientific, sociocultural, political, historical, and ethical issues at stake. Considering one of these dimensions separately, without seeing the larger whole, would only produce "half-truths." Rejecting the perils of reductionist thinking, Father Arana has written that "Quilish is more than Quilish." What was at stake in the protests, he explained, was not only the protection of this mountain; for Quilish also symbolized the protection of local people's right to water, their cultural identity, and the democratic right to prior consultation (Arana 2007).

Evoking Quilish's multiplicity was fundamental for making the struggle known nationally and internationally.

Although he has tried to play down his leadership role, no other individual has had as much of an impact on mining debates in Cajamarca or incited as much controversy as Father Arana. When I met him in 2005, he was already a nationally and internationally recognized figure whose busy schedule took him from his office at GRUFIDES to campesino communities, and from giving Sunday mass to speaking at conferences in Lima and abroad. In 2004, following the Quilish protests, he received a human rights award from the Coordinadora Nacional de Derechos Humanos (a Peruvian human rights umbrella organization), the first of several awards recognizing him as a "hero of the environment" (as *Time* magazine called him in 2009) (Chauvin 2009). Then in his early forties, Father Arana had been born and raised in the city of Cajamarca. Driven by both spiritual and intellectual pursuits, he combined his theological training with studies in sociology, earning a master's degree from the Pontificia Universidad Católica del Perú. In public statements to the press, Father Arana displayed a calm eloquence and spoke in measured statements. It was easier to get beyond his serious demeanor in person. Usually dressed casually in jeans and a sports jacket, he exuded warmth, humor, and an easy disposition, but any discussion about Minera Yanacocha was sure to evoke passionate views and a quick temper.

When the Quilish controversy emerged, he was based at the Parish of Guadalupe, in the city of Cajamarca, along with two other priests with whom he shared a strong friendship and a commitment to social and environmental justice. The offices of GRUFIDES were on the property of the parish, directly below the priests' living quarters, and Father Arana's combined role of religious figure and NGO activist was one that made many people uncomfortable—particularly the Catholic Church hierarchy. The priests at the Parish of Guadalupe recognized the problematic consequences that their stance on mining issues could bring but remained critical of both Minera Yanacocha and the church as an institution. One of them told me: "We are priests *in spite of* the [Catholic] Church" ("*Somos curas a pesar de la iglesia*"), making clear their rebelliousness vis-à-vis the institution. They were particularly critical of the current bishop of Cajamarca and priests who appeared to protect the interests of the wealthy and the mining corporations.

It was a radical change from the time when José Dammert headed the archdiocese, between 1962 and 1992. Bishop Dammert was part of an international movement that sought to interpret the church's teaching through the eyes of the poor and the oppressed, and to work on their behalf. As in much of Latin America, the ideas of liberation theology that inspired the work of Bishop Dammert had a significant influence on NGOs and individuals whose work merged Christian teachings with issues of economic justice, human rights, and (more recently) environmental concerns. During his years in Cajamarca, Bishop Dammert devoted special attention to Cajamarca's rural poor and supported the work of the rondas campesinas, gaining friends and foes along the way. Father Arana met the bishop when he joined the Juventud Estudiantil Católica (a Catholic youth group). Bishop Dammert became a mentor to him and was instrumental in his decision to become ordained as a priest. Father Arana thus began his ecclesiastical life within an activist church that saw the poor as its main priority, and with the youthful optimism shared by a group that, as one of his close friends told me, wanted to build a better world.

As part of his efforts to serve the rural areas, Bishop Dammert created the Cristo Ramos parish in Lower Porcón and sent Father Arana to live there in 1991, shortly after he was ordained. It was around this time that Minera Yanacocha began its operations in Cajamarca, and campesinos contacted Father Arana with complaints that the company was encroaching on their property and pressuring them to sell their land. In 1994, he acted as mediator in an extrajudicial agreement between Minera Yanacocha and campesinos who claimed the mining company had begun exploration activity without their permission and caused damages to their property. Thanks to the intervention of the Porcón parish, the campesinos received monetary compensation for these damages. Already, Father Arana's criticism of the mining company was causing controversy, and the new bishop wanted him to leave the region to avoid causing problems. He left Porcón to continue his studies, including seminary studies in Italy. But it was during his time as a rural priest that Father Arana made contacts with people and established a reputation in the countryside that would last beyond his years in Porcón, and even when he was no longer there, people would seek him out to request his help.

Father Arana's position as a trusted authority figure allowed him to hear firsthand about campesinos' initial altercations with the mining company and to intervene on their behalf. In the process, his day-to-day experiences in rural communities convinced him that Cerro Quilish was more than what could be captured by the utilitarian value of the resources it provided (land, water, and pasturelands) and that might be compromised by mining activity. Campesinos told him they had always known Cerro Quilish contained gold and water and spoke of a "golden fountain" from which water sprung and flowed in two directions (Arana 2007). This, according to Father Arana, was an apt description of Cerro Quilish's location in the area of the continental divide separating the watersheds that drain into the Pacific and Atlantic oceans. They also told of how, if the first clouds of October appear above the crown of Cerro Quilish, it will be a year of heavy rains and bountiful harvests (Arana 2007). For Father Arana, the significance of Quilish was evidenced in the stories passed on from generation to generation, and in the little "altars" made of rocks where campesinos would bring holy water, liquor, peppers, salt, candles, strands of lamb's wool, or little pieces of leather. "They prayed first to God Almighty, Father of Jesus Christ, and then came the libations and offerings to the earth with trickles of water," he wrote (Arana 2007), translating the practices of campesinos according to his understanding of religion. In this way, Cerro Quilish became a "sacred mountain," a designation that caught on in the media yet differed from what Cerro Quilish was to campesinos: an agentive being with whom people interacted and established relationships necessary to sustain life.

Like many priests working in the Peruvian countryside since the colonial period, Father Arana accepted the coexistence of Catholic saints and sentient entities, of special offerings left in rocky caves and processions in honor of Christ (like the Cristo Ramos celebrations held annually in Porcón). In his writings and reflections on Cerro Quilish, Father Arana seemed to tap into a consciousness of a world in which such mixtures were still possible, even if they were not always evident in peoples' everyday lives. In Porcón, Apus did not have the prominence that they do in the southern department of Cuzco, for example, where some mountains are the focus of yearly pilgrimages, or recognized as important protectors.

In the Cajamarca region, by contrast, the influence of Spanish colonialism prevailed over many precolonial practices. The indigenous Quechua language is spoken in only a few communities, and a significant number of rural people attend the evangelical churches that now predominate in the region. As in other parts of Peru and Latin America, evangelical Protestantism has grown rapidly since the 1960s. According to the 2007 departmental census, 14 percent of the population professed an evangelical religion (compared to 80 percent who identify as Catholic). While this is a relatively small percentage, the rapid inroads of evangelical religions in Porcón was evidenced by the proliferation of non-Catholic Christian churches. Also, since many Catholics are nonpracticing and regular church services were not available in each *caserío*, the majority of active churchgoers are evangelicals. Evangelism has had a significant influence on most aspects of everyday life, from politics and community leadership to personal habits, including the avoidance of alcohol. Evangelism also discouraged any behavior that could be seen as violating its monotheistic teachings (for example, making offerings to the dead, or being fearful of places where earth-beings are said to hide).

It was in this setting that Father Arana argued that Cerro Quilish was not only a mountain, and not just a source of water: it was an *Apu*, and a source of life. It was a message that became part of his writings, interviews, and sermons delivered during events organized in the defense of Cerro Quilish. On August 28, 2001, thousands of people marched to Cerro Quilish and symbolically demarcated an area that had been declared a protected area in a controversial municipal ordinance. The following are fragments of a homily given on Cerro Quilish during this event:

> Quilish, for campesinos here, is still the APU, the mountain that is protector of all earthly and heavenly life. Pantheist paganism, might say those who do not understand that the campesino's relationship with nature is the delicate thread that sustains all life. . . . Quilish is about to be seized from us[;] the destiny that the miners want to give Quilish is to transform it into some millions of dollars that will fill their pockets, without regard for the many people for whom Quilish is a source of water, and therefore, a source of life. Today we are here to tell ourselves, in the presence of God, that we renounce the avarice of gold; and that we will not allow others to transform our source of water into a handful of gold to satisfy their greed; that we will not permit that their idolatrous way of life, in which everything is sacrificed to a gold idol, continues without regard for how many lives depend on this, our source of water. (Arana 2002)

According to Father Arana, for "the miners" (meaning those involved with the mining company and, more generally, its supporters) Cerro Quilish was a source of minerals and profits. That it could also be an Apu and an aquifer allowed for the moral condemnation of the materialism and greed that goes along with the "idolatry of gold."

In addition, Quilish's identity as an Apu challenged any arguments that justified mining activity based on economic calculations about the utilitarian value of resources. In other words, the fact that Quilish was an Apu made it incommensurable, in the sense that it was irreducible to gold or other forms of material benefits. The question ceased to be: "How can Cerro Quilish be mined responsibly?" (as the problem is often framed by corporations promoting an image of Corporate Social Responsibility); nor could the dispute be described simply as a disagreement over how communities would "benefit" from the project. The multiplicity of Cerro Quilish disrupted the equivalences at the root of proposals to "manage" the impacts of mining activity with technological solutions and compensation agreements with affected communities.

Father Arana's interpretations of Catholic teachings and of campesinos' relationship with Cerro Quilish were certainly controversial, and many accused him of being a "false prophet" and of introducing the idea of the Apu where it had never previously existed. Fergus Bordewich (1997) describes a similar dynamic in *Killing the White Man's Indian*, where he tells the story of a conflict over the building of telescopes on Mount Graham, in Arizona. While opponents called it an Apache sacred mountain, others claimed that this was the invention of activists and their well-meaning but misguided non-Indian supporters. Bordewich argues that the success of the campaign to block the construction of the telescope rested on "the power of myth to sway the hearts of Americans who continue to see relations between Indians and whites as an unending morality play of predators and victims, of evil and innocence despoiled" (1997:238). Such narratives of indigenous peoples as environmental stewards fighting off evil interlopers may also have been at the root of the campaigns to protect Cerro Quilish and contributed to the romantic appeal of the Apu. Yet the binary opposition between "authentic" indigenous tradition on the one hand, and invented (and thus "fraudulent") interpretation on the other, does not capture the way Cerro Quilish came to matter as both an Apu and a source of water.

Father Arana's arguments were controversial precisely because they disrupted a "modern" understanding of politics that stems from the separation of Society and Nature (Descola and Palsson 1996) and relegates politics to the representation of humans (Society), and science to the representation of nonhumans (Nature). This distinction rests on what Latour (1993:13) calls the "crossed-out God, relegated to the sidelines." Through the process of purification (the ever-increasing separation of Society and Nature), God was separated from the realm of the profane and relegated to the sphere of "spirituality," where it could not intervene with worldly affairs. According to Latour, God was made transcendent, and also irrelevant, and thus did not pose a threat to the rationality of science.

In protests against mining expansion and subsequent media coverage of these events, activists and journalists sometimes defined Cerro Quilish according to a Catholic conception of the "sacred" or a romantic vision of ancestral knowledge, and relegated it to a "spiritual" dimension detached from its material properties. It could be said that Father Arana did this also and simply incorporated the idea of the Apu into his own (modern) understandings about Catholicism and environmentalism. Father Arana's translation suggests that an Apu was a "sacred mountain" according to "local beliefs," which maintains the dualisms that keep earth-beings (and the worlds to which they belong) confined to the sphere of spirituality. Treated as *belief,* Cerro Quilish does not pose "an epistemic alternative to scientific paradigms (ecological or economic)" (de la Cadena 2010:349), making it easier to dismiss from politics.

However, it could also be said that Father Arana tried to reject reductionist analyses that interpreted the defense of Cerro Quilish in terms of two incompatible spheres: that of the mythical, spiritual, romantic, and ideological, or that of the technical and scientific (Arana 2007). By refusing this ontological separation, Father Arana connected the plane of the secular with that of sentient entities like Apus and infused his critique of capitalist mining with both religious teachings on morality and hydrological studies of aquifers. Thus, it could be said that Father Arana brought the "crossed-out God" back into the world of the secular (and hence, into the realm of politics), making it impossible to settle the controversy solely through economic, technical, and scientific arguments.

The campaigns in defense of Cerro Quilish evoked an animate landscape that was part of campesinos' experience of the Cajamarca countryside. People's relationship to the beings that populated that landscape was not always expressed in everyday practice, but it nevertheless inspired the campaigns against mining and contributed to their success. I went to Porcón with the hope of understanding people's relationship with the neighboring mine, the resources that enabled their subsistence, and the mountain that had become so emblematic in debates over mining.

Knowledge Encounters in Porcón

The communities that dot the main highway leading up to the Yanacocha gold mine have changed political and administrative jurisdiction through the years but are part of an area that locals have generically designated as "Porcón." As in other communities around the mine, Porconeros have an ambiguous relationship with the mining company, one that oscillates between dependence and rejection, resistance and cooperation. The water used in many of these communities (for domestic and agricultural activities) originates in Cerro Quilish, and it is for this reason that many people from the area participated in the 2004 protests against the mine. Following the Quilish controversy, however, Minera Yanacocha's heavy investment in development projects and the number of people employed at the mine (either directly or through subcontractors) made many people more accepting of the company. In general, the people who continued to organize against the mine after the Quilish protests considered Porconeros to be "pro-Yanacocha" or, at least, apathetic when it came to mobilizing in opposition to the company.

Nevertheless, Porcón continued to hold particular significance for anti-mining campaigns. As one of the last remaining pockets of Quechua speakers in northern Peru, the region's distinctive characteristics—particularly its festivals, communal agricultural practices, and artistic traditions such as weaving and stonework—captured the imagination of many urban intellectuals, NGOs, artists, and activists, especially those critical of the mine. In the historical imagination, Porconeros were brought from what is now Ecuadorian territory during the Inca reign. The Incas used the practice of *mitimae*, or displacing a group of people into another area, as a strategy to weaken enemy groups, maximize their resources, and expand their empire. Many people in Cajamarca attributed the cultural distinctiveness of Porconeros to this early history of displacement, as well as their subsequent marginalization and relative isolation from surrounding communities. Porcón's unique qualities became part of the imaginary of both rural and urban actors involved in the defense of Cerro Quilish, while the changes they saw in Porcón became the focus of criticisms against Minera Yanacocha. For example, when cement houses with ceramic-tile façades built by campesino mine workers began to appear among typical adobe constructions, people criticized what they saw as ostentatious behavior, growing social disparities, and a break from local customs. In anti-mining narratives, Porcón stood for a way of life being effaced by the mine's influences, and one of the last remnants of a precolonial past.

I went to Porcón with the intention of exploring these narratives around mining and the role of "the countryside" (what people call *el campo*, contrasting it with the city) in the emerging conflicts. My first contacts in the area were made through Ernesto, a friend in the city who had worked with Father Arana in the Porcón parish high school. His fascination with what he termed the "Andean worldview" (*la cosmovisión andina*) inspired his involvement in the Quilish campaigns. He illustrated educational materials produced by NGOs, including little storybooks about the consequences of mining activity. In one of our conversations, Ernesto explained that he incorporated what he learned about the rural reality and Andean worldview in Porcón into his drawings and stories, which were intended for a campesino audience. What he wanted me to see was that in spite of the changes and conversion to Adventism, this cosmovisión was something that people carried with them and expressed in subtle ways, even if they had to outwardly behave according to the evangelical teachings (which included strict codes for dress, diet, and behavior). Just as evangelical Christians could no longer participate in the Catholic festival of Cristo Ramos but still watched from a distance, he told me, the fact that people could not talk about the sun and water being "sacred" did not mean that people did not treat them as such.

Ernesto introduced me to Salvador, who was in charge of the Quechua Academy in Cajamarca, one of the many organizations that had also lent its support to the anti-mining campaigns. The role of the Quechua Academy was to promote the language by offering classes (primarily to teachers) in the city, as well as by organizing activities in Quechua-speaking communities intended to foster pride in the Quechua language. This was not an easy task in an area where, as I was frequently told, parents preferred that their children learn English, thinking that this might help them get a job at the mine.

Salvador, who was in his early thirties, had an earnest expression and soft-spoken manner. His unassuming nature inspired trust in those who met him. Salvador had studied to be a teacher and learned Quechua from his grandfather. He and his two sisters were raised by his grandparents after his mother died when he was a month old. His father worked at the Porcón Farm, which took him away for long periods, and he later re-married and started another family. Salvador was close to his grandfather but said that when he was young, he didn't understand or value his grand-father's teachings. It was only when he was nineteen or twenty, training as a teacher and getting involved with the Quechua Academy, that he began to appreciate them. He was the only one of the grandchildren who felt some affinity with his grandfather's ideas and accompanied him on trips to the mountains to conduct what Salvador called *rituales*, rituals that involved presenting coca leaves and other offerings to the mountain as a way of giving thanks.

Salvador's work with the Quechua Academy put him in touch with people in Peru and abroad working to promote the Quechua language, and he became a kind of spokesperson for "Andean culture." He was once invited to Canada (where he passed up the opportunity to stay and teach Quechua at a university) and took some typical Porcón artifacts as a way to share aspects of the culture with his hosts. However, when he visited his native Cochapampa, his work and beliefs were at odds with his family, all of whom had adopted the Adventist religion. "Salvador worships [*adora*] the moon, the sun, everything," a neighbor once commented as she told me about the friction that this sometimes caused with his father, who was actively involved with the local Adventist church.

During my stays with his grandparents in Cochapampa, a small caserío consisting of some eighty families that is part of Upper Porcón, Salvador's family provided me with a glimpse of the many facets of life in Porcón. Traveling to Cochapampa simply required riding one of the many *combis* (minivans used for public transportation) that travel from Cajamarca to different points along the main highway. It took approximately forty min-utes to reach Km. 16, the last stop on a route with regular daily service. This fluidity between the city and countryside was also an effect of the mine's arrival, and people had grown used to frequent trips to the city—to shop for groceries, visit relatives, deal with administrative matters, or attend school. From Km. 16, it was a twenty-minute walk to the house of Salvador's grandparents, just behind the primary school.

Cochapampa was typical of communities within Minera Yanacocha's "area of influence," a designation that made it eligible to receive various forms of support. The company made yearly donations of classroom supplies to the primary school, and children could be seen carrying backpacks that read "Yanacocha loves you"—presents from the previous year's Christmas gift giving, personally delivered by Yanacocha employees who volunteered their time as part of the company's community outreach. In rural communities such as this one, people have long combined subsistence farming and small sources of income with support from a number of state-run assistance programs: mothers take turns cooking breakfast with food donations provided by PRONAA (National Program for Nutritional Assistance), and both the Wawa Wasi nursery program and Vaso de Leche (Glass of Milk) program provide mothers with staples such as sugar, powdered milk, and oatmeal, as well as occasional opportunities for income-generating activities. Minera Yanacocha was one more donor that had been integrated into this wider network of assistentialism that people depended on.

In the rainy season, the path from the highway to Cochapampa turned to mud and was traversed by small streams that swelled with the heavy rains. The elementary school teachers, who came up from the city each day on transportation partially paid for by Minera Yanacocha, complained about the wet trek to the school. The rains also gave the landscape a green lushness, a deceiving image of fertility given that the fields didn't produce like they used to and there was not enough pasture for the animals. Most families grew grains, tubers, and some vegetables adapted to the high altitude and complemented agriculture with the sale of milk. In addition to cows, some people also kept sheep and small animals (chickens, ducks, and guinea pigs) for sale or consumption.

Compared to other communities in the vicinity of the mine, Porcón was an area with a high population density and land divided into small plots. The story of Salvador's family exemplified the pressure on land resources that is typical of Porcón. His great-grandparents lived on what used to be the Porcón Hacienda, paying rent to the landlords in exchange for using a parcel of land. Before the agrarian reform of the 1960s, which put an end to the hacienda system, they purchased the land that now belongs to the family. When they were too old to work the land, it was passed on to Salvador's grandfather, who in turn divided his two hectares of land among his four children. Salvador's father, Mariano, had established his household on the property that corresponded to him and had to divide his property among six children from his two marriages. Salvador showed me the property that he would inherit, a strip of land about 20 by 50 meters, large enough to build a small house but certainly not to farm. Salvador lived in the outskirts of the city on land belonging to his wife and had no intention of moving permanently to Cochapampa, but some of his siblings had already started to build their houses. "It's beginning to look like a little village [*pueblito*]," he commented with an ironic laugh when we approached the cluster of houses, lamenting that it was more and more difficult to live from the land—and that perhaps this was not what people wanted anymore.

This was a typical story repeated across Porcón, as fields decreased in size with each generation. Campesinos struggled to subsist on small plots, battling *rancha* (potato blight), low soil fertility, and unpredictable weather. It was also difficult to sustain livestock on small plots of land, and having enough grass or fodder to feed the animals was a constant struggle, especially in the dry season. When the grass shortage turned critical, toward the end of the dry season, Salvador's grandmother, Maria, walked more than an hour each day to Upper Porcón, where she rented some pastureland from a relative to feed her two cows.

Given the importance of having access to pasturelands, many campesinos have multiple properties and grazing areas. This way, animals can rotate between different communities, sometimes located at different elevations, to ease the perpetual grass shortage. This strategy was common among campesinos in the Cajamarca countryside and resulted in a constant movement of people as well as an intentional effort to maintain links to multiple places of residence. When mining activity exacerbated the pressure on existing resources, this fluidity of movement and people's attachments to multiple communities influenced the way people organized against Minera Yanacocha. Beyond simply defending the land where a mining project would be developed, people were concerned with defending an expansive network of agricultural fields, pastures, and water necessary to maintain the household economy.

People's negative reaction to the Quilish project was in part based on the increased pressures that the mine would have on land and water resources that enabled people to eke out a living. However, people did not necessarily have a clear position "for" or "against" mining. Minera Yanacocha was already part of a network of relations that at times contributed to people's livelihood, and at others, made it more difficult. Temporary wage labor, donations, and development projects were considered useful insofar as they had become integrated into people's livelihood strategies, but with the recognition that these benefits were short-lived. This contradictory relationship with Minera Yanacocha—its promises of employment and development on the one hand, and its failure to live up to people's expectations on the other—contributed to the conflictive and sometimes self-interested relationship that people had with the company. They utilized it for their benefit, whenever it was convenient, and resented it at other times. The Quilish protests were one instance in which people's discontent resulted in the rejection of the proposed project. Arguments about the importance of Quilish as a key source of water resonated among people in Porcón, who were already experiencing shortages of pasture land, and lower crop yields. But what of the arguments about "Apu Quilish" that also emerged from the experience of life in Porcón?

Scientists and Mountain Spirits

During the time that I spent in Cochapampa, children and adults told me many stories—about good and evil mountains, the creatures that emerge from water springs at night, the places one should not venture for fear of losing his or her spirit (*ánimo*), the dangers of rainbows, and the plants that cure *susto* (literally "fright," which afflicts young children in particular, when traveling in dangerous areas). Sometimes I would ask about Cerro Quilish, thinking that people's stories could help me understand why so many had joined forces in its defense. Most of the stories I heard were not about a benevolent protector that might correspond to an environmentalist narrative or to the image of a "sacred mountain" that tended to surface in campaigns against mining. Instead, they were about harmful spirits lurking in caves and water springs, especially in mountains which, like Cerro Quilish, concealed precious minerals and other treasures to entice humans into the underworld where evil spirits reside.

These stories coincide with those in a monograph by anthropologist

Ana de la Torre (1986) titled *Los dos lados del mundo y del tiempo,* which is based on research conducted in communities around Cerro Quilish in 1979 and 1980. Her informants described a *Shapi,* a being who emerges from the underworld through tunnels that end at water springs. From these water springs, the Shapi waits for its victims in order to steal their ánimo, tempting them with the promise of sweets, gold coins, livestock, and other offerings. "Bad" mountains are those associated with the source of rivers and water springs, since water is property of the Shapi. The danger of the Shapi lies both in its evil intentions as well as its ability to fascinate and entice humans with promised gifts; this contradictory nature, the tension between danger and desirability, destruction and fecundity, is what produces the natural order.

Salvador once explained to me that the water used in Cochapampa came from the Kunguna, a small mountain with a distinctive rock façade. At the top of the mountain was a wooden cross decorated with flowers and offerings from the few practicing Catholics that have not converted to evangelism. I once accompanied Salvador and a group of teachers from the Quechua Academy to the Kunguna, where Salvador conducted the rituals that he had learned from his grandfather and continued to do on his own, usually with groups of visitors such as this one.

The water from the Kunguna, Salvador told me, comes from Cerro Quilish. He explained the importance of Quilish and its relationship to other mountains: "The Kunguna is female, and Quilish is her husband—he's male. His brothers are Cerro Negro, Campanario, Qaqamarca. . . . The mountains talk to each other at midnight, to find out how they are doing. All of them have water, but Quilish has more of it. They are like veins: if you cut off one arm the water starts to diminish. They are like people." This is what his grandfather had told him, and I heard similar stories from others. The liveliness of the landscape remained even though many people had new religious obligations that discouraged such thinking. Mount Kunguna was considered one of those places that one ought to approach with care, since the presence of water springs and the entities that could emerge through them could bring danger to those who ventured near them. People described the beings that emerged from the water springs as demons or evil bird-like creatures.

During my time in Porcón, people's stories and accounts made evident their detailed knowledge about the location of water springs, the flow of rivers, the route of irrigation canals, and other details pertinent to their livelihoods. But my conversations with people also reminded me that the intimate, lived experience of everyday life that is often conceived as "local" or "traditional" knowledge is always born from encounters.[2] Julie Cruikshank explores three different types of knowledge encounters in her account of the socionatural history of glaciers in Alaska: encounters take the form of actual meetings between strangers; they are interactions between humans and a rapidly changing landscape; and they concern ongoing exchanges between stories and their subsequent readers and listeners (2005:16). Similarly, some of the knowledge encounters that shaped the socionatural history of Porcón include interactions among Porconeros and state agents, Catholic priests, evangelical missionaries, NGOs, and mining engineers. But knowledge encounters also involve elements of the surrounding landscape (both before and after mining's transformative effects) and the animate entities that make that landscape. Furthermore, encounters take place as stories about Cerro Quilish travel outside Porcón, and when these stories become translated, reinterpreted, and perhaps reincorporated into different knowledge practices.

I learned about these multiple encounters during a conversation with Margarita, a twenty-nine-year-old mother whose husband worked for a subcontractor at the mine. Margarita's family lived just above the path leading to the highway, and on my way to or from Cajamarca I would sometimes find her peeling fava beans or harvesting potatoes. It was not a good harvest; the *medicamentos* (pesticides) were too costly, and the potatoes were full of worms, which she picked out and tossed into the waiting mouth of the dog sitting beside her. The family shared just over half a hectare of land with her husband's sister, who lived on the other side of the field. One day we were chatting at her house while she washed the dishes in a large tub on the ground and were joined by her twelve-year-old son, Jaime. Jaime liked telling me stories about devils inhabiting the Yanacocha mine, which he had heard from his father and uncle who worked there. I asked Margarita what she knew about Cerro Quilish:

MARGARITA: The water that we drink comes from Quilish, they say. They say that in Quilish, there's a lagoon inside, which rises every which way.
FABIANA: Who says this, the elders?

M: The scientists. They study it, that's why they say this. This is what they tell us.

JAIME: It's also on the radio.

M, J: They talk to each other. The devils talk to the gringos.

J: [Mount] Kunguna also talks to [Mount] Aliso.

M: And Aliso talks to Quilish.

J: They recorded this, when they talked, and they play it on the radio. They speak in Quechua, in English.

F: What else do the scientists say?

M: Quilish has a lagoon inside, they say. It springs every which way.

F: That's where the water comes from?

J: Yes, it springs from the foot of the mountain. There they made a reservoir, and then it comes through the pipes. That's where they take the potable water, and it reaches our house.

F: So this water from the tap comes from Cerro Quilish?

M: That's what they say. A lagoon, they say.

F: Before you heard it on the radio, did people tell stories about Cerro Quilish?

M: No, we hear them on the radio. "Quilish is life." If it's mined the water will be contaminated, and we'll die, like chickens [*laughs*].

J: There used to be frogs, but these are dead now.

M: There are no frogs now, before there were, green ones.

J: Now the mine has contaminated them.

M: On the path, you'd find them . . . it's been seven, eight years that there aren't any. I used to be afraid to walk there; we'd find the little frogs, around the rocks, green ones . . .

Margarita went on to recount some stories her grandfather had told her, about mountains that contained gold. I asked if her grandfather had also told her stories about Cerro Quilish, and she replied: "They used to say Cerro Quilish was evil. It would eat you. Yanacocha couldn't get there, the water springs would suck you in. Quilish was such an evil one! Little boys would die, dried up. But not anymore. It's become tame. I don't know how. Now we can get there, we're not afraid at all. Before they used to believe, our grandparents. . . . And because of their beliefs, the children would die. But now we know the word of God, and we don't believe anymore [in evil spirits]. We're not even afraid." Margarita's account combines her grandfather's stories and NGO campaigns against mining with her own observations of water springs at the foot of Cerro Quilish and the experience of walking on paths full of frogs to the nearby community of Chilimpampa (named after the *chilin,* one of the types of frogs commonly found in the area). Many campesinos commented on the absence of frogs as a consequence of mining activity, and this concern was picked up by environmentalist campaigns and the mine's own countercampaigns. The "scientists" that she mentions could refer to members of local NGOs or international consultants that went to Cajamarca to lend support to the Quilish campaigns. For example, a public event held in March 2004 to present observations to Yanacocha's Environmental Evaluation Study included the participation of members of GRUFIDES, a lawyer from Lima, and an environmental scientist from Belgium. Radio spots, printed materials, and educational workshops run by NGOs usually made reference to studies carried out by local and international organizations, even though the information was translated into nontechnical language. Thus, the "lagoon" refers to scientific descriptions of Quilish as an aquifer that holds water, but this idea merged with stories told in Andean communities, which say that large subterranean lakes exist beneath mountains. While rivers, lakes, and water springs are obvious sources of water, mountains themselves can also be considered sources of water, even if they show no evidence of being so (Sherbondy 1998:229).

Jaime and Margarita attributed their knowledge about Cerro Quilish to what they heard on the radio, but in their accounts the radio spots (produced by NGOs to raise awareness about mining) became entangled with their own conceptions about mountain-beings. Mountains have human qualities and "talk to each other." They referred as well to versions of stories about gold-bearing mountains and greedy individuals who meet a tragic fate when they are confronted by evil spirits. In recent versions of this oft-told story, the "gringo" perpetrators are North Americans and Peruvians from the capital city working for Minera Yanacocha. The NGO campaigns drew from these stories in order to reach a rural audience, even though as Margarita claims, people who converted to evangelism "don't believe" in them anymore. At the same time, she continued to attribute agency to Cerro Quilish when she explained that the reason Cerro Quilish no longer harms people is that "it's become tame."

The stories told by Margarita and Jaime mesh "scientific" narratives about the importance of Quilish with a world of spirits and agentive mountains. Both were necessary in order for stories about Cerro Quilish to travel outside the boundaries of Porcón and the Cajamarca region. While hydrological arguments appeal to universalizing ideals of science and environmentalism, testimonials incorporated into anti-mining campaigns appeal to the particularities of local knowledge. As I was constantly reminded in the field, however, what are usually thought of as "scientific" and "traditional" knowledge are both the result of local-global encounters — encounters that are unequal and unstable and have unpredictable effects.

Neither scientific narratives nor local stories are fixed and unchanging, and as they become part of new transnational contexts — of global mining, environmentalism, and cultural rights — they are transformed and in turn help transform those contexts with which they merge. Sometimes these different types of knowledge connect, and sometimes they slide apart (Cruikshank 2005), but as the Quilish case makes clear, these knowledges do not have to be based on shared interests or a common understanding of the world. Divergent knowledges can also communicate and come together in unexpected ways. One of the ways in which noncongruent knowledges came together in the Quilish controversy was in discussions around water. As I will show, arguments about the importance of Cerro Quilish as a water source were important for the campaigns against the mine, but they also helped further the interests of those in favor of the project.

Traveling Knowledges

In Peru, spirits and other beings that inhabit the mountains (variously known as "Muqui" and "duendes," among other names) have long been part of mining activity, engaged in complex negotiations with mine workers facing the dangers of the underground mines.[3] The ideas about a sentient landscape that I encountered in Cajamarca were part of this larger socionatural world that remains present in the popular imagination in the Peruvian highlands. However, the Apu that Cerro Quilish came to represent was not already part of a "traditional Andean cosmology" but came into public view through multiple interactions as it was incorporated into anti-mining protests.

Father Arana's evocations of Cerro Quilish's "sacredness" resonated with people in the campo as well as urban residents, including those who were part of his congregation but also others who shared his Catholic background. The protection of the environment from mining pollution, and the defense of Cerro Quilish in particular, came to be seen by some within this group as an intrinsic part of their Catholic duty. One example of how these ideas were articulated comes from a bulletin produced in 2003 by the Asociación para la Defensa Ambiental de Cajamarca (Cajamarca Association for Environmental Defense), which included some members of Father Arana's Parish of Guadalupe: "We Christians of Cajamarca defend Cerro Quilish, the Sacred Apu, for the traditional campesino way of thinking. . . . To defend Quilish as a Mountain where campesinos can worship God . . . is a challenge for us Christians who are called to cultivate a spirituality, that is, a life according to the Spirit of Jesus Christ that recuperates the meaning of God, always present in nature, which speaks to us of its Creator." The idea of the "sacred" helped to translate the relationship between campesinos and Cerro Quilish into the language of Catholicism. At the same time, Cerro Quilish's identity as an Apu traveled beyond a religious audience, enrolling environmentalists, journalists, and other supporters—including campesinos themselves, who perhaps reappropriated the meanings of Cerro Quilish in ways that helped to strengthen their claims.

Narratives about "Apu Quilish" that were part of Father Arana's writings were quickly picked up by the media, as were the arguments about water that activists emphasized in their campaigns. National and international news stories that circulated about the Quilish protests consistently described the conflict as one that revolved around the defense of Cajamarca's primary source of water. For example, *La República*, a national daily with a liberal slant, referred to Cerro Quilish as an aquifer that supplies water to the city (*La República* 2004). Some national media reports also mentioned the need to conduct hydrological and hydrogeological studies of the watershed before any exploration work could continue, a point that was written into an agreement between the mining company and local leaders that put an end to the protests (*El Comercio* 2004).

In missives from organizations such as Oxfam America and the international press, descriptions of Cerro Quilish as a source of water were often accompanied by references to its local significance as a sacred mountain. An article from AFP newswire stated that "campesinos justified their attitude [against exploration activity] alleging that the mountain is sacred and that the gods of Andean mythology (Apus) gave it to them 'in concession' to take care of them" (Cisneros 2004). In another article, titled "Protests Continue against Gold Prospecting on Sacred Peruvian Mountain," a journalist from the Associated Press wrote that Cerro Quilish was "historically considered an 'apu,' or deity, by local Indian communities" (Caso 2004). In the national press the term *Apu* did not appear with great frequency, but the alleged sacredness of Cerro Quilish was nevertheless present in media coverage (e.g., Sandoval 2004) and influenced public opinion on the issue.

Before the Quilish protests, Apus and other entities were usually relegated to studies of "folklore" (or more recently, to tourism, and to "New Age" and environmentalist discussions) but were not taken seriously in political debates. Additionally, the idea that Cerro Quilish was an important aquifer set the conflict apart from earlier disputes around mining activity in the country. Certainly, water had previously been a concern in mining regions, particularly when rivers and streams were contaminated by mine runoff. However, the idea that a mountain needed to be protected *because* it was a source of water marked a shift in thinking about mining, water, and the environment. Water helped make the Quilish issue compelling and drew the support of people who did not necessarily identify with an "environmentalist" or "anti-mining" stance.

In part, the shift to discussions about water related to new technologies of open-pit mining that involve moving massive quantities of earth, using chemicals that could leach into bodies of water, and using large quantities of water in the mining process. In modern mines like Yanacocha, the unknown and unpredictable risks associated with mining operations are the most worrisome for neighboring communities: the lowering of the water table, the reduction of water flows in rivers and irrigation canals, and contaminants that are often undetectable to the naked eye. Once Cerro Quilish was identified as a key source of water for the region, these unseen and unforeseen hazards became more tangible. Activists used these arguments to put a stop to the project and made water a key element of future conflicts.

Quilish as Water

The Quilish anti-mining protests, unprecedented in the country's history, prompted Yanacocha's definitive withdrawal from Cerro Quilish. Bowing to public pressure, Minera Yanacocha asked the Ministry of Energy and

Mines to revoke its exploration permit. Following the protests, the mining company emitted a communiqué in which it recognized its mistakes:

> The events that took place in September have made us understand the true dimension of the preoccupations that our insistence to initiate exploration studies and activity in Quilish generated in the population, both in the countryside and the city.
>
> We have listened to the preoccupations expressed by people of the countryside and the city, with regard to the quality and quantity of water. In this respect, we will work jointly with communities with the objective of obtaining an integral and transparent solution that will allow us to protect this precious resource.
>
> We want to give testament to our willingness to always listen to the sentiments of the people of Cajamarca, recognize our mistakes, and promote positive changes in our behavior that will permit constructing our relationship with the population. (Minera Yanacocha 2004)

It was an unprecedented recognition of fault on the part of the company and explicitly evoked the importance of water. Activism against the Quilish project, including scientific arguments about the importance of Quilish as an aquifer, helped make water the common language in which mining issues were discussed. During the Quilish controversy and in subsequent mining conflicts, protestors maintained that mining "at the headwaters of the river basin" (*en cabecera de cuenca*) would inevitably affect the water of communities downstream, and should not be permitted.

The focus on water in mining debates emerged alongside a national concern about water issues that were not restricted to the impacts of extractive activity, but ranged from potable water and sanitation in urban areas to global water scarcity and privatization. However, "water and mining" became a prominent theme in the many water-related conferences, forums, and educational events that were organized in Cajamarca and throughout the country in the years following the Quilish protests. These conferences often saw the participation of international experts and key figures such as Father Arana and spokespeople from the mining sector. In May 2007 in Cajamarca, for example, the first of an ongoing series of "Water Forums" (organized by a coalition of actors that included the mining industry) brought together representatives from corporations, government, and civil society to discuss water-related issues and management strategies. In several conferences on mining organized by NGOs, water also took precedence in the presentations and discussions.

While arguments about Cerro Quilish's role as a source of water contributed to an anti-mining discourse, Minera Yanacocha also began to give water more attention in its public relations campaigns. These campaigns transformed Cerro Quilish into an object for technical and scientific management and sought to counter criticisms against the mining company. Much of Minera Yanacocha's public relations work focused on water issues that activists themselves had helped introduce into the debate: for example, the company disputed the claim that mining processes compromise water availability for local communities. Instead, Minera Yanacocha's educational materials and public presentations suggested that the problem was not one of water *scarcity*, but of water *management*. In its public relations materials, the company argued that Cajamarca had abundant water, but it was "lost" because it was not captured and used to its full advantage before it flowed into the sea. For example, a poster and video campaign promoting Minera Yanacocha's water management plans stated: "We are collecting some of the water that Cajamarca loses at sea. There is [enough] water. Let's all think about how we can collect more of it."[4] Thus, the solution lay in capturing more water by constructing water reservoirs, dikes, and water tanks. Other company-sponsored projects focused on improving irrigation systems by lining canals to reduce water loss and introducing spray irrigation technologies. The company also invested in various participatory water monitoring programs that involved state institutions and local communities. This emphasis on the technical dimensions of water issues reduced the complexity of Cerro Quilish and facilitated the company's efforts to refocus the debate to emphasize the management of resources.

Following the Quilish protest, the company focused its efforts on promoting an image of environmental responsibility, institutional transparency, and public participation, all legitimized by technical arguments. This strategy was apparent in the events that took place on the second anniversary of the Quilish protests. On September 2, 2006, the company installed a series of information panels around the stone fountain in Cajamarca's Plaza de Armas describing operations at the Yanacocha mine (see figure 3.3). The panels contained photographs of the mine's laboratories and plant facilities, water monitoring programs, and reclamation projects

FIGURE 3.3 A Yanacocha engineer explains the technical aspects of the mining process in Cajamarca's central square.

to restore vegetation around the mine. According to a Yanacocha press release from May 28, 2007, the idea for this event came from a group of mine employees and was embraced by the company because it aimed to show in a "transparent and direct way, through contact with mine workers, how work is carried out at Yanacocha." The visual displays around the fountain, along with the engineers on hand to answer people's questions, were meant to inform people about the complex processes that are involved in modern mining operations.

There was a festive feel to the event, as the engineers and other mine employees who had volunteered to come out that Saturday morning gathered to chat around the fountain and took turns engaging with the public. Yet the relaxed and festive ambiance in the plaza concealed what was in fact one of the most difficult periods for Minera Yanacocha since the company's arrival. Just one month prior, residents of Combayo had initiated a roadblock to protest against Yanacocha's plans to expand its mining operations in the area. Combayo leaders insisted that the primary reason for their opposition was their concern about the effects of mining activity on the quality and quantity of their water (and consequently, farming and agricultural activities). Company officials dismissed the claims of Combayo leaders, arguing that the conflict was driven by personal economic interests—in other words, that the protests were a way to coerce the company into providing jobs for people in the community and contracts for Combayo entrepreneurs wanting to work on development projects funded by Minera Yanacocha.

The information displays around the fountain were part of the company's efforts to overcome the tensions lingering since the Combayo protests began. But the timing of the event was significant for another reason. While news about Combayo circulated around the country, it was an earlier conflict that was on people's minds: Cerro Quilish. The company anticipated that some activists might attempt to commemorate the second anniversary of the Quilish protests, but the fierce backlash against NGOs and the Combayo protestors—expressed in angry editorials, pro-Yanacocha rallies, and even direct hostility toward key activists critical of the mine—thwarted the activists' plans. Instead, I listened to the mine's engineers explain to passersby that the mine does not pollute the environment or affect water quantity, even amid a few skeptical remarks and pointed questions from the public. The engineers' technical explanations were an attempt to diffuse the conflicts that plague the industry, and which they blame on irrational emotion, misinformation, and political manipulation. Their direct engagement with local residents was part of the mining sector's renewed efforts to minimize opposition through information sharing, replacing people's uncertainties and fears of environmental threats with technical arguments intended to dispel them.

Relating Multiple Worlds

"Will Quilish give its consent to be mined?" Herlinda's question highlights the challenge of understanding conflicts that are based on ontological differences. For many campesinos in the region, Cerro Quilish is part of a sentient, animate landscape disrupted by recent large-scale mining projects. However, Cerro Quilish did not already exist as an Apu according to a traditional "Andean cosmology"; rather, it came into public view through multiple interactions and knowledge practices that revolved around the anti-mining protests.

Salvador's own role in the campaigns gave me some insights into how he enacted the "traditional knowledge" that he was working to preserve.

When I visited him in 2012, it seemed that the years that had passed since the Quilish conflict had given him the distance necessary to analyze these emblematic events from a different vantage point. Salvador continued to work at the Quechua Academy, and he was writing a book about the history of Cochapampa from precolonial times to the present, based on the stories that his grandfather and others had told him. It was a slow process, since he worked on it during breaks between the Quechua classes he gave as part of the government's interculturality training for teachers. When I read Salvador's text—what he had managed to salvage after the latest computer crash—I noticed that Mount Kunguna featured prominently in his account. I asked him about the importance of the mountain, and if Kunguna was considered an Apu.

Salvador clarified that the word *Apu* was used only in the central and southern parts of the country, while *orqo* was the word that was used in the Cajamarca variant of Quechua. He also explained that not all mountains (*cerros* in Spanish) are orqo; some are *qaqa*. When I asked him to tell me about each kind of mountain, he said that orqo is a mountain with "plants, water, and animals. You can walk and sow crops. It has spirit (*espíritu*), and people try to respect it. This is what my grandfather used to say." Qaqa, by contrast, had the opposite characteristics: "There are no animals, plants, or water. You can't walk on it, or it's difficult to do so, and you can't sow crops. It's a mountain that isn't natural." I asked him to explain what he meant by "natural," and he answered: "When there are earthquakes or landslides (*huaicos*), they collapse; they are not stable, they change form. It's not the same as orqo, which is firm rock, it doesn't change, it's stable." To further clarify the difference, he walked up to the chalkboard and drew the different kinds of mountains. He illustrated qaqa as a row of overlapping pointed peaks, while orqo was rounded in shape, with a gradual slope. Kunguna and Quilish were orqo, since they had the characteristics he had described: They hold water, plants, and animals, and they also have espíritu.

Salvador's explanation made it clear that Apu had been a term used in other parts of the country, but not by people in Cajamarca. He said that the term was adopted by outsiders and journalists who reported on the Quilish conflict, and it took hold. He acknowledged the irony of this, and the advantages of using the term that was more "catchy," to express what is essentially the same idea. I noticed that in his own writing, he used orqo and Apu interchangeably, and I asked him why. "Apu is more . . . international," he responded with a laugh. He said this half-jokingly, but he was also being practical. What he cared about was that the stories get told, and that children learn about the history of the region. Salvador, like Father Arana, was performing his own kind of translation, and the changes needed to be made to preserve what he construed as the culture of Porcón.

The struggles over Cerro Quilish involved a large number of partici-pants whose interests both overlapped and diverged in productive ways, contributing to the strength of the campaign against the mine. As I have showed in this chapter, Cerro Quilish's multiple forms made it possible for the campaign to draw a diverse base of supporters and travel through international activist and media networks. I am not suggesting that Qui-lish's multiplicity was planned or intentionally fabricated; rather, the vari-ous actors and events I have described helped shape and bring to the fore-front the particular forms that Cerro Quilish was to take at various stages in the controversy.

When the movement was at its strongest, the multiplicity of Cerro Quilish posed a challenge for Minera Yanacocha. Yet as I have sought to show, "making matter" requires continuous effort, and the precariousness of those multiple worlds became evident at times when the movements against mining expansion became fragmented and activism weakened. Arguments about water quality and quantity that anti-mining activists introduced into the debates, along with the mining industry's techno-cratic solutions centered on environmental management, had the effect of destabilizing Cerro Quilish's multiplicity and enabling a singular reality (water) to take hold. This singularity seemed to obscure (at least tempo-rarily) other realities. Yet the potential for ongoing conflict remains, for those other realities do not cease to exist. An attention to multiple worlds reveals the collaborative processes of enactment that bring entities into being. Contemporary conflicts over mining can thus be understood as an ongoing process of contestation over socionatural worlds. This is always an unfinished process and will continue as Cerro Quilish's multiple forms are enacted and reenacted in an evolving context of mining expansion.

CHAPTER 4

IRRIGATION AND CONTESTED EQUIVALENCES

I set out from Cajamarca before sunrise with Mr. Santos, a campesino leader who had invited me to participate in the inspection of the Tupac Amaru irrigation canal. Spanning thirty-two kilometers (twenty miles) over four communities (Cince Las Vizcachas, Hualtipampa Alta, Hualtipampa Baja, and Tual), the Tupac Amaru canal was one of the most expansive within the Yanacocha mine's area of influence. In recent years, the canal had become the center of a series of controversies over the effects of the mine's operations on the quantity and quality of water in the region. In 2002, as the Yanacocha mine expanded its operations, the company diverted water from one of the streams that fed the canal, since acidic water discharges from the mine's waste rock pile had made it unsafe for human use. More than two hundred campesinos registered as *usuarios* (canal users) received US$4,000 each, plus the equivalent of US$6,000 per usuario in community development projects, as compensation for the damages.

The Tupac Amaru canal is one of six irrigation canals (out of thirty-five within the mine's area of influence) whose usuarios have reached similar agreements and received varying amounts of cash, work contracts, and development assistance. Additionally, Minera Yanacocha constructed the San José reservoir out of one of the open pits that was no longer mined. The reservoir was designed to accumulate around 6 million cubic meters of treated water, which would be pumped into the affected canals (this project was completed in 2008) (Minera Yanacocha 2006). In the specific case of the Tupac Amaru canal, water users and Minera Yanacocha signed the Cushuro Stream Extrajudicial Transaction in 2004.

As part of this agreement, the company promised to pave the total length of the unlined canal with cement, a measure intended to reduce water filtration and increase the availability of water for irrigation. Construction work contracts would be awarded to small businesses (*microempresas*) that were to be created by the affected canal users as a way to generate employment opportunities. Furthermore, Minera Yanacocha promised to pump chemically treated water into the canal to make up for the reduced water flows. The affected stream had provided a flow of 39 liters per second (L/s) to the canal, so the company would substitute water for water, returning 40 L/s from its water treatment plant to the canal. By consenting to these compensation and mitigation measures, Tupac Amaru canal users ceded their right to use the water from the Cushuro stream (MWH 2006:189). A year after the agreements were signed, however, people again began to notice a reduction in water flows, and canal users felt that the treated water being "returned" to them by the mining company did not adequately compensate for the water they had lost— neither in quality nor quantity.

My host, Mr. Santos, was an outspoken critic of Yanacocha. As one among a group of campesinos that initiated the construction of the canal in the 1980s, he was now intent on defending it. I met Mr. Santos through our mutual contacts with the NGO GRUFIDES, since he was one of the peasant leaders who had played an important role during the Cerro Quilish protests and had maintained a relationship with the organization. I participated in the canal inspection along with a Peruvian geography student doing fieldwork as part of a graduate program in Europe. For us, it was an opportunity to learn about changes in the landscape since the mine's arrival; for Mr. Santos, we were additional witnesses for the inspection.

After a short bus ride from the city and a call on his cellular phone, we met up by the side of the highway with a group of relatives and friends of Mr. Santos who had come from Tual, a comunidad campesina in the vicinity of the Yanacocha mine. We rode in their pickup truck as far as the road would take us, then walked toward the mine's installations. Joined along the way by another group of villagers, we walked against a frigid wind over clumps of *ichu*, the tough grasses that cover the mountains at this high altitude, more than 3,700 meters above sea level. The landscape appears monotonous and barren to one unfamiliar with it, but people living in the communities nearby are well acquainted with its water springs, plants of multiple uses, and paths discernible only through frequent travel.

As we approached a cluster of large boulders, one of the men in the group told me we were in "Las Viejas," so named because the rock formations resembled petrified old women. His familiarity with this terrain came from having followed countless times the routes of irrigation canals and grazing animals. This was a place *made* by the coming together of human and nonhuman phenomena: physical labor, rainfall, transnational capital, pastures, and livestock. Dairy farming, sheep herding, and small-scale agriculture were people's primary means of livelihood, and all depended on water—the heavy downpours of the rainy season, the lakes, ponds, swamps, rivers, and streams. Equally important were the artificial means devised to *control* these water resources and mitigate the effects of drought and heavy rains: irrigation canals, dams, and reservoirs. Water scarcity in the highlands posed a constant challenge that could be assuaged with an intimate knowledge of the landscape: changing weather patterns, types of grasses, fertility of soils, and most importantly, the origin of streams and their fluctuating water levels in the dry and rainy seasons.

Concerned about the diminishing quantity and unfamiliar appearance of the water reaching their fields, campesinos demanded what they called an *inspección ocular*, an "ocular" or visual inspection to verify their claims. In Spanish, this is a term used primarily in the context of police investigations and legal proceedings. In disputes with the mining company, the adoption of the term highlights the need for witnesses to attest to the campesinos' claims, as well as the reliance on vision and sensorial experiences in detecting the changes produced by the mine. This visual inspection would involve walking along the route of the canal to identify any changes that might have been caused by the mine's operations—changes for which canal users felt they should be compensated.

The inspections were usually coordinated by the regional Administración Técnica del Distrito de Riego (ATDR), a division of the Ministry of Agriculture in charge of administering the region's irrigation infrastructure. The ATDR set the date for the inspection, requested the participation

FIGURE 4.1 Measuring the canal's flow rate during a "visual inspection."

of registered usuarios and mining company representatives, and provided technicians to carry out the inspection. The inspection itself was a low-tech operation: At different intervals over the canal's course, the ATDR technician used a speedometer to time how long it took to fill a regular plastic bucket with water (see figure 4.1). The technician recorded the liters per second of water flow at each designated point, and this information was later compared with the canal's official registration records.

On this particular occasion, the Tupac Amaru canal users had added another component to the inspection. Their goal—without the approval of the ATDR or Minera Yanacocha—was to begin at the canal's point of origin, which was now located within the mine's property (see figure 4.2). The campesinos felt entitled to inspect the canal infrastructure and water springs that fed it, something they were accustomed to doing freely before the arrival of the mine. However, this now involved entering private property (and thus a security breach), so when we arrived, the mine's security guards awaited us. For the group of campesinos, the legal ownership of the land on which the canal's source was found did not determine the right of access. "This was where I once grazed my animals," one of the canal users

FIGURE 4.2 Source of the Tupac Amaru canal, located within the Yanacocha mine's area of operations.

said indignantly. The construction of the mine had not simply changed the ownership of the land; it had also altered different kinds of connections between people, land, water springs, and other features of the landscape that cannot be reduced to contests over property rights. Rather, they entail a reconfiguration of place and all the human and nonhuman components of that place.

At the water spring that was the source of the canal was a water tanker; for the campesinos, this was evidence that Minera Yanacocha was using water from the water spring for its own operations, and thus diminishing the canal flow downstream. After a tense but nonviolent confrontation with the security officers, a group of Yanacocha engineers arrived on the scene, along with a bus full of back-up security guards that remained parked nearby. The campesinos began to voice their concerns, some more aggressively than others. "Why does the water look yellow?" asked one man, pointing to the water we saw trickling down a rocky slope by the side of the road where we stood. An engineer replied that Yanacocha operated within the legal framework, and that the water met the legal water quality standards. He explained that the water was treated with chlorine gas, and a reaction with the concrete made it appear a yellowish color. The engineer admitted that this water was not suitable for human consumption but said that according to the law, irrigation water did not need to meet the same standards as drinking water. Furthermore, he argued that (because of their acidity or high mineral content) none of the naturally occurring springs in the area were technically fit for human consumption (meaning that they did not meet the legal standards for drinking water either).

During this tense confrontation, the canal users and the engineers seemed to be talking about the same thing—water quantity and quality— but speaking from a different set of assumptions. For campesinos, the mining company was "stealing" the water from the natural sources that once fed their canal, and the treated water being returned to them was not the same as the water they once had. For the engineers, the mine's responsibility was to ensure that the water met legal standards for water quality, and that the irrigation canals were replenished with water from its treatment plant to make up for reduced water flows. The engineers' assumptions rest on what I have been calling a "logic of equivalence": first, that water from a natural source is interchangeable with water from a treatment plant; second, that water quality is acceptable if proven to meet the established legal standards; and third, that the mine's effects on the canal can be reversed by "returning" the same amount of water that was lost and compensating canal users with monetary payments, temporary employment, and development projects.

In this chapter, I want to examine this contested logic of equivalence. I do so by focusing on the canal to make visible how a logic of equivalences worked: how it was established, what it concealed, and how it came to be accepted or disputed. The concept of equivalence serves as an analytical tool to make sense of the processes that were intended to resolve the disputes between the mining company and canal users but that contributed instead to the endurance of those disputes. I use the term *equivalence* to capture two related processes: First, equivalence refers to the scientific and technical tools used to make things quantifiable and comparable; and second, I take equivalence to be a political relationship that involves constant negotiation over what counts as authoritative knowledge (see Espeland 1998; Espeland and Stevens 1998).

For mining companies and government officials intent on resolving conflicts, equivalence was the goal of every proposed solution and implied a permanent settling of accounts: pumping water into the canals to meet established water flows, or compensating for pollution with employment contracts, for example. Disputes and disagreements were to be resolved through calculation (of economic costs, environmental risks, and potential benefits) and careful negotiation based on a logic of the market. For example, negotiations with canal users involved the "valuation of resources" (*valoración de recursos*) to determine the loss of income per square meter of land owned, as measured by economic indicators such as diminished milk production. Company officials hoped that these settlements would bring a permanent solution to the disputes that marred relationships with local communities, yet what I observed in Cajamarca was that these disputes had a way of proliferating.

The mining company's attempts to establish equivalence and render it legitimate expanded the number of actors involved in protests, negotiations, and compensation claims. Translating claims over damages to the canal into monetary compensation for usuarios had the effect of multiplying the number of people in the canal's registry of users (*padrón de usuarios*) in order to make them eligible for compensation. Disputes between canal users and the mining company also incorporated other actors, such as scientists, engineers, NGOs, lawyers, and other experts required to establish the legal and scientific legitimacy of competing claims. These multiplying relations were what the media, corporations, and the general public had labeled "conflicts," glossing over how these relations were made. Walking more than thirty kilometers from one end of the canal to the other during the two-day inspection allowed me to see the canal as a living network of relationships, knowledges, and histories that cannot be encompassed into the logic of equivalences and presents a challenge to it.

Making Evidence Count

Campesinos' claims about reduced water quality and quantity cannot be understood simply as conflicts over the use of "resources;" rather, they challenge us to think about how a landscape is experienced, how it comes to be defined, and whose evidence counts as valid in doing so. While canal users had numerous ways of detecting the mine's effects—the changing color and taste of the water, diminished flows, the cattle's refusal to drink the water, the strange specks on the pasture after it has been irrigated—they had to substantiate this evidence with scientific measurements, technical data, and expert witnesses. Ocular inspections provided an opportunity to create this evidence and make it visible for state and company representatives. Walking and seeing the effects of the mine firsthand took on particular significance for campesinos who wanted their experiential knowledge to be taken seriously. No one, they insisted, knew the terrain better than they, who walked it daily and could observe its subtle changes.

Ocular inspections were some of the few occasions in which campesinos felt they had the upper hand. During the Tupac Amaru canal inspection, campesinos demonstrated their knowledge about the area by guiding the way, determining the best routes and shortcuts to take, and insisting on certain monitoring points they wanted to have included in the inspection. They joked about how the team of Yanacocha engineers that joined the inspection struggled to keep up with the campesinos' swift pace and were visibly exhausted after hours of walking. They considered this a sign that the engineers hardly left their offices, and that their work was done with little hands-on knowledge of irrigation systems. For campesinos, the act of walking—maintaining one's balance on the treacherous slopes and a firm footing on uneven terrains, and the stamina to walk from one community to another in harsh weather conditions—was a marker of social difference and defined their experience of the landscape. Walking was crucial for determining who was qualified to speak about the changes that they saw occurring. Just like their ease for walking was acquired through daily activity over the course of a lifetime, campesinos argued, their knowledge about water sources and changing environmental conditions was also acquired through this close, lifelong interaction with the landscape.[1]

The data gathered on the inspection—flow measurements taken over two days at designated spots along the canal and the water springs that feed it—helped canal users strengthen their claims for compensation and solicit further support from the mining company. Complaints from canal users about water quality and quantity forced the mining company to make water issues a priority in their environmental management efforts and public relations campaigns. For Minera Yanacocha, the canal was a site of conflict, but establishing equivalence through compensation agreements also made it possible to turn a public relations fiasco into a showcase of the company's environmental management plans and commitment to local communities. For campesinos, the mine's effects on the canal made evident the possible threats of large-scale mining, but the canal also helped transform these possible threats into money, jobs, and social relations. The canal thus became the means to negotiate for benefits that contributed to their livelihoods: compensation packages, employment at the mine and on company-sponsored development projects, the creation of campesino-run businesses that provided services to the company, charitable donations, relationships of *compadrazgo* ("godparenthood") with Yanacocha engineers, and other direct and indirect benefits derived from the mining company.

In communities near the mine, people's ability (or willingness) to calculate the costs and benefits of mining activity and negotiate with the mining company made them into "rational" subjects in the eyes of corporate executives, politicians, and the general public. On the contrary, the unwillingness to accept the terms of equivalence or engage in negotiation branded campesinos as *ir*rational—and thus their political exclusion was legitimized while mining projects were justified in the name of progress. Those who benefited from the privileges that the mining company could provide were those who were able or willing to make calculations, such as community leaders and canal representatives, and their ability to negotiate required adopting the terms of equivalence. While these negotiations are the mining company's desired outcome, they create conditions that reproduce unequal relations of power, facilitating corruption, paternalism, and new forms of exclusion.

As the canal inspection demonstrates, the legitimacy of the claims made by canal users and Yanacocha engineers rested on public involvement, visual evidence, legal authority, and scientific recognition. Through the canal, water became a common point of contention and the focus of efforts to establish equivalences between environmental damages and forms of compensation. Attempts to make—and reject—equivalence have connected politics and science in new ways, creating not only different ways of seeing and measuring pollution, but also novel forms of political participation and exclusion. Mr. Santos's trajectory as a campesino leader illustrates some of the continuities and changes in rural politics before and after the arrival of the mine.

Politics "Old" and "New"

Mr. Santos lived in San Francisco, a neighborhood built about thirty years earlier in the sloping hills in the outskirts of the city of Cajamarca by campesinos who wanted to take advantage of the opportunities the city had to offer but could not afford to live in the urban core. He proudly wore a straw hat and *ojotas* (rubber sandals worn by peasants), refusing to leave behind these typical markers of campesino identity even though he was spending most of his time in the city. One of Mr. Santos's primary motives for moving was to educate his eight children in city schools. Mr. Santos headed the Potable Water Committee and had worked to bring basic services to the neighborhood. He was also involved with the urban rondas campesinas, continuing his longtime involvement with the rondas in Tual. His involvement in community organizations made him as well known and respected in his new neighborhood as he was in the countryside, something that was evidenced every time his neighbors and acquaintances stopped us on the street to greet him and seek his advice or assistance.

Sometime after the inspection, I accompanied Mr. Santos to Tual for a meeting of the Tupac Amarcu canal users' association. The canal, more than his house in Tual or the few sheep that he kept there under a neighbor's care, was what kept him connected to the community. Public transportation to Tual was irregular, since it was located off the main highway, approximately eighteen kilometers from the city of Cajamarca. Still, it would have been possible to take a taxi, but Mr. Santos preferred to ride the *combi* to the turnoff and walk the rest of the way. We walked along the unpaved road, and up the mountain between houses and barking dogs to cut across the zigzagging road, until we were able to hitch a ride in a passing car. As we walked, Mr. Santos told me about his long trajectory in the campesino movements of northern Peru.

Now in his fifties, Mr. Santos had dedicated most of his life to rural politics. By his own account, his political education began when he learned to read as an adolescent through improvised lessons from one of the older boys in Tual. As they took the animals out to pasture, the dirt became the blackboard on which he learned to form letters with a twig. As a youth, he went to the city to become a laborer and began to attend political meetings. He would take what he heard back to the community and talked about exploitation and the plight of the campesinos against the landholding class, only to face indifference or ridicule. At first, nobody took him seriously, but his charisma, perseverance, and self-motivation would eventually make him into an influential (if also controversial) community leader.

As his political contacts and experience grew, he became involved in the Campesino Confederation and was chosen as a regional representative to the national congress of the Peruvian Workers' Confederation (CGTP) in Lima. Through the years, Mr. Santos's allegiances shifted as he dabbled in various leftist or populist political parties (the APRA, the United Left, and more recently, the Nationalist Party of Ollanta Humala). But what remained constant throughout his life was his involvement with the Federación de Rondas Campesinas. His activities with the Federación took him across the country—and even briefly to jail. When Yanacocha arrived in Cajamarca, Mr. Santos was president of the regional chapter of the rondas and of his own base in Tual. His work as a campesino leader brought him into contact with international NGOs, state institutions, students, engineers, and others working to "develop" the countryside by providing technological expertise. Mr. Santos prided himself on having taught them a thing or two instead—about local technologies, agricultural techniques, and negotiating the difficult landscape of the Cajamarca countryside.

In the 1960s, engineers and state functionaries traveled to Cajamarca to construct irrigation canals, often with the use of expensive equipment and the advice of development "experts." In Mr. Santos's accounts, however, campesinos succeeded in constructing the Tupac Amaru canal with their own knowledge of the landscape and very simple tools—including what Mr. Santos called the "poor man's theodolite." While the theodolite is a costly surveying instrument consisting of a telescope mounted to swivel horizontally and vertically to measure angles, campesinos used simple wooden sticks and string, allowing them to trace the route of the canal that continues to provide them with water.[2] In their narratives about the canal's construction (as in the inspección ocular) campesinos privileged experiential ways of knowing the landscape. The canal was the product of labor, skill, resourcefulness, and the rigors of daily life. This way of thinking about the canal contributed to a system of valuation that was at odds with the company's offer of compensation money and treated water.

At the same time that he remained critical of "expert knowledge" and bureaucrats, Mr. Santos's close contact with the international community and the politics of NGOs would shape his own leadership role. What Mr. Santos learned alongside these agents of development was the ability to move between various spheres of politics—from leftist parties, to peasant associations, to international development circles, to community assemblies. This ability to act as intermediary between different political worlds made Mr. Santos into a key leader in recent anti-mining protests. His contacts and political savvy helped him unite campesino communities by mobilizing ronderos and irrigation canal users, the two groups that would become the backbone of all protests against mining.[3] He also built alliances with city people: lawyers, journalists, union activists, international supporters, and also Father Arana and the NGO GRUFIDES.

Mr. Santos was one of several key figures in the 2004 Cerro Quilish protest. Familiar with the campo as well as the workings of urban politics, Mr. Santos and other leaders voiced the concerns of campesinos and other marginalized groups. According to Mr. Santos, many people were initially pleased with the arrival of the mining company, believing that it could bring opportunities for local communities, but this began to change when animal deaths and problems with the canals raised concerns about the mine: "At first we didn't know, we just supported [the mining company] . . . they gave us food, they seemed like good people, right? But then the problems started, and we realized it wasn't good. That was when the frogs, the trout were dying, the cattle were dying . . . that's when we realized. Here in Tual many animals died."

Campesino testimonies strengthened the advocacy work done by NGOS like GRUFIDES that attempted to document the animal deaths and illness in herds with photographs and inspections. Collecting evidence linking these deaths to mining activity proved difficult, since it was not always possible to carry out the necessary laboratory tests to prove a definite link, yet the captured images and campesinos' testimonies were crucial for their campaigns against the mine. Mr. Santos and others who decided to speak out against the mine did this by invoking a campesino identity forged through a connection to the landscape and a way of life that depended on agriculture and farming. He played an active role in organizational meetings and was a constant presence at protests and marches, where he addressed the crowd with his fiery rhetoric.

In his recollections of the past, campesinos had all the money and food they needed before Minera Yanacocha arrived to dirty the water and the animals started dying. Mr. Santos's statements, incorporated into local and international campaigns against mining, combined a radical defense of campesino rights with what could be interpreted as an ecological sensibility and a romantic vision of a rural past. His testimonies and those of other campesino leaders also provided anecdotal evidence about the location of water springs that were drying up or had disappeared and decreased productivity of animals and crops. These testimonies helped to connect mining to globally significant concerns such as biodiversity conservation, indigenous rights, and the health effects of pollution. Framing mining conflicts in "ecological" terms undoubtedly helped elicit the attention of international NGOS and the media and furthered the cause of campesinos who denounced Minera Yanacocha. Even if the language of protest was different from that used in peasant struggles for land, political activism against mining emerged out of a long history of campesino organizing. Campesino leaders with experience in the administration of their canals transferred this experience into organizing against Minera Yanacocha. Their struggle was not an "environmentalist" one in a conventional sense.[4] Nevertheless, land, water, and cattle were the basis of daily subsistence and, consequently, of campesino politics, including the work of the rondas campesinas and the water users' associations.

Situating campesinos' protest actions within these networks of political organizing and agricultural production counters Minera Yanacocha's claim that "environmental" concerns were introduced through the political manipulation of outsiders (such as NGOs like Oxfam and GRUFIDES). Far from suggesting that campesinos are intrinsic environmentalists or stewards of the planet, what I want to show is that the complex politics that emerged in conflicts over mining brought together local, national, and global discourses (about water, changes in the landscape, and development) that were nevertheless grounded in the materiality of the Cajamarca countryside. In this particular case, that materiality was embodied in both the concreteness of the irrigation canal itself and the fluidity of the relationships that revolved around it. These relationships were shifting and unstable: at times, they connected people (and things) through affect, kinship, and necessity; at others, they produced antagonisms and frictions, even as people sought to cooperate and reach an agreement. The story of the canal, then, is not a straightforward story of cooptation or resistance.

When Minera Yanacocha's activities began to interfere with campesinos' use of irrigation canals and water resources, the canal's already vast network of relationships—organized through peasant and irrigation associations, family connections, and community membership—mobilized the countryside. The canals organized people into *juntas de usuarios* (water users' associations), and the relationships forged through participation in the administration of the canal often overlap with those of other associations: rondas campesinas, community leadership, or participation in local and regional politics. The canal also binds people through kinship ties, as the number of hours assigned to each canal user is passed on to his or her children. Furthermore, the canal is a crucial element of community membership, since it requires each user to fulfill obligations related to the maintenance and administration of the canal.

As a peasant leader, Mr. Santos was already embedded within these established relationships and worked to strengthen and multiply them. While firmly entrenched in the "old" politics of the Left and campesino organizing, he was able to carve out new political spaces that helped make the campesinos' complaints public. His ability to engage multiple worlds allowed him to simultaneously embody many roles: left-leaning revolutionary, peasant hero, environmentalist, and most recently, campesino entrepreneur providing services to the mining company. While each of these roles gained him both friends and foes, they need not be seen as contradictory. Rather, the relationships and alliances built around the canal (and enabled by it) are fluid and contingent, for they reflect the multiple layers of a controversy that cannot be broken down into "pro-" and "anti-"mining camps. More than a mere piece of infrastructure, the Tupac Amaru canal bound together water, campesinos, and the mining company into a knot of relationships that were shaped by past events, present conflicts, and an uncertain future.

Tual's Irrigation Canals

Tual is a community in the shadow of Cerro Quilish. The pyramidal mountain stands as a backdrop to the scattered adobe houses and dairy cows grazing on the pastures. But the looming presence of Cerro Quilish also stands as a constant reminder of the 2004 protests, which mobilized campesinos from all the communities in the vicinity. Canal usuarios from Tual went out in full force to protest against Minera Yanacocha's proposed mining expansion project, since the water springs on Cerro Quilish feed two of the three canals that pass through this community. After the protests, however, Tual residents came to be seen by its neighbors as *"aliados de la mina,"* or "allies of the mining company," a term that people often used pejoratively to describe relationships of cooperation with Yanacocha. The construction of school buildings, a rural health clinic, roads, and other development projects had been sponsored by the mining company, and many people were employed in these projects or at the mine itself. Additionally, monetary compensation gave usuarios access to luxury goods (such as vehicles for personal and commercial use) and opportunities previously unimaginable, like establishing a small business. Critics of Minera Yanacocha and many usuarios themselves pointed out that this kind of assistance came at the cost of compliance with the mining company. And, some would argue, at the cost of compromising one of their most precious resources: water.

Water had always posed a challenge for Tual. The relative scarcity of this resource in the highland region made it necessary to channel water from distant sources. Those who recounted the story of bringing water to Tual did so with unabashed heroism. Building a canal across the slopes and valleys of this difficult terrain required hard physical labor, resourcefulness, and a detailed knowledge of the landscape. One of the men involved in the canal's construction was Teofilo, who had also participated in the canal inspection and like Mr. Santos had a long history as a community leader. When I visited him in Tual a few months later, he was recovering from an illness but nevertheless had the energy to talk about the canal, a topic that always got him worked up. Sitting outside his house, his straw hat shielding his face from the sun, he described the arduous process of bringing water to Tual. With a stick in hand, he made marks on the ground and took me through the motions of measuring, leveling, and tracing the route of the canal using the simplest of tools and much perseverance.

It began with long walks to identify possible sources of water and viable routes that avoided the most rugged parts of the terrain. Little by little, the group began to dig the canal, laying down wooden planks and covering them in cement. Sometimes the water that was channeled would begin to flow, and then peter out. They had to prevent its filtration by blocking any holes with clumps of grass or stones. The heavy rains posed another challenge, but they had to work in spite of the inclement weather, bringing along food to get through the day and sometimes even the nights that they would spend far from home. The women prepared and sent food to the workers, staying at home to care for the children and the animals.

For those involved in its construction, the canal became a symbol of campesino ingenuity, sacrifice, and hard work. In popular accounts of the canal's history, it is these qualities that prevailed over the technical expertise of engineers and limited government resources, and continued to influence campesinos' relationship with Yanacocha engineers. "We have suffered very much for our canal," said Teofilo, explaining why he now had to defend the canal at all costs and denounce the consequences of mining activity:

> We've had more water, but now the mine is screwing us over. And it will keep doing so, it's going to leave us without water. Before, we used to have 163 liters [per second]; since the mine has been operating, it's been going down, down. Now we barely get 100 liters. Nothing more. And that's considering that they are pumping water [into the canal], otherwise we wouldn't even have 50 liters. From the Quebrada Shillamayo, we used to get 4½ liters [per second]. They say they are going to pump [treated water]. Now they are giving us 1½ liters, sometimes one liter, sometimes nothing. That's why we yell at the engineers. As if we didn't know our water, didn't know how much water there is, for them to tell us: "Hey, we give you more water, cleaner water." It's a lie! That's why we yell at the engineers, worse than at dogs!

We are demanding our rights. We are not asking them: "give us your salaries." I'm not sitting there at your [negotiation] table waiting for you to give me a piece of bread. For our water, we've worked, we've eaten our own sweat and [from] our own land.

Teofilo went on to explain that people in Tual had grown crops like potatoes, *oca* (a native tuber), wheat, and barley, but now the earth was spent and produced nothing without fertilizers. This is why they had switched to pastures and dairy farming. Teofilo associated the arrival of the mine with a shift from agriculture to increased dependence on dairy farming and on the mining company itself. The canal was an accomplishment that represented campesino self-sufficiency, a self-sufficiency that many people felt they had lost. As Teofilo's comments also make clear, campesinos felt cheated not only by Minera Yanacocha's inadequate attempts to compensate for reduced water flows, but by the engineers' unwillingness to recognize their knowledge about the water, the work and effort that went into building the canal, and all that they have sacrificed.

According to Teofilo, constructing the canal was a slow, frustrating process of trial and error that involved more than one failed attempt and took more than five years to complete. Along the way, there were disagreements and feuds, and the constant struggle to find people willing to put in the time to work. They began construction with about twenty people who worked regularly, and at most there would be thirty to thirty-five people working each week. Only much later, when it was more certain that the water would reach their communities, more people began to join in the effort. By the time they finished, more than eighty people were involved in the construction. This, too, became a source of conflict, since those who got involved earlier on resented the latecomers who did not put in as much time and effort but wanted to benefit from the canal. In an attempt to reach the most equitable solution, everyone who participated in the construction of the canal became an usuario, but the number of hours they received depended on how much they had contributed to the construction process. Those who contributed more to the construction efforts were likely those with more land and hence would derive a greater benefit from getting more water. In an assembly, each of the original "founders" of the canal received between two and ten hours of irrigation time based on the labor and resources they had put in.

This way of collectively distributing water rights, based on each usuario's investment in the irrigation system, did not necessarily correspond with a technocratic distribution that aimed to increase productivity (Gutierrez and Gerbrandy 1999:261). Rather, access to water depended on a usuario's work on the canal, including its day-to-day maintenance and an annual cleaning (*limpieza del canal*) that continued to be an important communal gathering. In Cajamarca, the yearly limpieza was a technological and social event that used to involve two days of drinking, playing music, and dancing. The event lost its former festive character once a majority of people had converted to Evangelism, which forbids these activities, but the limpieza continued to be a social event and a responsibility shared by all usuarios. In addition, usuarios had other duties: attending meetings, taking on administrative positions (such as president, treasurer, and *repartidor* or water distributor), and volunteering for nightly patrols to prevent water theft. The canal convened people and enabled relationships that, like the canal's infrastructure, required ongoing labor and attention.

When Minera Yanacocha compensated all usuarios with US$4,000 for damages to the canal, it disrupted the system of water distribution that had been established among canal users. While the compensation agreements were intended to settle disputes, many people felt that they created more inequality and injustice. First, the compensation packages benefited only usuarios, and those who were not usuarios felt left out. Second, the agreements went against a system in which access to water was determined on the basis of belonging to a collectivity and on the usuario's involvement in activities related to the canal. While water use had previously been determined through the usuarios' active participation and collective decision making, the negotiations with Minera Yanacocha shifted the emphasis toward individual usuarios, who were compensated the same amount of money regardless of how many irrigation hours they had.

Decision makers within the company drafted the agreement based on two assumptions: (1) that the monetary compensation was equivalent to the financial losses incurred from the damage to the canal, and (2) that all usuarios were equally entitled to the same benefits. For campesinos, however, monetary compensation did not reflect the fact that usuarios were not all equal when it came to rights over the canal's water. The equivalences contained in the agreements did not capture the power asymmetries that were already part of the canal's history, nor did they compensate for the dramatic changes that people had lived through in the span of a couple of decades since the canal's construction.

The construction of the canal between 1980 and 1986 was only the first of a series of events that together transformed the landscape and economy in Tual. Once irrigation water became available, there was a gradual shift from small-scale agriculture to dairy farming. This shift in the local economy was made possible by three other major changes that reconfigured connections between people and the canal. The first change came about when the mining company constructed a road in the mid-1990s leading to its installations. The road passed through Tual and connected it to the city of Cajamarca. Second, the road provided access for delivery trucks from the transnational dairy company Gloria, facilitating the transport of milk from peasant farmers to the market. Once the trucks were able to reach Tual's dairy farmers directly to purchase their milk, people were encouraged to increase production and devote themselves fully to dairy farming. Third, once dairy farming intensified, communal lands were divided into plots of one to two hectares as part of a shift from communal to individual property. Since its establishment as a communidad compesina in 1976, some of the land in Tual was managed collectively, an arrangement that had worked well for sheep pasturing (since the animals can graze on wild, uncultivated pastures). However, some leaders (including Mr. Santos) felt that dairy farming required individual investment into the cultivation and improvement of pastures (primarily rye grasses, as well as clover and alfalfa), and that the land would be better utilized if it was individually owned.

By 2006, 68 percent of land in Tual was irrigated (MWH 2006a). The sale of milk provided most families in Tual with a small but steady income. The construction of the canal enabled the switch to pastures and gave usuarios an advantage over non-usuarios, who continued to rely on small-scale agriculture for their livelihood. Because of the low productivity of the land and the small profit margin derived from the sale of agricultural products, usuarios gradually devoted less land to food crops and intensified dairy production; the cash income they earned from the milk enabled them to buy potatoes, rice, noodles, vegetables, and other staples in the city, which was made accessible by the many transport vehicles that traveled on the road from Tual to Cajamarca. These key events—the construction of the road, the division of communal lands, and the switch to dairy

farming—intensified people's dependence on irrigation water and competition for it. As I will show through the story of Wilmer and Herlinda, the
effects of these changes were evident in Tual's household economies and
in the way people responded to the arrival of the mine.

Wilmer and Herlinda

At the canal inspection I met Mr. Santos's nephew, Wilmer, who was actively involved in the administration of the canal and community assemblies. When I visited Tual some months later, Wilmer invited me to stay
at his house with him and his wife, Herlinda. The young couple, who were
in their late twenties, had an infant son, and a daughter who lived with
relatives in Cajamarca so she could attend school in the city. Wilmer and
Herlinda owned a couple of hectares of land used primarily as pasture for
their dairy cows and had recently constructed a large two-story house. For
the most part, however, we would spend the day in the old house, sitting
in the kitchen as Herlinda prepared the day's meals on the wood stove, or
just outside the house warming up under the afternoon sun.

After the canal inspection, Wilmer became an important leader in the
"nueva junta" (new committee)—the self-denomination of the group that
began to challenge the legitimacy of the *"vieja junta"* (old committee),
meaning the community leaders previously engaged in negotiations with
Yanacocha. Herlinda did not take part in any committees, but she could
have made a good community leader; she was opinionated and eloquent
and kept up-to-date on everything that transpired in the meetings, which
she heard about from Wilmer. When we talked about the latest events in
the community, she was usually serious and thoughtful but punctuated the
conversations with humor and a burst of laughter. She joked that, having
more years of education than her husband, she was qualified to get involved in community politics, but said she was not interested in doing so.
According to the division of labor in the campo, men were generally considered to be in charge of farming and in control of the administration of
irrigation canals. As in other Andean communities, women in Tual could
be registered as canal users but did not usually hold positions of authority
in community assemblies or in water users' associations.[5] In general, men
were more likely to be literate and have a higher level of education, which
was necessary for dealing with the long paper trails of letters, meeting
minutes, and petitions that usually accompanied interactions with city

bureaucrats and company officials. As a result, women often felt the consequences of mining activity on irrigation water most acutely (because they were in charge of dairy farming and household chores), but they did not fully participate in meetings and negotiations related to the canal.

The dairy farming economy produced a new division of labor in which the women were primarily in charge of the day-to-day milking and caring for the cows, while many men no longer engaged in agricultural activities that used to occupy them before they turned the fields into pastureland. Wage labor and mine-related employment was usually temporary and unstable, so some men might work only two or three months in the year. In this uncertain economy characterized by chronic male underemployment, any opportunity to work was welcomed. Yet even when Wilmer was working, Herlinda bragged that she "beat him" by making more money selling milk than he earned with his subcontracting jobs with the mine. With four dairy cows, Herlinda could make about 1,100 to 1,200 soles per month (US$305 to $330 at the time), which was similar to the wage of a manual laborer. The advantage was that she could count on getting paid punctually every two weeks, while subcontracted mine laborers had no certainty of when their paychecks would arrive.

The land where Wilmer and Herlinda lived used to be communal land, until it was parceled out to members of the campesino community. Wilmer received one hectare and bought an adjacent one with money from the sale of another hectare that he had inherited from his father. Herlinda recounted that when the couple first established their household, they used the land to grow potatoes and other food crops, both for personal consumption and for local sale. Later, when this was no longer profitable and the canal provided irrigation water, they turned their *chacra* (a parcel of land used primarily to grow food crops) to pastureland and bought some animals to start dairy farming. It was around this time that the problems with the mine began.

In 2002, Minera Yanacocha constructed a waste-rock deposit near the Quebrada Cushuro (Cushuro Canyon), which affected one of the tributaries that feeds the Tupac Amaru irrigation canal. The runoff was produced as the rain washed over the waste-rock material and flowed into nearby streams, causing changes in the irrigation water. People said that after irrigating their fields, the grass seemed to glimmer with yellow specks that looked like *chochoca* (ground corn). The water had an unusual coloration and a different taste, which led some campesinos to diagnose this as pollution. They also connected these changes in the water to animal deaths and damaged pastures. Herlinda recalled that "the canal was clean, but then it wasn't anymore. It was a different color. . . . The animals were dying, and we said: [it must be] the water. A group of usuarios went to see the water [on an inspection]. It was already contaminated, the Quebrada Cushuro. Sheep and cows were dying, but not our own. For us it was the guinea pigs." Herlinda irrigated the grass with water from the canal and gathered this grass to feed the guinea pigs, so she blamed their deaths on the contaminated water.

In 2003, the canal's elected representatives filed a complaint against Minera Yanacocha demanding compensation for the damages and corrective measures to stop the water pollution. In a letter dated May 30, 2003, the company recognized "the impact generated on the quality of water in the Quebrada Cushuro . . . which shows values exceeding those established in Class III [water for agricultural and farming use] of the General Water Law." It stated that in an extrajudiciary settlement, the company offered forty sacks of chicken manure (*gallinaza*) for each canal user, to be used as fertilizer in their fields. Having followed through with this commitment, the company argued that further compensation was unwarranted given that subsequent water monitoring results were within the permissible limits. Minera Yanacocha also claimed to have addressed the problem of reduced water flow in the canal, since it had been pumping water from its treatment plant to compensate canal users.

This letter—signed by Minera Yanacocha's then manager of community relations—was circulated widely by activists and NGOs as a way of denouncing the company's practices. The letter's explicit acknowledgment of the problems with the canal, as well as the company's attempt to resolve the issue by giving canal users sacks of manure, provided evidence that Minera Yanacocha's critics could use to make the social and environmental consequences of mining known in Cajamarca and beyond.[6]

Following this controversial compensation agreement, representatives of the canal were suspected of siding with Minera Yanacocha in order to acquire personal benefits and were accused of betraying the interests of the usuarios, since they negotiated with the company without full community participation. Even though these representatives had been elected by the usuarios, people began to feel they could not trust the board members of the junta de usuarios because of their connections to the mining company; the president of the canal, for example, was a Yanacocha employee. This led to the organization of a political faction (instigated by Mr. Santos) that sought to replace the board members and demanded to be included in future talks with the company, which gave rise to a new set of disputes and negotiations. These usuarios rejected the logic of equivalence implicit in Minera Yanacocha's way of dealing with the canal. They challenged the claim that the "impacts" generated had been reversed by pumping water from the mine's treatment plants and were outraged that the company would offer forty sacks of manure to compensate for their loss, as if fertilizer for their fields could make up for the mine's permanent alteration of their primary water source.

As the problems with the canals gained notoriety, the company established a *mesa de diálogo* (dialogue table) for five canals affected by its operations to negotiate agreements with the usuarios. In these discussion meetings, usuarios and mining company representatives negotiated the terms of compensation, the amount of water that would be returned to the canals from the mine's treatment plant, and community projects that the company committed itself to undertaking. Company officials assumed that signing these agreements signified a successful resolution to a conflict, but what they did not take into account was how canal water and the relationships built around it disrupted the equivalences on which those agreements were based.

"The Water Is Not the Same Anymore"

Like other campesinas in Tual, Herlinda organized her days around the care of her dairy cows, which provided the family with a regular source of income. It meant waking up early in the morning to milk them and having the canisters out by the side of the road before the milk truck arrived. Throughout the day, she walked to whatever field she was using for pasturing, moved the stakes to which the cows were tied to ensure they had enough grass to eat, and refilled their water buckets. She liked the rhythm that these activities gave to her days and told me she got bored when she spent too much time in the city with her relatives.

From the house, I could spot Herlinda in the field across the canal, and I walked over to join her. Her layered skirts, pink blouse, and bright blue sweater stood out against the grass, and her straw hat lay beside her, revealing her tightly parted hair and a braid running down her back. As she milked the cows, Herlinda told me about the changes that led people in Tual to begin noticing the problems with the Tupac Amaru canal. Usuarios complained that their pastures were drying up and turning yellow from the canal water and the *polvadera*, the dust produced by the mine's constant movement of earth, which was carried by the wind onto their fields. She also added: "The water didn't taste good anymore" (*"ya no era rica"*). People used to drink from the canal when taking the animals out to pasture, but they stopped doing so if it could be avoided and began to rely on the other two canals that go through Tual and have not yet been affected by the mine.

The potability of canal water was a key point of contention in mining controversies, since Yanacocha argued that irrigation water was never fit for human consumption, and was not safe for drinking even before the mine's arrival. By *legal* standards, canal water is not fit for drinking. According to the General Water Law, water is classified into three types: Class I and II are for domestic consumption (with different degrees of treatment), and Class III is for crop irrigation and drinking water for animals. According to the law, canals are not, and are not required to be, safe for drinking. However, these legal standards did not always coincide with the campesino's use of the water. Herlinda knew that water should be boiled before drinking and said that people usually did so. "We drink boiled water, but when there isn't any, what are we going to do? If we're out with the animals, when there isn't potable water, we have to drink [canal water]." In an area where water had always been scarce, drinking from the canals when one was away from home or far from natural water springs was part of life in the campo—it was just the way it was done: *costumbre,* people said, or force of habit. Before they got running water, about five years earlier, people had no other choice but to drink water from the canals or natural water springs.

Wilmer recognized that canal water, according to its legal classification (in Peru and internationally), was not for human consumption, but was only to be used for irrigation and drinking water for animals. But he added: "Of course, we have drunk that water and know that nothing is going to happen to us." Before the mine's arrival, the Tupac Amaru canal was used not only for irrigation, but also for cooking, washing clothes, and other household activities. Alicia, Herlinda's sister-in-law and neighbor, told me that she used to wash clothes in the Tupac Amaru canal, but stopped doing so when she noticed that the clothes seemed oily and had a white film on them when they dried. She began using one of the other two canals not yet affected by the mine, from which she sometimes also drew water for cooking. The outdoor sink that provided her family with potable water was not close to her newly built house, so she continued to rely on the canal water to cook things like rice and lentils—though when making soup, she made sure to use potable water from the sink. Alicia differentiated between the different types of water and their suitability for each task, but these uses still went against Minera Yanacocha's recommendations. Regardless of its legal classification, campesinos had developed their own criteria for determining if water was apt for human consumption: its taste, its coloration, its source, and its effects on animals and pastures.

In addition to the changes in the water quality, usuarios began to notice that the water flow of the canal had diminished. As part of the compensation agreement that was reached in 2004, Minera Yanacocha agreed to pump water from its treatment plant to meet the flow registered in the records of the ATDR. But for Herlinda, this compromise had not increased water flows to their previous levels. "It's not the same," Herlinda told me. "If the machinery breaks down, the water doesn't come"; on those days, the only water feeding the canals came from the *ojitos de agua*, or natural springs.

One day, while discussing the negotiations with Minera Yanacocha, I asked Wilmer if entering into a compensation agreement with Yanacocha essentially amounted to "selling" the water to the mining company. He replied that this was not the case: they simply wanted the company to return the water that was taken. "*That's* called compensation," he said. But, I asked, if Yanacocha were to give back the same amount of water (from its treatment plant) that they took away, why should they agree to pay them, in addition, thousands of dollars in cash? To this Wilmer replied: "The water is no longer the same. It's treated. It's no longer natural ("*El agua ya no es la misma. Viene tratada. Ya no es natural*").

Though Wilmer claimed that the water was not the *same* water, he did concede that the water they received from Yanacocha was "clean" (in other words, not "polluted") since it came from the mine's treatment plant. This coincided with Yanacocha's own arguments when confronted with criticism about the quality of the water in the canals. For Minera Yanacocha, the water was "clean" because it had been treated to meet the legal permissible limits. Yet for Wilmer, the fact that the water was "clean" did not mean it was the same water, and hence he required additional compensation.

Wilmer's views pointed to the various ways in which water quality was measured and evaluated. For usuarios, the water returned to the canals was not the same because water quality was not determined solely by its chemical composition and mineral content, but by everyday practices that involved its use: the care of livestock, household chores, or a drink of water on an afternoon working in the fields. While the agreements signed between Yanacocha and usuarios implied that the dispute had been settled through equitable compensation, it was clear that this was not the case— neither for canal users for whom the water was *a different water*, nor for Yanacocha, which was obligated to provide more money and development projects each time a new "conflict" arose. In the rest of the chapter, I examine attempts to forge equivalences through negotiations between usuarios and the mining company, as well as efforts to subvert these equivalences.

Negotiating with Pollution

Wednesday morning, once a month, Tual experienced a flurry of activity. Yanacocha's vehicles pulled up into the community center that served as a meeting place, and fifty delegates prepared to attend the month's meeting. The rules were strict. Knowing that meetings had the potential to go on for hours, Yanacocha had set a time limit, and the engineers left punctually at noon regardless of where they were on the agenda. The canal users and engineers seemed to be operating with different conceptions of time. The engineers focused on the outcomes of the negotiations, and on the need to come to a consensus within the time assigned. For the canal users, on the other hand, community assemblies were an opportunity to make one's voice heard, and to reach decisions based on lengthy deliberations that often stretched for hours on end (and might remain inconclusive). The meetings were not simply about the agreements reached; they were also a way to create relations, maintain them, and make them visible. Usuarios observed each representative's level of participation and how well they articulated their arguments in order to evaluate their ability to represent the canal. Likewise, the meetings were an opportunity to get to know people from the company, to judge their trustworthiness, and to develop ties that could later be used to secure employment opportunities.

The appointment of the fifty delegates was one of the results of the inspection that I had witnessed, as well as more direct pressure tactics. Some months after the inspection, a group of people including Mr. Santos, Wilmer, and others associated with the nueva junta disrupted a meeting between Minera Yanacocha and the canal's elected representatives. Protesting against what they saw as "closed door" negotiations and corrupt dealings, the group demanded that the interests of the larger community be taken into account. The group and company representatives came to the agreement that fifty people would be elected in a communal assembly to meet with Minera Yanacocha (the group that was elected consisted of forty-nine men and one woman). Further, these meetings would no longer take place in one of Cajamarca's fancy hotels, as had been the custom, but in the community of Tual. Finally, it was agreed that these fifty delegates would take a paid twelve-hour shift on a rotational basis to act as canal "security guards" (vigilantes). Guarding the canal meant looking out for any irregular activities, such as water "theft" by canal users, and contributing to the general maintenance of the canal (cutting the grass around it, pulling out stones, etc.). More importantly, however, it meant ensuring that Yanacocha abided by its commitment to keep a regular water flow and did not damage the canal with its machinery, road building, or other activities.

The role of the vigilantes bore some resemblance to the rondas campesinas, where groups of men conduct a night watch around the community to prevent animal thefts and other crimes. The rondas began as a way for peasants to protect their livelihoods; patrolling the canals shifted the focus from cattle theft to water theft, and from the transgressions of other campesinos to those of the mining company. The irony of getting paid by Minera Yanacocha to watch over the company's own actions was not lost on the canal vigilantes, but both sides saw it as a win-win situation. Minera Yanacocha could claim that it was creating transparency and building trust (and some might also add, silencing the opposition), while the guards received a much-needed salary for their duties. At 900 soles (US$250) per month, this job was comparable to any temporary job that unskilled laborers might be offered by companies in the area.

Wilmer had been elected as one of the fifty delegates. When he returned home from one of the meetings, he explained that the delegates were asking for an increase in the 40 soles (US$11) per diem they received for attending each meeting. They reasoned that they should be paid more for their time, especially considering that Yanacocha was saving money by having the meetings in Tual instead of hosting them in Cajamarca. But more important issues were also on the table. They were trying to reach an agreement about the amount to be given in compensation for the mine's impact on the Quebrada Shillamayo, as well as the development projects that would be executed as part of the compensation package. A cheese-making plant, improved irrigation technologies, and tourism development were some of the possibilities being considered. Based on its previous experiences negotiating with canal users, Minera Yanacocha was shifting its policies to promote long-term development rather than cash settlements. It was also implementing land-for-land swaps (giving people an irrigated plot of land on the coast) with the hopes of reaching a permanent solution to the ongoing demands of affected communities.

As one of the fifty delegates negotiating with Minera Yanacocha, Wilmer was fighting for a compensation package that would bring development projects to Tual. Minera Yanacocha presented these development projects as a long-term investment that would provide people with a source of livelihood into the future. When I spoke to Wilmer about his visions for the future, however, he insisted that there *was* no future in Tual—the mine was going to leave them without water, he said, and the land was already worthless. Without enough water and abundant pastures, life in Tual was not imaginable. Like many others in the community, Wilmer considered that rural life no longer held any promise for his two children, especially if the canal, land, and other resources were compromised by mining activity. Yet to him, the negotiations were an investment in the future, for development projects would increase the value of land that he assumed Minera Yanacocha would eventually buy to keep expanding its operations. The benefits he sought did not involve a return to a pre-mining past, but a new beginning that was not necessarily tied to the way of life he sought to defend. The canal did not bind people to an agricultural, pastoral present but opened up a new imagined future; it also signified new investments and entrepreneurial dreams made possible through negotiations with the company.

One way of interpreting these compensation agreements would be to say that campesinos rejected attempts to reach a fair deal, and that their demands were duplicitous, unreasonable, or excessive. Certainly, some of the Yanacocha engineers I spoke with expressed such views and suggested that the proliferation of compensation claims was an attempt by campesinos to manipulate the company for personal gain. However, it is also possible to see that the changes brought about by mining activity were incommensurable with the compensation agreements.[7] Neither money nor chemically treated water could be made equivalent to what had been lost. Accepting the terms of the agreement did not mean that usuarios accepted the logic of equivalence implied in them. Knowing that water and land would not be as available as they once were, they had to make the best of their options and accept the company's proposals in the hope that they would lead to other opportunities for the future. The canals in Tual thus became much more than a source of irrigation water; they also brought opportunities for employment and compensation and were embedded in relationships that were being transformed by the mine's operations.

Canal Water

The canals around the Yanacocha mine—and the problems and opportunities they generated—mobilized kinship connections and shaped the way people related to each other. At the same time, the mine's operations altered those relationships as well as people's everyday activities and ways of using water. This was especially evident when the canal provided Wilmer and Herlinda with a promising—but short-lived—work opportunity.

Herlinda's family was from Llushcapampa, a caserío located between Tual and the main highway. Her father, José, was an usuario of the Arcuyo Canal, which originated at Cerro Quilish. This is why, like so many campesinos, José participated in the protests to defend Cerro Quilish from being mined—a patched-up hole in his jeans was evidence of the confrontation with the police, when he was hit on the leg with a tear-gas canister. A small part of the Arcuyo Canal was damaged by Minera Yanacocha's machinery, and following complaints from usuarios, the company accepted responsibility and offered to provide construction materials and one month's salaries for fifteen campesinos to carry out maintenance work on the canal. José formed a microempresa and was awarded the work contract. Minera Yanacocha encouraged the creation of microempresas as a way to improve its community relations, yet this initiative also had some unintended consequences: it created more microempresas than the available work contracts, resulting in a system where *empresarios* were pitted against each other, and those with little experience risked going bankrupt. The competition over work opportunities led some empresarios to protest against the mine or mobilize in its favor—depending on the circumstances at the time.

José's contract involved providing a minivan to transport the workers to and from the work site. He was responsible for the workers' meals, so he hired Herlinda to cook daily lunches for them. This kind of opportunity was highly coveted in communities near the mine, for it signified a secure income for several people in the household. Wilmer and Herlinda would have to make weekly shopping trips to Cajamarca to bring groceries and supplies back to Tual. Herlinda called on her younger sister, her sister-in-law, and a neighbor to help with the cooking. In addition to her father's project, Herlinda was hired by her uncle (another campesino *microempresario*) to cook for another fifty workers who were installing a drip irrigation system. This, too, was a project sponsored by Minera Yanacocha as part of its community development programs. Both contracts would provide Herlinda and Wilmer with two months of work, with the possibility of an extension.

Soon after they had begun the cooking operation, I joined Herlinda and her team in the kitchen. They had been working since 6 AM so that the lunches would be ready to be picked up as the minivan drove past Tual at noon. Each packed lunch consisted of soup, rice, lentils, and a small piece of meat, making it a better meal than some of the workers would have received at home. The kitchen was a frenzy of activity as vegetables were chopped, pots stirred, and the food divided into plastic containers. Suddenly, everything came to a halt as the minivan pulled up to the house earlier than expected and a woman wearing a Minera Yanacocha jacket appeared at the kitchen door.

The visitor was what Minera Yanacocha called a *prevencionista* ("preventionist"), usually a young engineer from the city of Cajamarca hired to accompany the campesino workers of a microempresa subcontracted to carry out a project. The job of the prevencionista was to remain at the work site and ensure that environmental, health, and safety measures (as established by Minera Yanacocha) were being met. When the prevencio-nista walked into the kitchen, Herlinda became visibly nervous. In the rush to prepare the food, she had not had time to sweep, and the kitchen was in a state of disarray. Worse, a neighbor's donkey left in her care was wandering loose outside the house and had made a mess outside the kitchen. With these things preoccupying her, she neglected to think about a more important problem: there was no running water. Perhaps a pipe had burst (not an uncommon occurrence), and there was no water in the sink outside the house that was the family's only source of running water. When the prevencionista asked where they were getting water, Herlinda was completely caught off guard and quickly replied: "from the Quilish Canal." That was where her sister was washing dishes at that very moment. There was, after all, no alternative, if they wanted to get the food ready in time.

Herlinda realized her mistake as soon as she answered. Canal water was not to be used for household activities, and the prevencionista would dutifully report this fault to her superiors. Almost as soon as the minivan left, Herlinda knew that she had lost her job. Indeed, that same evening she got a call from her uncle, informing her that he had no choice but to cancel her contract and hire someone else. When she analyzed the events of that day, Herlinda was able to laugh about the donkey and her bad luck but blamed herself for what she considered her biggest mistake: telling the prevencionista outright about using the canal water. It was the fact that she said it so quickly that proved this was not an isolated event, but something they were used to doing. If only she had hesitated, Herlinda lamented, or said they were waiting for the water to come back, perhaps things would have turned out differently.

Damages caused by mining operations created opportunities for people like Herlinda and her family to secure employment, which at the same time changed their relationship to the mining company and limited (at least temporarily) their participation in protests and claims against the company. At the same time, Minera Yanacocha changed people's habits relating to water use by compromising the water quality of the Tupac Amaru Canal and by stressing that canal water in general was not fit for human consumption. The new rules of water use were defined, monitored, and sanctioned by the mining company itself, through its educational campaigns, environmental management programs, and health and safety guidelines. Yet the company's warnings did not change the reality of water use in rural communities, since people were sometimes left without any alternatives to the use of canal water. This dependence on the canals reinforced their desire to protect sources of water not yet affected by mining activity, including those coming from Cerro Quilish.

Multiplying Relations

Upon the arrival of Minera Yanacocha, the canals around the mine generated relations of cooperation and antagonism, contributing to the creation of microempresas, committees, mesas de diálogo, and family alliances that worked for and against the mine. Even as people complained that the agreements did not compensate for what they had lost, they approached these negotiations pragmatically and sought to make the most of the new opportunities that the canal afforded. After the first compensation payments, Tupac Amaru canal users found a way to extend alliances by expanding the registry of canal users (padrón de usuarios) to increase the number of people who might potentially benefit from Yanacocha's compensation schemes.

The padrón de usuarios is a document that lists the names of people with access to the canal's water, as well as the number of irrigation hours that correspond to each person. The padrón is submitted to the ATDR, but in effect it is usuarios themselves who control the distribution of water rights, based on what is recorded on the padrón. The increase in the number of usuarios in recent years is evident if we examine the padrón (see table 4.1). In 1985, when the canal had just been constructed, there were ninety people registered as usuarios. In 2002, when Yanacocha gave out the compensation packages for the damages to the canal, there were 205 usuarios. In 2004, there were 460 usuarios, and by the end of the next round of negotiations in 2011, there were 650.

The increase in usuarios from 1985 to 2002 reflects a general pattern of inheritance in which parents tend to divide their irrigation hours among their children. However, the fact that the number of usuarios doubled between 2002 and 2004 is a result of the compensation given out by Minera Yanacocha. The negotiations between the mining company and usuarios of the Tupac Amaru canal created much controversy in Tual and in surrounding communities. The compensation created a marked division in communities, with usuarios having access to a range of economic

TABLE 4.1 Tupac Amaru Canal Users

Year	Number of Usuarios
1985	90
2002	205
2004	460
2011	650

benefits that were out of the reach of non-usuarios: not only the compensation money, but also employment opportunities that were part of the compensation packages, such as the improvement and lining of the canals or the installation of sprinkler irrigation systems. Minera Yanacocha awarded compensation to each usuario (regardless of the number of hours each had), while non-usuarios benefited only indirectly from community projects. Non-usuarios felt that they, too, should have received more assistance from the company.

The growing padrón de usuarios could be seen as a way to challenge the company's efforts to limit its liability for environmental damages to the canal by restricting the number of relations it was willing to recognize. Anthropologist Stuart Kirsch (2006) describes a similar situation in his work on the Ok Tedi mine in Papua New Guinea and the efforts of communities to seek compensation from the BHP mining company. He argues that compensation claims reveal competing assumptions about responsibility and liability that might be compared to the differences between ideas about property and ownership. In some contexts, property rights are established by "cutting the network" (Strathern 1996), as when practices like patents and copyrights restrict the number of claimants to an object of value. In the case of the compensation claims, strategies of ownership incorporated a wider range of claims on persons, which had the cumulative effect of "keeping the network in view" (Kirsch 2006:126). Similarly, the padrón provided a way for campesinos to keep in view the many relations between people and the canal that were concealed or excluded from Minera Yanacocha's negotiations and compensation agreements with communities.

While the politics of irrigation had always been an important aspect of

TABLE 4.2 Tupac Amaru Canal Irrigation Turns

Community	Number of Usuarios	Total Hours	Average Number of Hours Per Usuario
Cince Las Vizcachas	58	147	2.5
Hualtipampa Alta	16	40	2.5
Hualtipampa Baja	193	339	1.75
Tual	193	338	1.75
Total	460	864	1.88

rural life, the arrival of the mining company gave renewed importance to the administration of water rights. As the treasurer of the junta de usuarios, and perhaps because he was likely the only person in Tual with a home computer (acquired with the compensation money), Wilmer was given the task of ensuring that the padrón was up-to-date. Looking over the records on an Excel spreadsheet, he asked me to help him enumerate the usuarios and make sure that their hours added up correctly. Table 4.2 indicates the number of usuarios relative to the duration of water turns (*turnos de agua*) for the Tupac Amaru canal. It shows that usuarios now had, on average, less than two hours of irrigation time, which reflects the extent to which water rights had been subdivided in order to maximize the number of usuarios on the padrón.

Before the problems with the canal, water distribution was sometimes determined internally, meaning that someone could be given watering time by the repartidor without being inscribed in the official padrón that is submitted to the ATDR. Any disputes over water were discussed and resolved in general assemblies, and this was also the space where usuarios could detect any irregularities in water use (i.e., water theft) and determine whether the people listed on the padrón were legitimate usuarios. Minera Yanacocha's compensation programs put more at stake in these procedures, and the new power of irrigation authorities and community leaders over the padrón and negotiations with the company led to constant political struggles among different factions.

The compensation also created tensions within families. Herlinda's account about how Wilmer inherited water rights from his father reveals how mining changed people's relationship with the canal:

When my father-in-law was alive, he attended the meetings and the limpiezas. When he died, there wasn't anyone to take over for him. There wasn't anyone who irrigated; there was no [cultivated] grass. So when my father-in-law died, his children wanted one of the brothers to be in charge. So they said, let's give [the irrigation hours] to Wilmer, since Father said we should give the water to Wilmer. And they gave him all the hours. They didn't think we would get money. They gave them to him, drew up the documents; Wilmer had the water for eleven years. As soon as they gave the compensation, $4,000, that's when all the other brothers wanted to get water. But it was their fault. They didn't want to attend the meetings or the limpiezas.

According to Herlinda, the reason why she and Wilmer were more entitled to the compensation was that they had put in time for meetings and canal maintenance, and because they used the water for irrigation, while Wilmer's siblings did not. Her comments also point to the changes in people's relationship to the canal: when campesinos began to focus on dairy farming as a main source of livelihood, the irrigation water became crucial for growing grasses to feed the cattle; and once they realized that being an usuario could make them eligible for compensation money, the role of the canal was again transformed. The compensation agreement created much resentment in Wilmer's family and led to a family feud that resulted in the eventual distribution of the irrigation hours among his siblings.

The compensation programs and the new value of water formalized water distribution, since only usuarios who were "officially" registered became eligible for compensation. The need to be included in the official registry led to a surge in demand for *empadronamiento* (being added to the registry), not only in the case of the Tupac Amaru canal but also other canals in the mine's area of influence. There are two ways in which this was done. Those who already had irrigation hours could choose to divide these among their family members. Since *turnos* were divided between children, spouses, and other relatives, it was not uncommon for an usuario to have a mere half hour of irrigation time, which they may or may not have used to irrigate their land (the minimum length of time that could be allotted to an usuario was also a point of contention; the Tupac Amaru canal maintained a one-hour minimum, while others lowered it to half an hour to allow for increased membership, and some were even considering quarter-hour water turns). Another way to get on the padrón was to purchase hours from a registered usuario. I encountered cases of people who had paid 2,000 soles for an hour of irrigation time, though Wilmer said the going rate was about 5,000 soles. The legality of these transactions was questionable, and there was potential for abuse: people who hoped to benefit from future compensation programs were willing to pay for irrigation time without being able to guarantee that they would actually be registered in the official padrón.

The Quilish Canal, which also passed through Tual, had not yet been affected by the mine, but some people expected that Minera Yanacocha would eventually expand its operations onto Cerro Quilish, which increased the number of the people on that padrón as well. Herlinda was an usuario of the Quilish canal, since her father had given irrigation time to her and her husband. Her father divided his eleven hours among his children and their spouses, even though he was the only one that used the water for irrigation. Herlinda saw her inclusion into the padrón as a way of covering her losses in the event that the Quilish canal was also affected by the mine. The division of hours was specifically intended "to have the company pay all of us." She clarified that for the mining company, the number of usuarios on the padrón did not make a difference in its compensation plans, since whatever amount of money they agreed to give would be divided evenly among all the usuarios. The responsibility was thus left to the juntas, who determined the rules of membership.

Multiplying the number of Quilish Canal users was a form of insurance, given the likelihood that it would eventually be affected by the mine's expansion, but ultimately, Herlinda hoped that this would not happen. The compensation money would be better than being left with nothing (which would be the case if they did not become usuarios), but it would be quickly spent, as she had already seen with the previous compensation agreements. The money would never be equivalent to that which would be lost, for receiving compensation signified permanently severing a productive relationship with the canal.

Multiplying Conflicts

For campesinos living in the vicinity of a mine, extractive activity produces dramatic changes that are altering ways of life and relationships between people and elements of the landscape, including the irrigation canals on which they depend. Yet as I have tried to show, these relationships and the conflicts that they generate do not relate solely to the utilitarian value of water. Water is also part of a relationship that emerges from particular experiences and ways of understanding the landscape. Furthermore, people's way of assessing and responding to environmental changes are based on observations and experiences that do not necessarily correspond with scientific studies or legal norms that establish water quality standards. The logic of equivalence disqualifies these ways of knowing and delegitimizes opposing viewpoints, making it possible to justify mining projects in the name of progress and development.

Equivalences could thus be seen as a way to create consensus by negating disagreement and producing a dominant form of knowledge. Looking at how equivalences are established makes evident a set of connections that remain unexplored in the analysis of conflict. Conflict needs to be understood as a set of relations—and not simply in terms of rupture. These relations are always fraught with friction or antagonisms that equivalence seeks to neutralize but cannot negate.

Problems with the canal—which Yanacocha publicly acknowledged and which were not foreseen in the company's environmental impact studies—helped make visible many of the criticisms about Yanacocha's environmental practices that had been circulating since the construction of the mine. It was *through the canal*—its physical infrastructure as well as the relationships that revolved around its administration, use, and maintenance—that people forged relationships with the mining company. People's membership in irrigation associations allowed campesinos to organize protests against Yanacocha, seek compensation for damages, and benefit from the company's community relations projects. The inspección ocular was one of the ways in which campesinos could make their claims against the mine verifiable and scientifically valid, strengthening their bargaining power in future negotiations with company representatives.

In a conversation about the mesa de diálogo, Wilmer once told me: "You can't put a price on water, but we need to calculate the value of what is being lost." The oscillation between the incommensurability of water and efforts to calculate the damages caused by mining activity were at the root of negotiations with the company. Equivalences helped to establish consensus and agreements, but these agreements were necessary (and only temporary) compromises for an irreparable loss.

In all of its dealings with affected communities, Yanacocha's strategy was to limit the number of actors involved—negotiation meetings did not permit the participation of NGO mediators or government representatives, and agreements were discussed with elected delegates rather than in community assemblies. However, campesinos found ways to push at these limits of exclusion. Expanding the padrón de usuarios made use of already-existing relations around the canals to expand networks of association. "Everybody now wants to be an usuario," I heard many people say, and this was even acknowledged by a Yanacocha community relations officer who was familiar with the politics of irrigation in Cajamarca. The mining company was well aware of this trend, yet there was little that it could do to prevent it.[8] In this way, the canal—its material infrastructure as well as the social relationships that were both brought into being and maintained by irrigation systems—enabled campesinos to demand forms of compensation from the mining company.

The canal created and maintained relationships in a number of ways. In the past it did so by expanding water rights through inheritance, while more recently, people have tried to become usuarios through family connections as well as monetary exchanges. These connections allowed campesinos to protest against the mine and pressure the company for benefits. Once obtained, the benefits derived from the canal also had a way of proliferating relations, since being an usuario brought employment opportunities and social connections that allowed many campesinos to become empresarios. By the end of my fieldwork in 2006, Mr. Santos, his son-in-law, and Wilmer had formed a microempresa to provide transportation services for Minera Yanacocha. They purchased a van to transport workers from the city to the mine's installations and set up a small office in Cajamarca to run the operation. The Tupac Amaru canal association also formed a microempresa, which provided some economic opportunities for usuarios. In some cases, the campesino-empresarios purchased vehicles or equipment that were rented out to Minera Yanacocha, so the contracts involved no actual labor on their part but tended to only last a few months.

This new role as empresarios changed their relationship with the company and with the canal. The relations around the canal, then, are not stable but constantly shift as usuarios, campesinos, and empresarios acquire different roles and move between them. Alliances are formed and transformed through the actions of NGOs, the mining company, campesino organizations—and the canal itself. These shifting relations call for ways of analyzing social movements and environmental politics that do not rely on predefined social categories such as "peasants," "corporations," "environmentalists," or "anti-mining activists"—as if each of these groups were motivated by shared interests. These groups are neither internally coherent nor unchanging. Rather, they are a set of connections in movement and are often characterized by contradictions, ambivalence, and ambiguity. What I have tried to do instead is to think about mining controversies not in terms of "stakeholders," a term sometimes used in studies of environmental conflicts and in corporate rhetoric, but in terms of connections—connections between people, and between people and *things* like the canal itself. As the case of the ever-growing canal registry illustrates, the canal's effect of multiplying relations can also lead to the multiplication of conflicts.

PART III   ACTIVISM AND EXPERTISE

CHAPTER 5

STEPPING OUTSIDE THE DOCUMENT

Early one morning in April 2006, a group of protestors gathered outside an auditorium in the city of Cajamarca to express their opposition to the expansion of the Yanacocha mine. A large contingent of police officers guarded the building, where government officials, company representatives, mine workers, engineers, and other attendees were taking part in a public hearing to evaluate the proposed project. Outside the auditorium, tensions escalated as protestors (many of them campesinos from nearby communities) considered whether their most effective form of resistance was to enter the auditorium and voice their opposition in the meeting, or to refuse to participate in a process they felt would inevitably lead to the project's approval.

In the media and academic analyses, the proliferation of conflicts over resource extraction in Peru is often attributed to an "absent" or "weak" state.[1] Corporations, too, blame the state for its inability to resolve the conflicts or control its insurgent populations. An emphasis on the absence or weakness of the state, however, glosses over the complex ways in which the state and its legal structures operate in controversies over mining activity. As Timothy Mitchell (1991) has suggested, the state cannot be analyzed as a fixed, monolithic entity that stands apart from society; rather, it is the sum of structural "effects" that are continuously enacted (through the establishment of boundaries, policing, documentation, or other social practices) in ways that make the state seem both powerful and elusive. Although mining conflicts in Peru are often analyzed in terms of the state's absence, I propose to take a different approach by examining how the state's regulatory structures facilitate resource extraction in the context of neoliberal governance.

In the 1990s, neoliberal restructuring in Peru was aimed at liberalizing trade, privatizing the public sector, and deregulating the economy. Without suggesting that neoliberalism is a single, overarching, or uncontested political project, I contend that these economic reforms brought with them new knowledge practices, including mechanisms of accountability that have become central in state and corporate rhetoric on mining activity. Couched in a language of transparency, environmental management, and democratic participation, these practices are both pervasive and difficult to criticize.[2]

This chapter examines a key process in the making of social and environmental accountability in mining projects: Environmental Impact Assessment (EIA). According to the International Association for Impact Assessment, the EIA is a process of "identifying, predicting, evaluating, and mitigating the biophysical, social, and other effects of development proposals" (IAIA 1999). I will focus on the EIA for the Yanacocha West Supplementary Project (or PSYO, its Spanish acronym), which would expand the Yanacocha gold mine.

In conflicts over mining, people often demand public mechanisms of evaluation and record keeping that they can use to hold corporations and governments accountable to citizens. However, I argue that practices of accountability prioritize mining interests and enable corporations to define the standards of performance that governments will use to establish compliance. "Accountability" relates to but differs from the broader notion of "responsibility," a term that is commonly used in discussions about mining (i.e., Corporate Social Responsibility). Both terms are generally translated into Spanish as *responsabilidad*, though accountability could be more literally translated as *rendición de cuentas*, meaning a "rendering of accounts." In this chapter I maintain a distinction between the two terms: *accountability* refers to a corporation's obligation to answer to citizens and the state and provide evidence to show that certain outcomes have been achieved. By contrast, *responsibility* can refer to initiatives that do not necessarily require rendering accounts to a specific entity: for example, a company can claim to act *responsibly* by implementing voluntary social and environmental programs of its own design but not be held *accountable* for their outcomes. In other cases, *corporate accountability* can be transformed into a sense of *shared responsibility* as citizens, state institutions, and NGOs are incorporated into participatory forms of environmental monitoring, management, and audit.

My discussion of the EIA considers this document as well as the knowledge practices that both shape and result from its elaboration and approval. This approach is inspired by a body of literature that treats documents as "paradigmatic artifacts of modern knowledge practices" (Riles 2006:2), and takes an ethnographic approach that moves away from a textual or discursive analysis to focus on what a document *does*—the actions that it anticipates and enables.[3] Documents are not only about information or direct representation but may be something different than what they say.[4]

Drawing on these theoretical insights, I argue that the *form* of the documents produced for the EIA (i.e., their required components, as established in legal frameworks) and the *process* of making them public (participatory meetings and public forums) can take precedence over their *content*. Two aspects of the EIA make this possible. First, the risks that are identified in the EIA are those that a company deems to be technically manageable based on the kinds of solutions and interventions that the company has to offer. Second, the participatory process of the EIA creates collaborative relationships among state agents, corporations, NGOs, and communities. These forms of collaboration strengthen the EIA's claims of accountability while circumscribing the spaces for opposition to a proposed project.

My aim in this chapter is not to point out the weaknesses of the EIA or to suggest that the state and corporations have failed to address the public's concerns. Rather, I am interested precisely in those mechanisms of "good governance" that are being implemented in response to public pressure and in accordance with international guidelines aimed at transforming the state into an entity that is efficient, transparent, and accountable to the public (Anders 2008). Undoubtedly, the participatory component of the EIA has opened up the document to public scrutiny, and in some cases this has enabled activists to draw attention to their concerns. However, contesting the approval of an EIA has proved to be a difficult endeavor.

To date, only one major mining project at the EIA stage has ever been halted because of public opposition: the Tambogrande project in northern Peru, in 2004. In this case, three North American NGOs (Oxfam America, the Mineral Policy Center, and the Environmental Mining Council of British Columbia) hired hydrologist Robert Moran to conduct an independent assessment of the mining project, which was being developed by the Canadian company Manhattan Minerals. Using Canadian environmental standards and mining guidelines to evaluate the Tambogrande project, Mr. Moran argued that the "extremely poor quality" of the company's baseline studies would not be acceptable in Canada (Moran 2001a:9). Mr. Moran also challenged the company's assertion that mining and agricultural production could coexist, given the risks posed by water, soil, and crop contamination from mine wastes. While Mr. Moran and other critics of the mining project pointed out fundamental inadequacies in the environmental assessment work presented by Manhattan Minerals, the Ministry of Energy and Mines cited the company's inability to meet financial (not environmental) requirements as the reason for its failure.

In this chapter, I focus on a specific EIA presented by Minera Yanacocha, yet the processes I analyze apply more generally to environmental assessment and other mechanisms of corporate accountability. I begin by describing the proceedings of a public hearing to show how the EIA *defines* the potential risks of mining activity. While the EIA is intended to guarantee environmental accountability, I suggest that what is contained (and not contained) in the EIA is defined by mining interests. I then turn to a workshop that took place six months before the public hearing to discuss the EIA's preliminary findings and respond to questions from the public. I show that the EIA's emphasis on "participation" can in fact limit public critique and disqualify opposition to mining activity. In the final part of the chapter, I return to the public hearing to consider how techniques of accountability have led some activists to *step outside the official document* by adopting political strategies that resort to *non*participation and a refusal to be informed.

Documenting Accountability

On the day that the EIA was to be presented in the city of Cajamarca, people arrived at the Ollanta Convention Center well before 7 AM and began lining up in front of the entrance (see figure 5.1). A group of about

FIGURE 5.1 People lining up outside the entrance of the auditorium where the public hearing was to take place.

twenty campesinos from nearby communities had spent the night outside the auditorium where the EIA public hearing was to take place, hoping to voice their opposition to a project they believed would further impact the region's water resources. As with most demonstrations against Minera Yanacocha, this protest was loosely organized through community ties, canal users' associations, and rondas campesinas. Since mining activity tends to create divisions within communities, it is likely that people from the same communities were inside and outside the auditorium, either as workers supporting Minera Yanacocha or as protestors opposing the project. Other supporters who joined the protestors included urban professionals, students, and journalists.

A team of police officers in riot gear soon arrived and positioned themselves in front of the auditorium's imposing wooden doors. The group of protestors grew as others arrived to join them, but they were vastly outnumbered by those forming long queues on both sides of the auditorium doors: Yanacocha engineers, mine workers, employees, and others that the protestors considered to be "allies" of the mining company.

Though delayed by more than an hour, the public hearing got underway even as people continued to demonstrate outside the building. Since I chose to remain outside with the protestors, my analysis of the proceedings inside is based on videotaped footage of the public hearing. EIA regulations stipulate that the hearing must be filmed in its entirety and made available to the public. Several months after the public hearing, I presented a written request for a copy of the footage, and Minera Yanacocha complied with my request.

Inside the auditorium, representatives of Minera Yanacocha were present, along with consultants from MWH (Montgomery Watson Harza), the firm that the company had selected, hired, and paid to conduct the studies that formed part of the EIA (according to Peru's EIA framework, mining companies must commission and pay for a written technical evaluation that outlines the company's mitigation plans). Like mining itself, environmental consulting is also a transnational operation: MWH is based in the United States, but according to its website, it has over six thousand specialists with a variety of disciplinary backgrounds working in thirty-six countries. Environmental consulting has grown alongside the mining industry, creating new professions and transforming existing ones (including those in the fields of environmental science, anthropology, and sociology) as professionals are increasingly drawn to mining consultancy work.

In the auditorium, officials from the Ministry of Energy and Mines (MEM) and municipal and regional government officials made their way to the head tables set up on the stage. The presentation about to take place was the second of two public hearings and was intended for Cajamarca's urban residents. Another hearing had taken place two days earlier in a peasant community in the area that would be affected by the proposed project and was also marred by protests. Presenting the EIA in the district that would be affected by the project was a recent modification to EIA legislation, since before 2003, public hearings were only held in the capital city of Lima.

The moderator welcomed the attendees and stressed the importance of this participatory aspect of the EIA. Participation and democracy are learned through practice, he stated, as he explained that the presentation of the EIA would be followed by oral and written rounds of questions. The moderator pointed out that the objective of these meetings was not simply to answer people's questions, but to give people an opportunity to

"improve the quality of their questions, allowing them to better participate in the decision-making process" (partial transcript translated from
videotape). All questions would be recorded and addressed by the mining
company in the final document submitted to the MEM, thus becoming
part of the EIA dossier (*expediente*). Once the dossier had been submitted,
the public would have thirty days in which to make observations. The company would then have a chance to respond to those observations, and with
all this information, the ministry would make its deliberation.

The hearing began with an overview of the EIA and legislative frameworks pertaining to mining activity. The EIA was first established in the
United States in 1969 and has since been implemented in many countries
around the world. Indeed, the EIA is a global tool of accountability, having
been adopted by multilateral development banks, bilateral donor agencies,
and United Nations agencies. Two key events contributed to the international dissemination of the EIA: in 1989, EIAS became a requirement for
all World Bank–financed projects, and in 1992, the Earth Summit resulted
in a series of international laws and policies that encouraged signatories
to undertake the EIA as a national instrument (Sadler 1996). The transnational reach of these practices of accountability means that they are not
restricted to a particular part of the world or to a single set of institutions
(Strathern 2000b; Power 1994).

In Peru, the EIA came into existence in 1990, when the Peruvian government implemented legal and economic reforms to attract foreign investment. In particular, the Law for the Promotion of Investment in the
Mining Sector guaranteed a series of benefits for mining investors (fixed
tax and exchange rates, freedom of capital movement, etc.). As part of the
conditions set by international financial institutions that backed these reforms, the government was also required to introduce new environmental
regulations including the EIA, which was put under the jurisdiction of the
Ministry of Energy and Mines (de Echave and Torres 2005).

Moving on to the specific objectives of the EIA, a woman representing
the MEM's Environmental Affairs Division explained: "What an EIA seeks
to do is to identify what the place where the investment project would be
developed is like. The baseline study is . . . a description of this particular
place: flora, fauna, socioeconomic activities, all the physical characteristics of the place. . . . This description of the project [will serve to] identify
what would be the positive and negative impacts or effects that the project

could have and then see what technical measures are necessary to correct or prevent these impacts." The studies conducted for this EIA resulted in a document comprising a 530-page "Technical Component" and a 130-page "Social Component," as well as numerous appendices with additional maps, figures, survey results, interview guides, and other data.

One of the main functions of an EIA, then, is to map out the terrain. In a literal sense, this involves creating maps that indicate the location of water springs, canals, monitoring stations, and archeological sites. Other maps indicate soil types and land-use patterns, air quality, underground and superficial water flows, and other features of the landscape. These maps (more than fifty in total) are based on studies carried out by the mining company and its consultants. Though they are produced for and become property of Minera Yanacocha, the information acquired through mapping, measuring, and classifying elements of the landscape contributes to the sense of technical rigor that the EIA is intended to convey, allowing it to circulate as an "objective" source of scientific knowledge (cf. Latour 1988, 1999).

In addition to mapping the physical terrain, baseline studies conducted for the EIA provide an inventory of the area's natural resources and local communities and establish the characteristics of an area *before* a mining project begins. Social baseline studies are an inventory of the communities within the project's area of influence and their socioeconomic features: rural health clinics, educational institutions, common illnesses, availability of basic services, and so on. Biological baseline studies enumerate animal and plant species and identify sensitive habitats and vulnerable or endangered species. Water baseline studies establish flow rates in irrigation canals and streams, subterranean water levels (based on modeling technology), and the presence of heavy minerals in the water.

According to Michael Goldman, environmental assessment can "precisely delineate the parameters of a project, its measurable impact, and the backers' liability" (2005:119). It determines where the project area begins and ends, defines what counts as a natural asset, and establishes what constitutes an impact. In this way, it allows companies to minimize the project risk—for example, by establishing that an area was *already* degraded. This information can be crucially important in disputes with local communities. To counter claims about the contamination of water resources, Minera Yanacocha has turned to the baseline studies to argue that concentrations of copper, iron, lead, and other trace minerals in rivers and streams are not the effect of the mine but are naturally occurring, since they were present before the development of the mining project. Creating this inventory makes the socionatural landscape quantifiable and intelligible in scientific terms, and thus subject to mechanisms of environmental audit (e.g., periodic water monitoring) that contribute to an image of corporate accountability and stringent government control.

Impacts and the Management of Risk

A second function of an EIA is to identify the "impacts" that an activity will produce. The term *impact* has become ubiquitous in discussions on the environment, but it has acquired a specific meaning in the context of Minera Yanacocha's mining operations. In public presentations and environmental educational materials, the mine's environmental specialists differentiate between "pollution" (*contaminación*) and "impacts." They point out that every human activity generates an *impact*; by contrast, they define *pollution* as a deleterious, critical, and irreversible effect on the environment:

> The word "pollution" tends to be confused with the concept "impact."
> The latter is a change in nature provoked by any type of human activity,
> which, if it is not significant, can be absorbed by nature. It is possible
> to speak of pollution when this impact becomes significant or critical,
> the point in which nature itself cannot cope with the changes produced
> around it and this has a negative repercussion on the established "natu-
> ral order." (Minera Yanacocha 2007:4)

A diagram from a Minera Yanacocha publication shows a spectrum that goes from "irreversible impacts" (on the far left) to "significant and critical impacts" to "control of significant impacts" (in the middle) (see figure 5.2). Moving toward the right side of the spectrum, we have "No Pollution," meaning impacts of "no significance" and "zero impact" (at the far right). Minera Yanacocha claims to operate within the range of "impacts" that are not considered "pollution" because they fall within the legal maximum permissible limits (the threshold of "pollution"). But even those activities that generate a "significant impact," and sometimes surpass the maximum permissible limits, can be controlled or reversed through its environmental management programs. According to the company, instances where

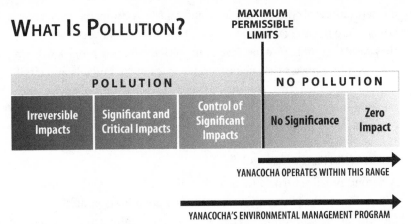

WHAT IS POLLUTION?

MAXIMUM PERMISSIBLE LIMITS

POLLUTION			NO POLLUTION	
Irreversible Impacts	Significant and Critical Impacts	Control of Significant Impacts	No Significance	Zero Impact

YANACOCHA OPERATES WITHIN THIS RANGE

YANACOCHA'S ENVIRONMENTAL MANAGEMENT PROGRAM

FIGURE 5.2 Minera Yanacocha's definition of "pollution." Adapted from Minera Yanacocha 2007.

the maximum limits are exceeded represent isolated events that do not imply a sustained level of pollution, and thus these "impacts" are not considered critical or irreversible. From this perspective, the changes produced by mining activity are not considered "pollution," but *manageable risks*; and for every potential risk described in the EIA, there is a mitigation plan in place.

In the Technical Component of the EIA, the "potential impacts" that are identified include things such as "alteration of habitat for flora and fauna," "changes in subterranean water levels," "change in the quality of groundwater," and "soil erosion" (MWH 2006b). Each of these impacts is classified as being of "major," "moderate," or "minor" importance (or "without importance"). This designation is based on a set of criteria including probability, magnitude, duration, and reversibility. None of the fifty-seven potential impacts for the PYSO are classified as being of "major" importance, while only eight are considered to be of "moderate" importance.

As I showed in chapter 4, peasant farmers who rely on dairy farming and small-scale agriculture for their subsistence argue that mining activity reduces flow levels in their canals and the water springs that feed them. These controversies surrounding irrigation canals can help to illustrate how "potential impacts" are made visible and neutralized through the EIA. In the Technical Component of the EIA, "change in water flows" is identified as a *probable* impact, since in order to mine safely, groundwater must be pumped from beneath the mining pits to lower the water table and prevent flooding. Lowering the water table reduces the amount of groundwater that discharges into surface water sources such as springs, marshes, and streams (MWH 2006b:385). However, this potential impact is classified in the EIA as *reversible*, since the company promises to return the same volume of water that it pumped out of the ground to the affected water basin. This water would come from the mine's treatment plant and would have to meet the legally established water quality standards in order to be released into the environment. Since "returning" the water makes this impact "reversible," it is classified as being of "minor significance."

Turning "pollution" into "impacts" rests on a logic of equivalence that informs the company's environmental mitigation plans. For Yanacocha, replacing the water and meeting the legal permissible limits represented a successful environmental management strategy that put its operations within the range of "no pollution"—the range where equivalences are possible. These legal maximum permissible limits, endowed with the authority of the law, are assumed to be transparent and objective and establish the threshold between "pollution" and "impacts."

Consumption versus Management

In addition to the distinction between "pollution" and "impacts," Minera Yanacocha's informational campaigns also differentiated between "water consumption" and "water management." In an interview, a Yanacocha engineer and water specialist emphasized this distinction: "We *manage* the water level, we don't *consume* the water," he said. In addition to the technical aspect of his work, he spent time talking to campesinos and the public in order to dispel what he called "misunderstandings" about water. One of the arguments made by activists is that mining lowers the water table. He explained that the mining process requires drawing water from wells around the pits in order to mine safely. However, since the company treats this water and then discharges it downstream, he does not consider this water consumption, but a "water management issue." Further, he argued that the reduction of groundwater levels is not in itself a concern, because it does not mean that the mine is reducing the amount of water that people use for agricultural and household activities: "My concern isn't that the groundwater is lowering. My concern is that the groundwater lowers, and there's less water coming out of the ground downstream of the mine.

Therefore there has to be a mitigation plan, a water management plan put in place, to make sure that that activity is not reducing the flow of downstream water."[5]

In public presentations and published materials, Minera Yanacocha steadfastly denied the claim that its operations were depriving campesino communities and city dwellers of water. Minera Yanacocha countered this claim with the following explanation:

> Yanacocha pumps subterranean water to carry out mining activities, but it does not *consume* this water. Yanacocha has permits from the corresponding authorities to use approximately 900 liters per second of subterranean water; however, this does not mean that Yanacocha consumes or uses all this water, since most of this water is pumped, treated, and discharged directly into the same water basin. The total annual use of water is approximately 52 liters per second . . . this water is consumed in the control of dust, that is, in watering the roads in the operation zones in order to ensure [good] air quality around the mine and not generate discomfort in the neighboring population. Water for all other uses (mining processes, kitchen, camps) is *managed, treated, and discharged* into the environment: this is water that is not lost, *that is not consumed* [emphasis added]. (Minera Yanacocha n.d.)

This explanation of water use assumes equivalences between inputs and outputs, or between water that is drawn from subterranean sources and what is discharged into the water basin once it has gone through the mining process. As long as this water is returned into the environment, it is not affecting the overall water balance in the watershed—and therefore, it does not count as "consumption."

Some skeptics saw this kind of explanation as a simple manipulation of language to deceive the public and resented the company for this. Yet I would argue that what is at play are competing ways of making equivalences that reveal a fundamentally different understanding of water flows. For the company's engineers, the management of water negated any potential problems that might accompany the mine's operations. Mitigation plans aimed to maintain the hydrological balance of the watershed and assumed that equivalence could be achieved if water is retained and discharged in the right amounts.

For critics of the mining company, however, the groundwater drawn by

Minera Yanacocha directly affected the water level of aquifers, rivers, and subterranean flows. According to activist organizations such as GRUFIDES (Arana 2006), mining activity substantially altered the water cycle: it changed not only the quantity of water, but also its quality (through the treatment process) and location (for example, by deliberately diverting streams or by altering surface and underground water flows through the continuous movement of earth that modern mines require).

Hydrologists often conceptualize the water cycle as behaving in a consistent, uniform manner (Budds 2009), and mining companies require a regular flow of water in order to sustain their operations. Campesinos, on the other hand, are acutely aware of the uncertainty, unpredictability, and irregularity of water flows. A mine's water needs place extra pressure during the dry season, when water scarcity poses a grave problem for rural communities. This awareness of seasonable variability, changes in the quality of water, and disruptions in the water cycle caused by mining processes is at odds with the logic of equivalence embedded in the company's didactic materials and mitigation strategies.

Following a similar logic of equivalences, the environmental consultant presenting the EIA at the public hearing assured the audience that if an irrigation canal's flow was to decrease, the company would pump water from its treatment plant and return the flow to previous levels (as defined by fixed, uncontestable measurements recorded in the baseline studies). Another mitigation plan he presented was the construction of the San José reservoir (made out of an old pit no longer being mined) that would accumulate water during the rainy season in order to make it available during the dry season.

As these examples show, the EIA is an instrument through which risks become visible and are introduced to the public. However, the risks that are disclosed in the document are those that engineers deem to be technically manageable. As Beck (1992:29) points out with reference to nuclear reactors, safety studies "restrict themselves to the estimation of certain *quantifiable* risks on the basis of *probable* accidents. The dimensions of the hazard are limited from the very beginning to *technical manageability*." By linking each risk to the availability of a mitigation plan, the EIA's way of diagnosing potential problems is contingent on the kinds of solutions and interventions that experts have to offer (Murray Li 2007; see also Ferguson 1997). But as critics have pointed out, the EIA conceals other risks that are more difficult to ascertain, quantify, and control. Campesinos complain that water springs they used to rely on have disappeared, and that canal flows have not returned to their previous levels. Other critics worry about the long-term effects of the mine's cyanide leach pads and waste deposits and wonder how the company will continue to chemically treat the water and pump it into the canals "in perpetuity" (as it promises to do in the EIA) once the mine closes.

The EIA is intended to guarantee a company's environmental accountability to local communities. However, by entrusting companies to create an inventory of the socionatural landscape, establish the "baseline" characteristics of the site, and link each potential risk to a mitigation plan, the *form* of the EIA implicitly facilitates a project's eventual approval. Furthermore, as one of the few public sources of technical, ecological, and demographic data, company-sponsored studies often became a definitive source of technical information about a region. EIAS and related studies conducted for one project became references for future projects, thus reinforcing the information that becomes part of a company's vast library of publications. These libraries were "open" and accessible to the public, as Minera Yanacocha's Documentation Center (CENDOC), located in Cajamarca's city center, demonstrated. The CENDOC was frequented by schoolchildren, high school students, and the general public. It hosted mining-related and academic talks; held a collection of books, EIA documents, reports, and magazines; and had computers to access the company's digital library. These materials were also used by academic researchers, journalists, and NGOS.

The CENDOC and other strategies for disseminating information were part of the company's efforts to make mining operations more transparent. At the same time, these practices enable the corporation to define and ultimately enforce the terms of accountability. The EIA sets the parameters that the state's regulatory institutions will use to evaluate environmental performance, which will be measured against data from studies the mining company funds and oversees. The EIA's explicit function of establishing an environmental management plan "shapes public perception of the very problems for which it is the solution" (Power 1994:7). In the EIA, science becomes an instrument that allows corporations to create an image of "clean" modern mining and establish the standards of "good practice" in the industry, all while claiming neutrality.

By making explicit the ways in which a mining company will manage the risks revealed in the document, the EIA produces the conditions necessary for corporations to check themselves—in terms that they themselves create. This is an effect of neoliberal governance, where the state's concern is not to impose day-to-day direction, but to ensure internal controls, in the form of monitoring techniques, are in place (Strathern 2000b:4). Practices of accountability, from public hearings to participatory studies and the dissemination of information, must be made explicit in order to allow people (and in this case, corporations) to monitor themselves. It is not that the state is absent, since its intervention has already taken place "in the social adjustment which corporations, public bodies and individuals have already made to those self-checking practices now re-described as evidence of their accountability to the state" (Strathern 2000b:4).

The EIA serves as a self-regulatory regime that contributes to state legitimacy while limiting the regulatory responsibilities of its institutions (Szablowski 2007). Through participatory mechanisms like the public hearing, the role of ensuring compliance shifts from the state, to corporations, and eventually to communities and individuals who are called on to monitor and safeguard "their" natural resources. The responsibility to care for the environment becomes a *shared* concern. Meanwhile, mining companies are able to shape the terms of accountability, leaving the state with the "perfunctory role of checking indicators of performance" (Strathern 2000b) that the EIA helps define.

Collaboration in the Making of the EIA

In the hope of preventing the kinds of conflicts that mining activity had been generating, state institutions placed particular emphasis on public participation, and Minera Yanacocha made this a key aspect of its social and environmental programs. The participatory nature of the EIA was part of these larger efforts to incorporate public participation into corporate and state practices. A ministerial resolution from the MEM outlined the participatory requirements at each stage of the process: *Prior* to the elaboration of the EIA, the MEM was responsible for carrying out information sessions to inform citizens of their rights and obligations, environmental legislation, and technologies to be used in the proposed project. *During* the elaboration of the EIA, the project proponents were obliged to inform the public of its progress, while the regional office of the MEM was responsible for informing about relevant legislative frameworks. *After* the EIA was presented to the MEM, the project proponent had to inform the authorities and general public of the contents of the study. For the PSYO EIA, Minera Yanacocha organized forty-nine workshops prior to the elaboration of the EIA. Thirty-two workshops were held in the city and seventeen in rural communities, involving a total of 1,676 participants. An additional 3,489 people participated in sixty-seven participatory workshops during the elaboration of the EIA.

As part of this participatory framework, Minera Yanacocha organized a workshop in Cajamarca to present its preliminary findings for the PSYO EIA. The meeting took place in October 2005, approximately six months before this EIA was to be completed and presented in the public hearing. This particular workshop was held in one of the city's large hotels and was intended for NGOs (including some of the mine's strongest critics), educational institutions, governmental organizations in the city, and others that the company had invited. There were forty-two people in attendance, and a team of about a dozen Yanacocha engineers were on hand to present the EIA and answer questions from the audience. The gendered dynamics of the meeting were similar to those of other mining-related events: key participants (e.g., mining engineers, government representatives, and community leaders) were predominantly male, but women played an important role in many NGOs.[6] In this particular workshop, the audience was almost entirely made up of urban professionals. In other workshops intended for a rural audience, low literacy rates (particularly among women) would have added another barrier to the dissemination of the EIA's technical information.

The workshop began with a presentation by the newly appointed regional director of energy and mines, who spoke about the legal requirements for mining projects and highlighted new laws that have led to more stringent environmental standards. Visibly nervous, the director admitted that he was not very articulate but was good with numbers. He proceeded to illustrate his points with a series of formulas and commented on the state's dependence on mining revenues. Though the regional director opened the event, the dominance of Minera Yanacocha's team was evident—not only in the dynamics of the meeting, but in the contrast between the state's representatives (local professionals) and the mine's personnel (mostly from Lima, with one engineer from Canada, and thus of a higher status in Peru's racialized socioeconomic hierarchy).

Using PowerPoint slides, the team of engineers described new modeling technology to measure changes in groundwater levels and progress with water monitoring and baseline studies. But these explanations did not favorably impress the audience, which included Father Marco Arana and other members of GRUFIDES. Father Arana initiated the question-and-answer period with the following comment:

> I understand that my participation here is for you to listen, to take notes, but what citizens and institutions might have to say is not in any way [legally] binding. . . . You say that everything is within the permissible limits—so who is lying? . . . Just recently, results from the CAO [Compliance Advisor Ombudsman] water monitoring program were published showing that there are heavy metals in the water, and you have just said that there are no such problems. . . . Our constitution guarantees the right to a healthy environment. How can you guarantee this, when at this moment we know that the water from various irrigation canals has either disappeared or is being contaminated? . . . If the ministry has not been able to guarantee the quantity and quality of the water, how will you be able to do so with this new project? These problems will only deepen and intensify. If the norms don't change, if the legislation doesn't change, this project will not represent an opportunity for development, but an environmental threat.[7]

An engineer from the mining company responded:

> This is a space in which we need everyone to participate. Maybe the meeting is going to take us four hours in total, but that's the idea. The only way to obtain participation is by conversing with everyone. With regard to the [water] study that was mentioned . . . this is the result of collective work that is being done. It's very good that it was published. This opens up spaces where we can talk about these issues. The strange thing would be if nothing was published, what would be bad is if we didn't have that access to information. . . . But in this [water study] perhaps there are many points that need clarification: One important point is that the problems cited were isolated problems, and the month in which they occurred is specified. It would have been good to note that

these problems were resolved immediately. . . . But what's redeemable about this study is that the information is being given out, it's not being hidden. Now, is this in Yanacocha's best interest or not? That doesn't really matter, what matters is that the information is being published, and it's allowing us to resolve problems that might exist.

Father Arana's comment was a direct critique of the EIA's participatory process, since it implied that company and state representatives were there to "listen and take notes," but the public's participation did not have any concrete effects. His questions simultaneously addressed the company and the state, accusing Minera Yanacocha of presenting false information about water quality while criticizing the state's inability to protect citizens' right to a healthy environment.

The engineer's answer to the question evaded the critique of the mining project by emphasizing the importance of public participation: everyone must be heard and included in the process, regardless of how long it takes. Significantly, the engineer dismissed the water quality problem as an isolated incident that had been managed and was no longer cause for concern. Based on the company's definition of "impacts," exceeding the permissible limits for heavy metals in the water was a single *event* that, because it could be reversed, did not constitute "pollution." The engineer never addressed the audience member's critique of the project (that it posed an "environmental threat"), choosing to focus instead on lauding the company's efforts at transparency. What was important, according to the engineer, was that information (whether favorable to the company or not) was being disseminated.

New practices of accountability like the EIA are based on the assumption that the spread of information will help to build more positive relationships among state, corporate, and community actors (and thus enable mining to continue unimpeded). The giving of information is equated with "participation," and "transparency" with trust. Yet as Strathern points out, the term *accountability* implies that "people want to know how to trust one another, to make their trust visible, while [knowing that] the very desire to do so points to the absence of trust" (2000a:310; see also West and Sanders 2003). In Peru, it is precisely the lack of trust in mining companies and the state that has led to an emphasis on transparency. This is why Minera Yanacocha's constant attempts to produce *more* information (in the form of newsletters, magazines, radio shows, internet resources, participatory monitoring programs, workshops, etc.) have not corresponded with an increase in trust. Instead, for many people with a critical stance on mining, the question that remains is: what does transparency conceal? Making information explicit masks the absence of trust, uncertainty of risks, and outright rejection of mining projects that is expressed by mining's critics. The EIA's participatory process invalidates these criticisms even as it is intended to show a company's openness to critique and desire to improve performance.

The use of the EIA as a practice of accountability has multiple consequences. It could be argued that the quest for the manageability of risks drives companies toward some changes in their environmental practices. There is no doubt that companies are focusing unprecedented attention on environmental management, in large part as a result of public pressure. It is also the case that growing public awareness of EIA regulations has helped mobilize local communities, whether to demand employment opportunities and better environmental safeguards, or to oppose mining activity altogether. At the same time, however, the language of "impacts" and "risk management" creates a process in which the very form of participation and critique is circumscribed from the moment in which the risks become visible in the EIA. After all, as long as they are *manageable* risks, they are not an impediment to mining development. But how does the EIA—from its very conception—acquire the authority to define a region, predict the consequences of mining activity, and "manage the risks involved"?

I would suggest that the scientific and political legitimacy of the EIA results in part from the collaborative process that goes into making it, which involves the participation of government institutions, corporations, NGOs, local communities, and even the mining company's staunchest critics. The collaboration that I refer to does not simply imply a sharing of information, nor does it assume that all participants have the same interests and goals (Tsing 2005:13). Rather, collaboration refers to the way the EIA enfolds individuals and institutions into itself regardless of whether or not they agree with its content. In spite of (or perhaps because of) the diverse and sometimes conflicting interests among the actors involved, the language of public participation, transparency, and risk management contributes to an image of consensus.

At the workshop, this collaborative process is evident in the way that questions and criticisms got incorporated into the EIA. During the question period, Minera Yanacocha's most outspoken critics did not hesitate to voice their questions and concerns: How much water will be used for this new project? How will irrigation canals be affected? What does "participation" really entail? One of the objectives of the workshops is to record all of the public's questions, concerns, and demands so that they can be taken into account in the elaboration of the final document presented to the MEM. Every person in attendance at this meeting received a CD containing 122 questions selected from previous workshops, along with the company's responses. The questions were grouped by themes (water, air, chemical products, social impacts, employment, development projects, etc.), and each question specified the name of the institution or community that posed it. The EIA regulations stipulate that questions collected from participatory workshops must be included as an appendix. In this way, every attempt to challenge or oppose the information presented risks being transformed into another page in the document.

The questions posed at the workshops illustrate how the EIA has contributed to new ways of talking about mining in Peru. Water flows, maximum permissible limits, impacts, baseline studies, and the EIA itself have become incorporated into political debates over mining, and have even influenced the language of protest against it. Increasingly, activists and NGOs must challenge mining corporations on issues that they helped bring into the debate, but that corporations ultimately define (such as water quality and participatory monitoring programs). For mining's critics, the EIA has the potential to be used as a political tool and can provide the foundation for what Ulrich Beck (1992) calls "solidarity science." For example, activists used information from Yanacocha's EIAs to calculate the amount of water that mining processes require, and these estimates became a key argument in campaign materials and anti-mining protests.

Activism and Solidarity Science

In Cajamarca, organizations like GRUFIDES have found themselves obligated to respond to the technical information presented by mining companies. In the EIA process, these organizations are often the only external actors that can provide a review of the studies carried out by the mining industry. Furthermore, in order to convincingly show the impacts of mining activity, they must produce their own studies and publications. During the time I spent as an informal volunteer and frequent visitor to the offices of GRUFIDES, I observed some of the ways in which the NGO engaged in solidarity science. Constantly vigilant of the company's ongoing expansion plans, GRUFIDES staff were devoting an increasing amount of effort to the environmental assessment review process. With the PSYO EIA still pending, the NGO was faced with another challenge.

In December 2005, Minera Yanacocha simultaneously presented two mining exploration projects for governmental approval: Exploration Projects Yanacocha East and Yanacocha West, called PEYZE and PEYZO by their Spanish acronyms. According to Peruvian law, projects at the exploration stage require the submission of an Environmental Study (EA). The EA is similar in form to the EIA, and the review process also includes a period in which the public can submit observations to the Ministry of Energy and Mines (MEM). The response of GRUFIDES and their work reviewing these projects show the possibilities and limitations of engaging in a technical critique of corporate documents.

The Municipality of Baños del Inca (one of the municipalities within the area of the projects) commissioned GRUFIDES to carry out an evaluation of the EAS. GRUFIDES staff produced a report describing the exploration projects (GRUFIDES 2006) and provided a series of technical observations to be presented to the MEM. From the outset, the process of reviewing the EAS was laden with frustrations. The time given for the observations— twenty-five calendar days from the date the project was submitted to the MEM—was too limited, as were the resources of the NGO. Reviewing the EA materials was an onerous task that involved combing through hundreds of pages looking for loopholes, missing information, and errors in calculations, as well as scrutinizing maps and figures.

It also required making new maps, since the ones presented were deemed to be unreliable. Maps can be used to change territorial lines, make communities invisible (by not identifying all inhabited areas), or skirt around legal requirements. For example, one of the points of contention in this case was Minera Yanacocha's claim that the expansion projects were within its already-titled property (and therefore did not require new agreements or land titles). GRUFIDES' maps and analysis of project coordinates showed this was not actually the case: 51 percent of the area corresponding to the PEYZE was *not* property of Minera Yanacocha, and 42 percent of the total area of the PEYZO belonged to campesinos (GRUFIDES 2006:5). Checking the maps also revealed that the information about archeological sites did not match up with the clearance permits from the Instituto Nacional de Cultura (National Culture Institute). Bodies of water can also be "hidden" in maps and hydrological information; GRUFIDES claimed that several water springs and canals had not been taken into account.

For GRUFIDES members, the serious flaws in the documents—including the fact that the two EAs were virtual copies, to the point that some geographic coordinates were identical for the two projects—reflected Minera Yanacocha's lack of professionalism and a disregard for environmental and community concerns. They argued that the technical errors and omissions identified and the potential risks posed by the projects should lead the MEM to disqualify the EAs. In the end, the PEYZO and PEYZE were approved, and this could suggest that targeting the technical and scientific aspects of a project was not an effective strategy. Indirectly, however, it could be argued that the increased vigilance of NGOs and the general public can—in the long term—lead to more rigor in the elaboration and review of environmental assessments.

The evaluation carried out by GRUFIDES could also be viewed as an educational tool. The report was intended to summarize the general characteristics of the project and make the basic process of mining exploration comprehensible to a general audience. GRUFIDES staff held information sessions on the PEYZO and PEYZE, and the information disseminated contributed to larger discussions against mining expansion that extended beyond these specific projects. The educational aspect of the NGO's work undoubtedly shaped the terms of the discussion and the arguments that people could use to challenge the scientific claims that the company presented. At the same time, it confirmed the distrust that people already felt about the company and government institutions. Thus, it could be said that environmental assessment does indeed involve the public and open up spaces for participation, discussion, and opposition—but not in the ways intended, and not within the legally established spaces created by the EA and EIA processes.

I do not wish to discount these possibilities for creative forms of activism and the importance of science as a strategic tool embraced by local and international NGOs. Indeed, NGOs and activists are increasingly relying on scientific expertise to strengthen their solidarity work. However, the use of science to produce counterinformation inherently creates an unlevel playing field where small organizations with limited resources face corporations that spend incomparable amounts of money conducting scientific studies. The only option for local NGOs is to rely on volunteer assistance, student interns, and professionals willing to work for a reduced fee. When larger international NGOs or foreign universities fund environmental studies or independent EIA reviews, such studies (because of budgetary and human resource constraints) may not be able to match the level of investment that goes into the information produced by the mining sector.

The EIA, including baseline studies and environmental monitoring, increasingly rely on the language and tools of large-scale, capital intensive science. The need for costly scientific studies and expert knowledge has changed the terms of the debate around mining, channeling activism toward *scientific* counterarguments. As a consequence, campesinos and NGOs are often put at a disadvantage, since their arguments can be dismissed as "uninformed" and "unscientific" in the case of campesinos, or "biased" and "inaccurate" in the case of NGOs. Both campesinos and NGOS may be forced to reduce a wide range of political, economic, and social demands and discontents into arguments that will be evaluated based on their "scientific" validity.

The dominance of science as a tool of accountability has helped direct the actions of NGOs and local activists toward scientific counterarguments in ways that may limit the effectiveness of their efforts. At the same time, the participatory emphasis of new processes of accountability leaves activists with few alternative courses of action, since *not* participating can be taken as an affront to the democratic principles that these processes claim to promote.

The Limits of "Participation"

In communities affected by mining activity in Peru, people often feel that the very processes that elicit their participation actually disempower and exclude them. It is in these cases that they seek alternative ways of voicing their opposition, even if these avenues are often considered more radical and, in some cases, more violent. At the Ollanta Convention Center, confrontations between protestors and the police delayed the start of the public hearing (see figure 5.3). In the turmoil, a police officer hit a female pro-

FIGURE 5.3 Protestors are invited into the auditorium, but they choose to remain outside as the public hearing gets underway.

tester on the head with his baton, further angering the crowd upon their seeing the woman's head covered in blood. When people began to enter the auditorium, the protestors did not do so. The MEM representative who was presiding at the hearing came outside to personally invite them into the meeting, but they refused to participate—not with an auditorium full of *mineros*, they argued, referring not only to mine workers but Minera Yanacocha supporters more generally.

While people inside presented the technical aspects of the mining project, people outside continued to protest. There was even an attempt made to set up large speakers to transmit the proceedings to the people outside, but the protestors' response was to throw rocks at the speakers until they were removed. The protestors' statement was clear: they were not interested in the information that was to be presented or the meeting's proceedings, because nothing they could say would prevent the EIA from being approved. Not only would their intervention in the meeting be futile, but the company would use their attendance to legitimate the EIA with the claim that it was democratically accepted. They decided that their best course of action was to *step outside the document*. I have chosen this phrase to indicate the protestors' need to eschew the boundaries established by the EIA process, and their refusal to engage with the information presented in the document.

By stepping outside the document, protestors were rejecting the EIA's way of defining them and their communities according to what they are deemed to *lack*: education, basic services, and employment opportunities. To elaborate the EIA's Social Component, consultants visit local communities to ask people about their "vision of development," "expectations," and "suggestions for improving the relationship with the Yanacocha mining company" (MWH 2006a). In the same way that each of the "impacts" revealed in the EIA corresponds to an environmental management plan, people's needs are defined by what the mining company can offer. Social baseline studies describe, quantify, and map socioeconomic conditions in local communities in ways that come to define extreme poverty, unsustainable agricultural practices, and inefficient social organization; in other words, a way of life that must inevitably give way to mining's progress.

Inside the auditorium, the EIA presentation was followed by a round of written questions. Some people also signed up to ask questions orally and took their turn at the microphone upon being called by name, institutional affiliation, and place of residence. Some speakers (including the mayor of one of the districts within the PSYO's area of influence) implored the company to keep its promises but emphasized the economic benefits and employment opportunities that could be derived from responsible mining. One of the few critical questions was posed by a regular participant in anti-mining protests, who brought up the issue of water quantity and the disappearance of water springs. His question was abruptly dismissed by a Yanacocha engineer: "It's very easy to say this but it has not been proven," the engineer replied, and repeated that the mine was not affecting water quality in communities. Few of the speakers referred to the EIA information that had been presented, and many did not pose questions at all; instead, they took the opportunity to speak favorably of the company's accomplishments to date. Addressing the audience rather than the presenters, one speaker made the following comment: "Today, we *Cajamarquinos* bear the enormous responsibility of deciding if . . . Cajamarca shall become a prosperous town, with education and employment, or if we will deny it this opportunity. What has happened outside has been regrettable and embarrassing. If [the protestors] had come inside they would have listened, and they would have understood; there would have been dialogue."[8] The participatory aspect of the EIA is more than an opportunity to ask questions. What the EIA "maps" as well are the relationships of individuals and organizations vis-à-vis the corporation: their attendance at meetings, their concerns, and their willingness to cooperate. Along with other mechanisms of surveillance (such as attendance sheets, filming company events, photographing people at protests, etc.), the information collected and made public through the EIA is essential for the establishment of alliances. These corporate strategies are often considered coercive and intimidating, and many people feel that speaking against Minera Yanacocha would put their jobs at risk or lead to other negative repercussions. Furthermore, making these alliances visible to the public reinforces the polarization between those with a purportedly "pro-" or "anti"-mining stance, pitting these groups against each other. As a result, the role of corporations and the state fades to the background while individuals and local organizations take it on themselves to monitor the activities of their fellow citizens and discipline them accordingly.

Following the public hearing, Minera Yanacocha's Institutional Relations and Communications Department issued a communiqué that described the day's events as follows: "From very early on people gathered at the Ollanta convention center. Groups opposed to mining activity tried to mar the hearing, without success. . . . Close to a thousand people filled the building. The event got under way at 10 AM, due to a delay caused by a group of protestors who refused to enter the building. . . . This group did not want to participate in the hearing. Furthermore, they generated acts of violence as they attacked some individuals and attempted to cause damage to the theater." Local newspapers also reported that the event was a success, and that only a handful of protestors (depicted as troublemakers with political interests) attempted to violently disturb the proceedings. These representations of the protests constructed an opposition between the "irrational subject" (driven by selfish interests, ignorance, or misinformation) and the "informed subject," who embraced participatory knowledge-making practices in order to come to an informed decision.

In response to these depictions of the public hearing, an anonymously written parody of Minera Yanacocha's communiqué was circulated by e-mail. It read: "The hearing was a total 'success' because in less than five hours the PSYO EIA's 5,098 pages were explained to campesinos and Yanacocha subcontractors. . . . The campesinos and subcontractors posed dozens of questions, demonstrating their prodigious and exceptional intelligence as well as their complete comprehension of everything that was presented in an extremely simple way, which only the ignorant campesinos manipulated by the NGOs who protested outside failed to understand." The mocking e-mail addressed precisely the criticisms of the EIA process put forth by campesinos and NGOs, as well as the stereotypical image of campesinos as passive subjects manipulated by outside interests.

In the context of modern mining, corporations, governments, and other actors operate on the logic that more information equals more public knowledge and therefore, more transparency. But public documents and hearings do more than create an image of transparency. Their effects are twofold: on one hand, they reinforce the corporation's alliances by giving people the arguments and the language to respond to criticisms against the mine. On the other hand, critics such as NGOs can use this same information to generate activism. While this counterinformation is fundamental for anti-mining campaigns, some local people feel that contestation through existing channels of public participation is largely ineffective. Sometimes, their best chance to voice their opposition is to take this counterknowledge outside the document. It is in these cases where the refusal to engage in dialogue and a stance of *non*participation become the most appealing forms of political action.

In Peru, controversies over mining activity have generated much discussion about promoting democratic participation and transparency as a way to resolve conflicts. Yet the introduction of mechanisms of accountability such as the EIA, including recent modifications to incorporate public participation and community consultation, have not eliminated the tensions generated by the continual expansion of extractive activity. In communities affected by mining, some people argue that the EIA only provides them with an opportunity to ask questions and make comments, which *may* lead to some modifications in the company's environmental mitigation plans, but cannot stop a proposed project from being approved.

The EIA for the PSYO was indeed approved by the Ministry of Energy and Mines on September 4, 2006. Since the project involved the expansion of an already existing mine (rather than the construction of a new mine), the EIA's approval attracted little attention beyond Cajamarca. In a newsletter, Minera Yanacocha stated that the EIA's approval gave communities a guarantee that the company's commitments would be met and provided the state with a tool for environmental monitoring and control. The proposed expansion went ahead as planned, and the San Jose Reservoir that was central to the company's water management plan was inaugurated by President Alan García in April 2008.

Conflicts still surface repeatedly in communities around the Yanacocha mine, and critics continue to fault the company's lack of transparency, inadequate processes of community consultation, and the absence of the state. In their critique of the EIA process, environmental activists in Peru and elsewhere focus on the benefits of participation and ways of making it more meaningful. Scholars also suggest that public participation has both direct and indirect benefits, including individual and community empowerment and social learning (Fitzpatrick and Sinclair 2003). In practical terms, changes to the EIA process could be made by providing adequate notice when a project is submitted for approval, facilitating access to information, providing government funding for the public to adequately participate in the review process, and involving communities in the decision-making process from the earliest stages of project planning (Sinclair and Diduck 2009). In Peru, public pressure has led to changes in the EIA process, such as an increased emphasis on the social impacts of a mining project, and requirements to hold information sessions in the communities affected by the project. These changes are desirable, and I am not suggesting that the solution would be *less* public participation, transparency, and accountability.

What I have suggested in this chapter, however, is that mechanisms of accountability require a different analysis of the role of the state, corporations, NGOs, and community actors. I have argued that the EIA entrusts corporations with the task of creating an inventory of natural resources and local communities that establishes the characteristics of a place and makes it knowable in scientific terms. The EIA reveals the potential risks of a proposed project, but making these risks visible is contingent on the company's ability to make them technically manageable. Once the company has established a management plan, the state is left with the perfunctory role of monitoring environmental indicators and checking standards of performance that corporations themselves have helped define. Nevertheless, the form of the EIA and the process of making it public create an image of consensus, cooperation with local communities, and state avowal.

This is the essence of collaboration that the EIA embodies, as it incorporates state institutions, corporations, consultants, communities, and civil organizations into its elaboration and evaluation. By including a wide range of "participants," collaboration deflects authorship and shifts the focus from *corporate* accountability to *shared* responsibility. The participant becomes complicit in the coproduction of the document and is thus expected to share in the benefits—*and* the risks—of the knowledge that it contains.

CONCLUSION

Expanding Frontiers of Extraction

I wish this wasn't a political march, but a technical one, that the [protest] leaders would really show the problem that they see in the water.

—PRIME MINISTER OSCAR VALDÉS, FEBRUARY 9, 2012 (REUTERS NEWS AGENCY)

They say that if a government minister says "technical" three times in front of the mirror, a fairy that resolves social conflicts appears.

—GREGORIO SANTOS, REGIONAL PRESIDENT OF CAJAMARCA, MARCH 2012 (POSTED TO TWITTER)

When I returned for a visit in May 2012, Cajamarca was the site of one more conflict to add to Minera Yanacocha's tarnished corporate image (see figure C.1). Protests were being held in the provinces of Cajamarca and Celendín, which would be affected by the company's newest project, Minas Conga. The Conga mineral deposits were discovered in 1990, and Minera Yanacocha began exploration work in 2004. In 2011, the company announced an investment of $4.8 billion, making it the largest investment in Peruvian mining history. Production was set to start in 2014, and preproduction activities were underway when protests against the project intensified. Like many other recent conflicts, protests against mining expansion focused on water. To reach the mineral

FIGURE C.1 Protestors and police meet again on the streets of Cajamarca during the Conga protests in 2012.

deposit, the company would have to drain two lagoons, and turn another two into waste-rock deposits.

In many ways, the Conga conflict seemed like a repeat of the many protests that had been taking place in Cajamarca and elsewhere in the country. But there were also some significant changes. A new president, Ollanta Humala, had been sworn into office in July 2011. A former army officer, Mr. Humala campaigned on a center-left platform that recognized the need to redistribute the country's wealth more equitably while maintaining an open economy. In a runoff election, he obtained a narrow victory over his opponent, Keiko Fujimori, the daughter of former president Alberto Fujimori. Humala's support came in part from the poor and marginalized sectors of the population, many of them campesinos dissatisfied with the unfulfilled promises of extractive activity. On a campaign stop in Cajamarca's town square in early 2011, Mr. Humala promised his audience that he would safeguard water resources from mining activity, "because you don't drink gold, you don't eat gold, but we drink water, our children drink water . . . agriculture needs water." The crowd cheered for Mr. Humala, and their support translated into votes that helped land him the presidency later that year.

At the regional level, regional president Gregorio Santos joined forces with groups opposed to the Conga project. In December 2011, his government passed Regional Ordinance 036 to protect land on the proposed mining site from development. The regional government's critical stance marked a shift from previous governments with a more favorable or ambiguous position on mining activity and provided resources and institutional support for mobilizations against Conga. By the time the Conga conflict erupted, mining was a key issue at the national level, garnering unparalleled attention from politicians and the press. There was also greater popular awareness of mining issues in Peru and beyond, as mining conflicts had become the focus of documentaries, alternative media, and international campaigns. In February 2012, the Conga conflict inspired a National Water March that began symbolically at the lagoons. Father Arana was one of the main organizers of the event, which drew people from various parts of the country who congregated in Lima's city center. Additionally, Conga inspired a number of protest actions including international petitions and solidarity activism involving NGOs in Spain and Belgium.

The Conga conflict encapsulates the politics of extraction that I have described in this book. Like other conflicts discussed in previous chapters, the Conga controversy was a mix of science and politics, yet efforts to address the problems tried to separate the technical from the political. In the first opening epigraph, then-Prime Minister Oscar Valdés expresses his desire for protestors to focus on "technical" evidence to back up their claims about water pollution instead of staging a "political" march. Meanwhile the ironic comment from Gregorio Santos in the second epigraph mocks the assumption that technical arguments will resolve the conflicts, pointing to an over-reliance on scientific expertise over moral and political claims (see Grieco and Salazar-Solier 2013).

One of the most noteworthy aspects of the Conga conflict was the way that the project's Environmental Impact Assessment (EIA) came to monopolize debates over mining expansion. The government's response to the unrest in Cajamarca was two-pronged: on one hand, it commissioned experts to review the Conga EIA and evaluate the project's potential environmental impacts. On the other, it deployed police and military personnel to the areas of conflict and called for a state of emergency in an attempt to quell the protests. Like previous conflicts, the Conga controversy also focused on water, which helped to mobilize communities and generate public solidarity. Specifically, the lagoons at the center of the conflict enabled arguments for and against the project to take shape. In this concluding chapter, I want to elucidate the ways in which arguments for and against the project were deployed as "science" or "belief," and how expert and nonexpert knowledges came together and diverged in debates over the Conga project. I also continue to explore the making of equivalences in environmental controversies, and the nature of politics in a context of continued mining expansion. Finally, I reflect on what the conflicts discussed in this book can tell us about the future of resource extraction and political activism in the Latin American region.

Water in Conflicts over Mining

One of the most widely circulated photographs during the Conga protests showed people gathered around the Laguna El Perol. Some of the men wear straw hats and ponchos, the distinctive clothing of Cajamarca's campesino communities. A Lima-based blogger called it "the embrace of the lagoon," noting the powerful impact of the image and the significance of a protest so different from those in urban streets and plazas more familiar to city dwellers (Ilizarbe 2011). Conga's lagoons (Lagunas Azul, El Perol, Chica, and Mala) became emblems of the conflict, and the "guardians of the lagoons" emerged as their heroic protectors. These guardians were campesinos who came from the provinces of Bambamarca and Celendín to protest against the mining project and included a small group that had set up camp near the lagoons to ensure that the mining company did not proceed with any work in the area. Groups of policemen from the DINOES (Special Operations division) were sent to protect the area that Minera Yanacocha considered to be its private property. Observers have noted the problematic conflation of state and corporate interests as mining corporations contract out security companies that hire off-duty police officers, who are permitted to use state property such as weapons, uniforms, and ammunition (Kamphuis 2011). Around the lagoon, the policemen entered a precarious stand-off with campesinos, each group observing the other.

The lagoons became a site of pilgrimage, as activists staged protests and invited journalists and observers to see firsthand the area that would be destroyed by the mine. One of these visits was organized for two priests, Gastón Garratea and Miguel Cabrejos, who were appointed by the government to facilitate a dialogue intended to put an end to the conflict. They set out in a caravan of thirty vehicles transporting representatives of the local government and activist organizations, and met with some three thousand campesinos from nearby communities waiting for them at the lagoons to express their concerns about the project. "The people defend what God has created, we will not exchange water for all the money in the world," said a resident of El Tambo, noting that their irrigation canals would be affected by the project (Matta Colunche 2012). The mayor of Bambamarca offered the priests trout caught in the lagoons to counter the company's claims that the water was not apt for human use and consumption.

Prior to the delegation's trip to the lagoons, other visits were facilitated by the regional government and activist groups that provided transportation to take people from the city and other communities to an area that most had never seen. Through this experience of witnessing, visitors gained a greater sense of connection to the area. Conga's lagoons became as central to the conflict as did Cerro Quilish in the 2004 protests against Yanacocha's expansion project. As I described in chapter 3, debates over mining in that case centered on whether Cerro Quilish was an Apu or "sacred" mountain. Many people, including company representatives, accused activists of introducing the idea of the Apu where it had never existed. I have argued that Cerro Quilish was neither "invented" nor pre-existing; rather, its identity as Apu-aquifer-sacred-mountain came into being and acquired political significance in ways that helped the movement against the mine. Water is a web of relations among humans and other-than-human beings that are sustained through everyday practices. If water is analyzed as a set of relations, rather than as a stable substance with inherent properties, we can see how resources are made and change form, reconfiguring the collectives around them. Lakes, watersheds, rivers, canals, and pollutants are not fixed, unchanging features of the landscape. Their importance—and their physical properties—changed as the company altered the landscape, and as people's relationship with that landscape and with Minera Yanacocha also changed.

Similarly, in the Conga case, the lagoons emerged as important entities over the course of people's interactions and confrontations with the mining company. Like Cerro Quilish, the lagoons were different things to different actors. In activist campaigns, the lagoons featured prominently for their role as a source of water and pastures for animals. The project area, activists noted, was at the headwaters of five watersheds. Also evident in the way that people talked about the Conga project was the affective dimension of the lagoons—their beauty, significance for life in the campo, and other intangible properties that made them worthy of protection.

For the mining company, on the other hand, the lagoons were a repository of water that could be replaced with artificial reservoirs and a system of water management. In response to this proposal, activists argued that the lagoons' value could not be offset with reservoirs or economic benefits. Education materials produced by NGOs, including calendars, pamphlets, and websites, featured photographs of a deep blue lagoon and wildflowers, images that coincided with narratives of pristine nature unspoiled by industrial development. Added to these activist narratives were the lived experiences of campesinos and their interactions with an agentive landscape. I was told that people from nearby communities, when traveling long distances by foot, were afraid to spend the night near the lagoons, for all the chatter of voices in the middle of the night. In translating such stories, activists invoked the special significance of the lagoons for local people. As with the Quilish campaigns, the language of the "sacred" occasionally appeared in media coverage and activist missives to describe the lagoons. In this way, various forms of knowledge and experience came together with the interests of activists and narratives against the mine. These knowledge encounters were produced as these various actors were brought together in response to the mine's expansion.

Like the Quilish protests, the Conga conflict could be understood in terms of ontological differences, where lagoons and mountains are not mere repositories of water and minerals, but are agentive beings that command respect. However, the conflict's focus on the lagoons should also remind us that what is often glossed as "local knowledge" is not a fixed entity. Rather, arguments that appeal to "indigenous knowledge" and "Andean traditions" are always made from local-global encounters. People's arguments about lagoons and mountains are not based on already established knowledge or cultural practices but emerge from their interactions with other actors (including corporations, politicians, and environmentalists). Their claims are efforts to speak across difference and engage with a wider public who can address their concerns (Brosius 2006).

At the same time, what is glossed as "science" in both activist and corporate campaigns should also be understood as forms of knowledge that are coproduced in the course of the conflict. Like "local knowledge," scientific claims are not preestablished, objective, and fixed. Rather, information relating to the impacts of mining activity—whether about pollution, water management, or the hydrological cycle—was continuously reevaluated and challenged. Corporate public relations campaigns had to address the questions and concerns that activists raised, and the information disseminated by the company in turn shaped the way that organizations structured their own campaigns against the project. This process increased the reliance of all parties, including state institutions, on scientific and technical arguments around water issues.

The centrality of water in recent conflicts calls attention to the specific material effects of modern mining technologies, which also contributed to emergent debates. As the Conga conflict began to take shape, stories circulated about campesinos who noticed that water springs in the area of the lagoons had dried up. People did not talk about the lagoons in the same way before the conflict, just like Cerro Quilish took various forms over the course of the conflict with Minera Yanacocha. However, people's relationship with the lagoons was influenced by how they experienced the mine's effects on the landscape. Over the course of almost twenty years of coexistence with the mining company, people had heard about land usurpation, damages to irrigation canals, and animal and fish deaths. They had also directly witnessed the mine's gradual extension over the terrain, the reduction in water flows, and the disappearance of water springs. The mine's operations encompassed former grazing lands, water springs, and irrigation infrastructure; water from all stages of the mining process had to be treated before being released into the environment. These activities reconfigured people's relationship with water resources, and communities threatened by the Conga project feared that they, too, would experience the same effects on their ways of life.

These very tangible changes brought about by modern mining technologies produced a different type of conflict from ones previously experienced in the country's mining regions. Unlike underground mines or small-scale informal mining, open-pit chemical mining interrupted watercourses while introducing new elements into the debate: toxic substances, runoff, and threatened water springs and lagoons. The particular characteristics of the Cajamarca landscape were not merely a backdrop to the conflicts but animated them in unexpected ways.

Knowledge, Expertise, and Environmental Impact Assessment

In the popular memory, the movement against mining at Cerro Quilish was characterized as an expression of grassroots mobilizing, horizontal in its organization, and without a central leader. Activist friends who were involved in the protests remembered the coming together of campesinos and city folk, students and teachers' unions, young and old. For the Conga conflict, the panorama of protest bore some similarities with the Quilish mobilizations, but differences were also evident. This time, the rondas campesinas also played a key role in mobilizing the countryside. Unionized teachers and other city dwellers also joined in the marches in the city, but the rural participants were considered to be the central players. Day after day since the beginning of the general strike on May 31, campesino delegates congregated in Cajamarca's central plaza, and others gathered in the city of Celendín and the area of the lagoons.

The political climate in Cajamarca had undergone some significant changes, the main one being the creation of a political party called Tierra y Libertad (Land and Liberty), founded by Father Marco Arana. Father Arana's move from the church to organized politics displeased many people—not only Catholic authorities, but also his family, closest friends, and supporters. The party's national ambitions made Father Arana into a potential presidential candidate, although his intentions to run for president were only hinted at (especially by his detractors) and not confirmed at the time that the Conga conflict erupted onto the political scene. When he asked his superiors for permission to engage in political work, his privilege of giving mass at the Parish of Guadalupe church was revoked. Gradually, his activities with Tierra y Libertad took him away from his religious obligations, and he reduced his involvement with GRUFIDES.

Bertha, a lawyer who ran a small educational NGO and had been involved in activism against Minera Yanacocha since the mine's arrival, was disillusioned with what she saw as the politicking that accompanied the Conga conflict. "Political interests have become more visible," she said, and divisions by political parties were now more evident than during the Quilish mobilizations. Other friends who had participated in the Quilish protests made the same observations, and many of them stayed away from the demonstrations, even if they opposed the Conga project. Like others who had been close to him, Bertha continued to respect Father Arana, but after supporting the signature drive to enlist the party, she distanced herself from it. Some members of GRUFIDES and the NGO community also chose not to participate in the party, even though they had previously placed their hopes on building a political movement that could challenge the status quo. Bertha was discouraged by Tierra y Libertad's association with what she called "traditional politics," and its connection to an old guard in leftist parties. She was also unconvinced that their platform represented significant change in areas like women's rights and the environment. Bertha and others who originally lent their support were critical of the party's decision to go national, instead of building up a base of supporters and having candidates run for local and regional elections (in which many believed Father Arana could have achieved an easy victory). Many saw this as an error in judgment, and an indication that Father Arana and the party's top rung had their eyes on the presidency.

Father Arana was one of three people identified in the media as "leading" the Conga protests. Another was a lawyer who served time in jail for his association with the MRTA (Movimiento Revolucionario Túpac Amaru) guerrilla movement in the 1980s. Finally, there was Gregorio Santos, the regional president, who had a history of involvement in teachers' unions, the rondas campesinas, and the communist party Patria Roja. In various accounts of the conflict (from media reports to company communiqués to comments from city dwellers), the political interests of these key leaders were brought to the forefront. All three were said to harbor political ambitions that went beyond stopping the mining project. In some cases, accounts targeting the character of these leaders were an attempt to delegitimize the protestors by opposing "politics" with a technical approach to the conflict, one based on the examination of environmental studies and proposed mitigation strategies. The language of expertise was used to shift the discussion away from "politics" and toward their technical dimensions, something that was done by focusing on the Environmental Impact Assessment of the proposed project.

The Conga EIA was approved by the administration of President Alan Garcia in 2010, more than a year before activists called for an indefinite general strike on November 24, 2011. When tensions began to surface, President Ollanta Humala declared a sixty-day state of emergency in three regions in Cajamarca. Also in November 2011, critical comments by Environment Minister Ricardo Giesecke were leaked to the press, making public some methodological and technical flaws of the EIA. The report noted that the Conga project would "significantly and irreversibly transform the watershed, disappearing various ecosystems and fragmenting those remaining, in such a way that the processes, functions, interactions, and environmental services will be irreversibly affected" (Gorriti 2011). A key point of contention was the impact of the mine on four small lagoons in the project area. The report noted that using two of these lagoons as waste-rock deposits would be more economical for the company, but was not the only alternative available.

In order to appease protestors and reduce public opposition to the project, the government called for a *peritaje*, an Expert's Report that would review the results of the Conga Environmental Impact Assessment. Three consultants from Portugal and Spain had forty days to review the contents of the EIA and produced a report that made some recommendations while ultimately backing up the company's claims. The report was presented to the public in April 2012. Around the same time, NGOs hired hydrologist Robert Moran to provide his observations to the EIA. This alternative report was commissioned and funded by the Environmental Defender Law Center in the United States, with the logistical support of GRUFIDES. Mr. Moran based his report on a twenty-day trip to Peru, which included a visit to the project area, and a review of between nine thousand and ten thousand pages contained in the EIA (Moran 2012). He presented his findings in March 2012.

Why did these artifacts (the EIA and related reports) become the key actors in the conflict? Why did people buy into the idea of reviewing the EIA? Whose idea was it to do the peritaje? The peritaje could simply be seen as the government's way of justifying the project and "buying" the support of international consultants. The reports' predictable findings—according to Mr. Moran, they essentially mirrored those of the company—did not come as a surprise. And yet, the activists inadvertently contributed to the idea of the peritaje and helped to put it on the government's agenda. The EIA ended up being at the center of the conflict, even though activists recognized that the issues could not be addressed through their technical dimensions. The state, the company, and activists used the EIA and related studies with different aims, and with different expectations.

The EIA enabled the state to claim that the project was environmentally sound, and the experts' report strengthened the legitimacy of the document. As I showed in chapter 5, practices of accountability such as environmental assessment and audit, regardless of the actual content of documents such as the EIA, can have the effect of facilitating resource extraction. Through the EIA process, corporations establish the physical characteristics of a project and standards of performance, while leaving the state with a perfunctory role. Government ministries must show that corporations are complying with environmental measures and other standards of good practice, but these are standards that companies themselves have helped define through their own baseline studies, voluntary codes of conduct, and environmental mitigation plans. The Conga EIA enabled the company to present information about the project's effects and the mitigation plans in place to deal with them.

In the Conga conflict, the increased reliance on technical expertise led to a situation in which all parties—both for and against the mine—felt compelled to present their claims in the technical language of environmental management. Activists had long criticized EIAs for their inadequacy and continued to call for independent reports to be done. When I talked to a member of GRUFIDES, he recognized that somewhere along the way his organization, too, might have contributed to the idea of undertaking the peritaje. He recalled that in their many meetings with government and company representatives leading up to the conflict, GRUFIDES and other community organizations suggested that the EIA should be reexamined, and this proposal was taken literally. Various local organizations formed a committee to propose solutions to the conflict, and their recommendations ended up being the blueprint for the Expert's Report. The collective making of the peritaje is an example of how unintended collaborations take place in the context of mining conflicts, bringing together actors with divergent viewpoints and allowing their interests to cohere.

The emphasis placed on the EIA, water monitoring, and other environmental studies have channeled the energies of activists toward technical counterarguments. This is not always a good avenue for activism, since it requires resources and expertise that NGOs often lack. At the same time, activists are obliged to respond to the technical arguments presented by corporations, and to use their own data to give their position more validity. In spite of their skepticism about the EIA process and corporate-sponsored science, many activists placed hope on expert knowledge and counted on allies who might help strengthen their claims against the company. More specifically, the faith in the use of counterscience was based on previous successful experiences, such as Robert Moran's (2001a) review of the Tambogrande EIA. Since that time, Mr. Moran had acquired an international reputation for his work with communities opposing mining activity, and he began to provide his services to a number of NGOs dealing with mining issues.

Performing the conflict through the EIA offered all parties the legitimacy of technical data and the language of expertise. For those who opposed the project, the EIA represented an opportunity to challenge the mine's viability. The science mobilized by the anti-Conga movement and alternative studies like Robert Moran's was as much of a performance as the peritaje. Activists did not necessarily believe that an independent report would change the outcome of the conflict, nor did they believe that it would yield trustworthy observations and recommendations. Indeed, for many, the project was simply unviable, and no amount of technical data could have changed that. For activists, the review of the EIA was a way of stalling the project, a desperate measure in the face of a pressing and seemingly unstoppable threat.

Meanwhile, the company hoped that by focusing the conflict on technical aspects, it could convince the public of the benefits of the project. The company's public relations efforts reflected the assumption that giving more information would dispel what they saw as half-truths and erroneous ideas—in other words, as "beliefs" that were not founded on solid science. This was especially evident after the publication of the Moran report, which the company responded to in detail on its website. Company officials that I spoke to also attributed the spread of misinformation to the intervention of local and international actors. Like company officials, Humala's government hoped to gain the public's trust by providing them with more information, but in fact, the way the conflict developed points to people's lack of confidence in the authority of the state. As Wynne notes, "Public responses to risks and risk information are rationally based upon their experience and judgment of the credibility and trustworthiness of the institutions who claim to be in charge" (Wynne 1992). Even before the results of the peritaje were made public, people's lack of trust in the government made them unlikely to accept the experts' observations as legitimate.

Given that critics and allies of the company had already-established positions, the technical reports did not provide any new or different information but ended up reinforcing those positions and added to their incommensurability. Instead of leading to dialogue and a resolution of the conflict, as the government hoped that it would do, the reliance on technical studies and reports helped to solidify opposing, incommensurable viewpoints. Both sides further entrenched themselves instead of finding a middle ground (Wynne 1992).

The EIA process and the Conga conflict's focus on the technical aspects of the project rely on what I have called a "logic of equivalence." Environmental mitigation assumes the possibility of equal inputs and outputs, and a conciliation of positive and negative outcomes. The increasing focus on the environmental aspects of a project, including disputes over water quality and quantity, have meant that technical solutions often take precedence and are presented as evidence of social responsibility. In the Conga case, the debate revolved around the lagoons at the site of the project and the amount of water that they contribute to the local communities downstream. For the company, the solution to the problem was to present a water management program that included the construction of four reservoirs, based on the amount of water held in each lagoon. The arguments presented by the company and its critics were based on different ways of apprehending the significance of the lagoons, their connection to other bodies of water, and the amount of water that they contributed to the watershed and the communities in the vicinity. Each of these perspectives was backed up by the technical studies and documents produced by actors for and against the project.

Local people, and the NGOs and environmentalists that supported them, argued that the project would destroy water springs crucial for communities downstream. They also saw the lagoons as part of a larger system, rather than isolated entities, as they were described in the EIA. A pamphlet distributed by GRUFIDES, produced with the collaboration of two Spanish NGOs, emphasized the threats to water sources in a highland ecosystem characterized by bunchgrass (*ichu*) and wetlands. The project area is described as follows: "This ecosystem acts as a water sponge (*esponja hídrica*), since it allows for the capture and filtration of rain water and humidity from the mist, recharging the water table and generating water springs and rivers downstream. Therefore, this system is completely interconnected and any affectation at a single point implicates the entire system." The ideas of an interconnected system and a "sponge" that holds water were also made during the Quilish campaigns, and these arguments against the mine were commonly repeated in subsequent conflicts.

Robert Moran's alternative EIA review also emphasized that surface water and groundwater, as well as springs, are interconnected. His report reads: "Beneath a large part of the project area, there are volcanic and karstic rocks, with faults and fractures, together with glacial sediments, all of which conducts water. Satellite imagery and structural geological studies show that many of the lagoons in the area are located on faults and fractures, some possibly related to collapsed volcanic structures [*calderas*]. All this information shows that surface water and subsoil water would be interconnected, especially if they are submitted to a long-term hydraulic stress" (Moran 2012:3). Contrary to Robert Moran's view of an interconnected system, the Conga EIA suggested that the rock beneath the proposed waste deposits was impermeable. Mr. Moran argued that the EIA did not provide adequate evidence to prove this point. Yet this was the argument repeated in the company's public relations materials and by Yanacocha engineers.

In an interview, Minera Yanacocha's water specialist challenged the veracity of the claims made by Conga's opponents. He argued that some people think there are water springs (*manantiales*) everywhere, when in fact they are just "*charcos de agua*" (water puddles). In the rainy season there are many puddles, but this doesn't make them a source of water. Upon further discussion, he did recognize that some manantiales exist in the area, but he turned to the company's oft-repeated argument that everything generates an impact, and these impacts simply need to be managed. The loss of some manantiales that he considered insignificant (in terms of water flows) did not mean that people downstream would not have enough water. Indeed, he stressed that the aim of the company was to improve conditions for local people by providing "more water, more irrigation, more pastures, more animals, and higher incomes." He saw both the lagoons and water springs as stagnant water that would not otherwise be used, or that would simply disappear in the dry season.

In his view, the lagoons exist in isolation from the larger ecosystem, a perspective that isolates water from its connections and relations. He said the lagoons sat on top of an impermeable clay-like material, which prevented water from filtrating into the water table. The lagoons are thus disconnected from other bodies of water, and from the human and nonhuman relations that make up life in the countryside, and on which people depend in order to sustain that way of life. The image of the lagoons as isolated entities contradicts how local people presented the lagoons in campaigns against the mine. Isolating water from its relations (whether in the case of the lagoons, water springs, or irrigation canals) was necessary to make technical (or monetary) equivalences. However, such equivalences did not account for underlying differences that made it impossible to reconcile opposing points of view.

Equivalences have the effect of disqualifying discrepant arguments, which are discounted as "belief," while privileging the knowledge of experts (even if the information they present is necessarily partial). A common way of presenting arguments critical of mining activity is to dismiss them as either "politics" or as "belief." In the first instance, anti-mining activism is an attempt to manipulate for political, personal, or economic gain. In the second instance, arguments against the mine are a stubborn neglect of what the company presents as undisputable facts. During our conversation, Minera Yanacocha's water specialist asked me a hypothetical question: "Do you believe in God?" he asked. What he meant to say was that the protestors' claims were beyond reason—belief is not something that can be argued about, since it is not based on factual information or empirical evidence. However, for him, technical evidence is free of politics *and* belief.

Corporate and state rhetoric centered on the idea that ignorance and political interests invalidated activists' arguments against mining expansion. Furthermore, company representatives did not see all "expert" knowledge as equivalent, since they also considered technical arguments presented by activists and NGOs to be tainted by bias and political manipulation. At the same time, activists doubted the validity of corporate data and the state-sponsored peritaje for the same reasons. But regardless of the skepticism about expert knowledge variously expressed by activist and corporate actors, the prevalence of a technical discourse influenced their respective arguments and how the conflict took shape. What the Conga case illustrates, then, is that expert knowledge that is deemed to be scientific (and thus opposed to "belief") is not part of a stable, preestablished worldview but is emergent, contested, and shaped by the interaction of different actors.

Extractive Futures

Andrew Barry writes that by focusing on social movements and ideological conflict, scholars have tended to neglect the objects, technologies, and practices of political action, which have the potential to "open up or close down the space of the political" (2001:196). The chapters in this book have examined how the objects, technologies, and practices related to mining activity provoke political action and reshape political terrains. I have written about how water and pollution mobilized protestors throughout the country and contributed to the organization of political groups. People organized not only through political parties and associations but were also connected by irrigation systems and linked through shared waterways. In Cajamarca, some Yanacocha spokespeople saw the urban opposition to the Conga project as evidence of manipulation by "outsiders," people disconnected from the communities directly affected by the mine. In reality, however, the city became connected to the campo through the mine's effects on water. Watersheds became a newly relevant unit of organization, and the mine's impacts (manifested as changes in water quantity and quality) came to define the territory of action. Water connected and divided people, places, and issues in ways that furthered the goals of different actors at various times, including the company, which was also able to mobilize water to further its own interests.

As I have shown, focusing on water makes equivalences possible and shifted the debate over Conga toward its technical dimensions. As a result, technocratic solutions to the conflict replaced a more explicit critique of the extractive model of development driving the economy and policies in Peru (and beyond). At the same time, this emphasis on the technical may have contributed to an intensification of protests rather than their dissolution. After the Expert's Report and independent observations to the EIA, one of the Conga protest leaders talked to me about the upcoming general strike, which organizers were calling an "indefinite" strike at the regional level. Recognizing that this mass mobilization could lead to violence, he argued: "We already have five reports, so what else is there? We've done everything possible, we don't have any other option [than to call a strike]." In the end, five people were killed by police bullets during the confrontations between police officers and protestors.

In the words of a friend and longtime local activist, "weapons are the most powerful nonhuman actor." He recognized the powerful role that water was playing in the conflicts and in ways of mobilizing people to protest against mining activity. Water and other nonhuman actors had enabled protestors to make their claims heard, but Conga provided an evident reminder about the limits of these strategies. Even as we pay attention to the mobilizing power of water, we cannot neglect the force of the state and the role of corporate and state-sponsored violence in suppressing opposition and limiting possibilities for political action.

In the years leading up to the Conga conflict, activists had grown increasingly concerned with strategies used by mining companies and their government allies to contain mining opposition. Many felt that President Humala's heavy-handed response to the protests and the state of emergency were uncalled-for, and were reminiscent of the Shining Path years. Indeed, accusations of terrorism and presumed linkages between activists against the Conga project and insurgent groups were used to justify the state's response and intimidate local residents.

Adding to the constant presence of corporate security forces and the police, activists remained shaken by the discovery, in late 2006, of a surveillance operation that tracked the movements of GRUFIDES staff and other critics of Minera Yanacocha. Father Arana and other activists were stalked, filmed, and photographed as part of a complex operation named "El Diablo" ("The Devil" was the moniker given to Father Arana by those tracking his moves). According to an investigative report in *La República* (Cruz and Romero 2006), e-mails connected the surveillance activities to an employee of Forza, the company subcontracted to provide security for Yanacocha. The surveillance operation was dismantled following a police investigation, but occasional threats, mysterious phone calls, and the increased polarization in Cajamarca continued to create a sense of insecurity for activists. According to Father Arana, the surveillance operation was an indication of Minera Yanacocha's dual approach to preventing conflict: outwardly, it focuses on corporate social and environmental responsibility programs; covertly, it is willing to engage in other tactics to suppress opposition.

In the Conga conflict, science and the law initially seemed to provide ways of dealing with the disagreements over the proposed project. However, people's sense of optimism was crushed by mechanisms that invalidated local opposition. Ultimately, science, the law, the state, and corporate security worked together to close avenues available for people to express opposition to mining activity. The peritaje sought to prevent any further challenges to the technical aspects of the project, while the EIA process closed legal avenues to oppose the project. Left without other options, protestors took to the streets. The police responded with excessive force to quell demonstrations, adding to a climate of intimidation that increased people's distrust of the company and the state. The result was an explosive mix of interests, including those of grassroots groups and new political parties wanting to force open a space of opposition.

The Conga case shows two sides of the conflicts that have emerged in the country over the past two decades. On one hand, it illustrates the openings that have enabled new actors to become visible in the political sphere, drive grassroots movements, and put new issues on the political agenda. On the other hand, the state's response shows a move toward the criminalization of protest, and a forceful advance of extractive activity in spite of local resistance. As long as mining continues to expand into new frontiers, the proliferation of conflict will also continue unabated.

The dynamics of mining controversies have marked the political terrain in Peru over the past two decades. While the events I have described in this book—from campaigns against lead pollution in La Oroya to the Conga conflict in Cajamarca—emerge from the specific historical heritage of mining in Peru and the political and economic policies in the country, some of the characteristics of the conflicts have been reproduced in various parts of Latin America and the world. What we are seeing, then, are processes that extend beyond national borders, and have been driven by the global demand for minerals, the high price of metals, technological changes in the mining industry, and policy and institutional changes favorable to extractive activity (Bridge 2004b). As Bebbington and Bebbington (2012) have noted, mineral, gas, and oil extraction in Latin America shows continuities across different types of regimes over time and across space. Throughout the region, from Peru and Colombia to Bolivia and Ecuador, governments of different political hues have promoted extraction as a pillar of economic growth. What these scholars point to is a common regional narrative of extraction in which mining represents a crucial source of government revenue.

Yet in spite of continued efforts by states and corporations to promote investment in extractive industries and criminalize any form of opposition, campaigns against mining activity have posed a significant challenge to the dominant narrative of extraction. The response of communities affected by mining activity has also reverberated across borders, giving mining unprecedented visibility in public debate. More specifically, the increased visibility of water and pollutants in public discussions around mining has influenced the formation of alliances and created new forms of political organization. Activism around mining issues does not conform to party lines or ideological positions, as grassroots movements have expressed their demands in terms of indigenous rights, claims to citizenship and democracy, environmentalism, or anticapitalist sentiments. This diversity of agendas challenged conventional political organizing, sometimes opening up spaces for novel forms of resistance and social transformation, and at other times, fragmenting and destabilizing the movements.

Though the outcome of activist campaigns has varied, some observers argue that mining conflicts play a constructive role and are an essential aspect of democracy, bringing about progressive changes in governance at the level of the state, civil society, and the private sector (Bebbington and Bebbington 2012). Corporations operating today can no longer ignore social issues and have placed greater emphasis on community relations. Simultaneously, conflicts could be seen as strengthening civil society and the capacity of communities to negotiate and engage in dialogue with the state and the industry.[1]

Of course, we need to be aware of the limitations of activist strategies, and the ways in which the rhetoric of transparency and corporate responsibility might contribute to the hegemony of the extractive model of development. Regardless of whether activists have been successful in getting their demands met, there is no doubt that grassroots movements have had a profound impact in the political sphere. Beyond the specific demands of groups and individuals involved in mobilizations against mining companies, these collectives of actors have unsettled dominant views of nature as inert resources to be controlled and managed. As the global demand for minerals keeps extending the frontiers of extraction, the conflicts that accompany mining expansion will continue to challenge—and perhaps help transform—dominant understandings of nature, politics, economy, and development.

NOTES

All translations from the Spanish are by the author.

Introduction: A Mining Company

1. For an overview of the literature on mining, including social organization and resistance to resource extraction, see Godoy 1985; Gedicks 1994; Ballard and Banks 2003; Bridge 2004a.

2. Scholars have documented the environmental consequences of mining in Peru (Bury 2005), with particular attention paid to the impacts of mining operations on water resources (Bebbington and Williams 2008; Budds and Hinojosa-Valencia 2012).

3. On the emergence of conflicts over mining in Latin America, see Bebbington 2007, 2009; Kuecker 2007; Perreault 2008; Holt-Himenez 2008.

4. The word for "pollution" most frequently used in Spanish is *contaminación*, while *polución* is used very rarely. In English, the two words are sometimes used interchangeably, though pollution and contamination are not necessarily the same thing. Pollution refers to the introduction of harmful substances or products into the environment, as in the case of toxic discharges from a factory. Contamination, on the other hand, can refer to the presence of extraneous materials or unwanted substances that would not necessarily be called "pollution" (as in the contamination of a lab sample by a foreign substance). In Peru, however, *contaminación* encompasses the meaning of both English words, and is the word more commonly used to refer to anthropogenic pollution of air, water, and soil. This ambiguity and the broad range of meanings associated with the term may contribute to its contested nature.

5. My approach is inspired by a multidisciplinary body of work that problematizes the divide between Nature and Culture (Descola and Palsson 1996; Ingold 2000;

Latour 2005) and draws attention to the power of *things* that are not usually recognized as agentive forces (e.g., Bennett 2010; Braun and Whatmore 2010).

6. This statement was part of an interview (Patriau 2007) published in the national newspaper *La Republica* eight months before Mr. Brack's appointment as Environment Minister.

7. The commission was made up of representatives from the Council of Ministers, the Ministry of Energy and Mines, the Ministry of the Interior, the Ministry of Agriculture, and the Ministry of Labor.

8. Red Muqui (Muqui Network) is made up of twenty local and national organizations, and was established in 2005 in response to the growing number of mining conflicts around the country. *Muqui* is the Quechua name of a mythical creature said to inhabit the mines.

9. Since the late 2000s, NGOs, academics, and activists have produced an extensive collection of publications on mining conflicts, analyzing the experiences of various communities affected by mining, comparing experiences in various parts of the country, and providing policy recommendations to prevent future problems (e.g., Observatorio de Conflictos Mineros 2007; Salas Carreño 2008; Scurrah 2008; Gil 2009).

10. Scholars who have examined the making of corporate discourses on social responsibility include Bendell 2004; Jenkens 2004; Frynas 2005; Raman and Lipschutz 2010. On corporate-community relations in the context of mining, see Welker 2009; Horowitz 2010; Kirsch 2010; Rajak 2011; Velásquez 2012; Himley 2013.

11. This saying is usually attributed to the Italian naturalist Antonio Raimondi, who arrived in Peru in the nineteenth century to study the country's diverse fauna, flora, and geology. However, no written evidence exists to indicate the origin of this oft-repeated phrase, which became part of the national popular imaginary.

12. Scholars have examined the relationship between neoliberalism and resource extraction (Bridge 2004b; Ferguson 2006; Sawyer and Gomez 2008). Bebbington and Bebbington (2010) suggest that conflicts occur not only under neoliberal regimes, but also in so-called post-neoliberal countries like Bolivia and Ecuador that have adopted policies that counter the neoliberal model.

13. Mr. Fujimori served as president until 2000. The son of Japanese immigrants, Mr. Fujimori fled to Japan in 2000 amid a bribery scandal and accusations of human rights violations. He was extradited in 2007 and sentenced to twenty-five years in prison for embezzlement and for authorizing death-squad killings and kidnappings during the Shining Path insurgency, including the "disappearance" of a professor and nine students at La Cantuta University.

14. According to the final report of the Truth and Reconciliation Commission, 69,280 people died during this period of violence. Massacres, forced disappearances, and other human rights violations were perpetrated by the Shining Path and the Peruvian military (as well as by another guerilla group, the MRTA [Mo-

vimiento Revolucionario Tupac Amaru]) (Truth and Reconciliation Commission 2003).

15. Scholars have suggested that nothing is self-evidently a resource, emphasizing the social and political dimensions of resource making (Ferry and Limbert 2008). For an overview of the anthropological literature focusing on the sociality, signification, and value of substances constituted as "resources," see Richardson and Weszkalnys (2014).

16. From a different perspective, classic works by Nash (1993) and Taussig (1980) explore how Colombian and Bolivian miners negotiate changes in modes of production through their relations with a sentient landscape that includes *el tío*, a nonhuman being that inhabits the underground mines.

17. On the plurality of nature, see Latour 2004; Viveiros de Castro 1998; Haraway 1997.

18. For a more extensive review of theories of value and exchange, see Graeber 2001; Guyer 2004; Ferry 2005; Guyer et al. 2010).

19. Lakoff (2005), Turnbull (2000), and Verran (2001) have examined the commensurability of knowledge practices. Equivalence is also examined in the science studies literature. For example, equivalence is necessary for the inscriptions (documents, maps, data tables) and circulating reference that "make worlds into words," or to turn matter into knowledge (Latour 1999).

20. Also because of the conflictive climate, I have declined to name most of the people mentioned in this book to protect their anonymity. Except in the case of highly public figures that could be easily identified based on their leadership roles and statements expressed in the media and other public forums, I have fictionalized all other names, including those of less publicly known leaders and officials.

Chapter 1: Toxic Legacies, Nascent Activism

1. The ten most polluted cities on the list were: Chernobyl, Ukraine; Dzerzhinsk, Russia; Haina, Dominican Republic; Kabwe, Zambia; La Oroya, Peru; Linfen, China; Maiuu Suu, Kyrgyzstan; Norilsk, Russia; Ranipet, India; and Rudnaya Pristan/Dalnegorsk, Russia (Blacksmith Institute 2006).

2. Journalist Marina Walker Guevara (2005) published an article with this title and received the 2006 Environmental Media Award given by Reuters and the International Union for Conservation of Nature (IUCN).

3. These by-products are zinc sulfate, copper sulfate, sulfuric acid, arsenic trioxide, oleum, sodium bisulfate, zinc oxide, zinc dust, and zinc-silver concentrates. The Cobriza copper mine (purchased by Doe Run in 1998), in the department of Huancavelica, supplies most of the copper concentrate processed by the smelter. Major suppliers include the most important mining companies in Peru, like Buenaventura, El Brocal, Milpo, and Atacocha, as well as smaller mines that depend on the smelter to process their concentrate, since La Oroya's complex is one of a few facilities in the world capable of treating the "dirty" (mixed) minerals

characteristic of the central Andes. For example, it can process lead and copper concentrates containing high antimony, arsenic, bismuth, and precious metal values in addition to a variety of residues (Doe Run 2001).

4. Doe Run Peru is owned by the Doe Run Resources Corporation, which is in turn part of the Renco Group, headquartered in New York City.

5. For a more detailed history of the mining industry see Kruijt and Vellinga 1979; Flores Galindo 1983; Dore 1988. Until they were nationalized by the government in the mid-1970s, mining interests were controlled by American companies. Aside from the Cerro de Pasco Mining Corporation, the most important of these were Marcona Mining (which began operating in 1953) and the Southern Peru Copper Corporation (which opened the Toquepala mine in 1960) (Laite 1981).

6. My account of the establishment of the Oroya smelter draws primarily from Laite 1981.

7. According to the communal organization that represents it, the Comunidad Campesina Oroya Antigua was founded in 1681, and officially recognized in 1928.

8. Decree Law No. 20493, Ministry of Energy and Mines (1973:9).

9. Perhaps one of the most confrontational organizations supporting the PAMA extension was the Multi-Sector Committee for the Socioeconomic and Historical Validity of La Oroya (Comité Multisectorial por la Vigencia Socioeconómica e Histórica de La Oroya), which argued that the identity of the town was intimately linked to the existence and permanence of the metallurgical complex.

10. Mr. Rennert purportedly built his business empire by selling high-yield junk bonds in the 1990s, which he used to finance a number of acquisitions that were controlled by his Renco Group. Mr. Rennert's business ventures included mines and processing plants that began to accumulate fines for environmental violations.

11. Fortun (2001) locates the institutionalization of "corporate environmentalism" in the 1960s. By the mid-1990s, Corporate Social Responsibility became a significant industry (with profit and nonprofit organizations, journals, guidelines, etc.) (Welker 2009:145).

12. Paley (2001) calls this the "paradox of participation." Drawing on the experiences of grassroots health promoters in 1990s Chile, she notes that participation "offered a sense of meaning to citizens at the same time as it limited avenues through which citizens could act" (2001:146) Participation operated simultaneously as a motivating force *and* a mode of control that is characteristic of democracy amid neoliberal economics.

13. The idea that environmental devastation is a shared concern disallowed the designation of a single culprit (cf. Fortun 2001). For example, campaigns to clean up the Mantaro River pointed to multiple sources of pollution: the metallurgical complex, agricultural chemicals, runoff from nearby mines, inadequate sewage treatment and sanitary landfills, etc.). Fortun (2001:333) notes that this logic of

being "beyond blame" is a key element of corporate environmentalism and helps deflect criticism from activist groups.

14. Encouraging frequent hand washing, a nutritious diet, and wet cleaning to remove dust is consistent with the recommendations of international institutions (see, for example, UNEP-UNICEF 1997). However, these actions should be part of a comprehensive set of local, national, and international strategies that emphasize the elimination of principal sources of lead and the long-term reduction of children's exposure to lead.

15. Based on the CDC's classification system, the children who attended the Casaracra Day Care were of Class IV and V, according to a study by the Convenio (MINSA–Doe Run 2006). This put their blood lead levels at 45–69 µg/dL, and 70 µg/dL and higher, respectively. In November 2005, five children out of 788 tested were identified as Class V and taken to Lima for a medical evaluation. Sixty-six children (8.4 percent) were in Class IV (45–69 µg/dL). The majority of children in the study (82 percent) fell into Class III (20–44 µg/dL).

Chapter 2: Mega-Mining and Emergent Conflicts

1. Between 1994 and 2007, Peru produced 1,857 tons of gold, of which 42 percent was produced by the Yanacocha mine (Apoyo Consultoria 2009).

2. A number of scholars have written about the prioritization of scientific models over nonscientific forms of knowledge; for example, see Bavington 2010; Wynne 1992; Raffles 2002.

3. *Jalca* is the term for one of Peru's eight natural regions, located at an altitude of 3,500 to 4,100 meters above sea level.

4. In response to public pressure, the company made an effort to increase the number of local people hired. In 2006, approximately 48 percent of workers hired directly by Yanacocha were born in the province of Cajamarca; 0.44 percent were foreigners; and the rest were Peruvians from other parts of the country.

5. Cyanide heap leaching is an old practice dating back to New Zealand in 1889 and South Africa in 1890 (Hilson and Monhemius 2006).

Chapter 3: The Hydrology of a Sacred Mountain

1. The company also asked Alois Eichenlaub, a Catholic priest during the time Yanacocha began operating, to conduct a blessing at the inauguration of the Maqui Maqui mine. Mr. Eichenlaub told me the gesture was an effort to establish good relations with the church.

2. See Raffles 2002; Tsing 2005; Lowe 2006.

3. June Nash (1993) illustrates these relationships in the context of the Bolivian tin mines.

4. Yanacocha Cajamarca 2008.

Chapter 4: Irrigation and Contested Equivalences

1. According to Tim Ingold, knowledge of the environment is based in feeling, consisting in skills, gained through experience and long-term learning. These "dwelling skills" are acquired through practical activity and constant engagement with the land and beings that dwell therein (2000:133).

2. Mr. Santos's account appeared in a document produced as part of the Andean Ecosystems Pilot Project (PPEA), created under the auspices of the United Nations Environment Program (UNEP) and financed by the German government. The French-language publication titled *Le paysan, l'expert et la nature* (The Peasant, the Expert and Nature) (de Zutter 1992) sought to evaluate and synthesize the PPEA's work over five years (1985–1990). Based on tape-recorded interviews and presented in testimonial format, Mr. Santos's contribution to the volume recounted the experiences that made up his education: his grandparents' teachings and his travels, work, and leadership experience.

3. Some ronderos and canal users also participated in marches and activities in support of Minera Yanacocha. The company, aware of the influence that these associations could have, tried to mobilize them in its favor. In some instances, rondero organizations were specifically formed to promote a pro-mining agenda.

4. Some theorists have suggested that such struggles are part of an "Environmentalism of the Poor," where the defense of livelihood may be expressed in terms of property rights and access to resources, but nevertheless represents a struggle for environmental justice and sustainability (Martinez-Alier 1991).

5. On the role of women in the organization of irrigation systems, see Gelles 2000; Lynch 1991.

6. For example, the letter was used as a supporting document in the case presented by the NGO GRUFIDES against Yanacocha at the Inter-American Water Tribunal, held in Mexico City in 2006.

7. According to Kirsch, out-of-court settlements reflect a neoliberal shift in policy that has "encouraged the transfer of responsibility for monitoring social and environmental impacts from states to corporations" (2006:128), leaving mine-affected communities with little option but to seek redress directly from mining companies. The result is a proliferation of compensation claims—and related conflicts—that challenged mining companies' attempts to limit their responsibility for the effects of their operations.

8. What the company is attempting to do is to push for the formalization of the canals, requiring each junta de usuarios to register the canal with the ATDR, acquire a formal government resolution, and pay for water rights (which constitutes a major change in an area where canal relations have been largely informal).

Chapter 5: Stepping outside the Document

1. See for example, Lanegra 2008; Alayza 2007; Lenka 2005; Defensoria del Pueblo 2005.

2. See Strathern 2000b; Paley 2001, 2008; Murray Li 2007; Coles 2007.

3. In addition to Riles (2006) such work includes Strathern 2000a; Hull 2003; Hetherington 2011.

4. The anthropology of documents examines the material and bureaucratic aspects of governance to shed light on the daily workings of the state, as well as the interactions among state institutions, NGOs, and transnational actors (e.g., McKay 2012). For an overview on the anthropology of documents and bureaucracy, see Hull 2012.

5. Tape-recorded interview with Minera Yanacocha water specialist, July 11, 2006.

6. In GRUFIDES in particular, women were well represented as founding members, full-time staff, volunteers, and supporters from the church. Within activist movements and NGOs more generally, female professionals (lawyers, scientists, engineers, journalists, etc.) also played an important role.

7. The Compliance Advisor Ombudsman was created by the International Finance Corporation (IFC) and Multilateral Investment Guarantee Agency (MIGA) to respond to complaints from communities affected by projects with IFC involvement, such as the Yanacocha mine. Exchanges from the question-and-answer period have been transcribed from a recording of the workshop proceedings.

8. Transcription from videotape of the hearing.

Conclusion: Expanding Frontiers of Extraction

1. For further analysis on the role of civil society in conflicts over extraction, see Bebbington, Scurrah, and Chaparro 2013.

REFERENCES

Agrawal, Arun. 2005. *Environmentality: Technologies of Government and the Making of Subjects.* Durham, NC: Duke University Press.

"Alan puso calma en bases de Cajamarca." 2004. *La República*, August 22.

Alayza Moncloa, Alejandra. 2007. *No pero sí: Comunidades y Minería: Consulta y consentimiento previo, libre e informado en el Perú.* Lima: Oxfam.

Alvarado Merino, Gina. 2008. "Políticas neoliberales en el manejo de los recursos naturales en Perú: El caso del conflicto agrominero de Tambogrande." In *Gestión ambiental y conflicto social en América Latina*, by Gina Alvarado Merino, Gian Carlo Delgado Ramos, Diego Dominguez, Cecilia Campello do Amaral Mello, Iliana Monterroso, and Guillermo Wilde, 67–103. Buenos Aires: Consejo Latino-americano de Ciencias Sociales (CLASCO).

Anders, Gerhard. 2008. "The Normativity of Numbers: World Bank and IMF Conditionality." *Political and Legal Anthropology Review (PoLAR)* 31, no. 2:187–202.

Apoyo Consultoría. 2009. *Study of the Yanacocha Mine's Economic Impact: Final Report.* Prepared for the IFC. Lima: Apoyo Consultoría.

Arana, Marco. 2007. *La Defensa del Cerro Quilish: Una cuestión romántica?* Cajamarca, Peru: GRUFIDES.

———. 2006. *La crisis del Quilish, la afirmación de los derechos ciudadanos, y la construcción de la democracia.* Cajamarca, Peru: GRUFIDES.

———. 2002. *El Cerro Quilish y la minería del oro en Cajamarca.* Cajamarca, Peru: GRUFIDES.

Arzobispado de Huancayo and St. Louis University. 2005. *Estudio sobre la contaminación ambiental en los hogares de La Oroya y Concepción y sus efectos en la salud de sus residentes: Informe de primeros resultados biológicos.* Huancayo, Peru: Arzobispado de Huancayo.

Asociación Civil Labor. 2008. *Primer encuentro nacional de comités de monitoreo y vigilancia ambiental participativo en ámbitos de influencia minera.* Lima: Asociación Civil Labor.

Ballard, Chris, and Glenn Banks. 2003. "Resource Wars: The Anthropology of Mining." *Annual Review of Anthropology* 32:287–313.

Barry, Andrew. 2009. "Visible Invisibility." *New Geographies* 2:67–74.

———. 2001. *Political Machines: Governing a Technological Society.* London: Athlone Press.

Basso, Keith. 1996. *Wisdom Sits in Places.* Albuquerque: University of New Mexico Press.

Bavington, Dean. 2010. "From Hunting Fish to Managing Populations: Fisheries Science and the Destruction of Newfoundland Cod Fisheries." *Science as Culture* 19, no. 4:509–28.

Bebbington, Anthony. 2009. "The New Extraction: Rewriting the Political Ecology of the Andes?" *NACLA* 42, no. 5:12–20.

———, ed. 2007. *Una ecología política de la minería moderna: Movimientos sociales, empresas y desarrollo territorial.* Lima: IEP.

Bebbington, Anthony, and Denise Bebbington. 2012. "Post-What? Extractive Industries, Narratives of Development and Socio-Environmental Disputes across the (Ostensibly Changing) Andean Region." In *New Political Spaces in Latin American Natural Resource Governance,* ed. H. Haarstad, 17–38. Basingstoke, UK: Palgrave Macmillan.

———. 2010. "An Andean Avatar: Post-Neoliberal and Neoliberal Strategies for Securing the Unobtainable." *New Political Economy* 16, no. 1:131–45.

Bebbington, Anthony, Martin Scurrah, and Anahí Chaparro. 2013. *La sociedad civil y las industrias en el Perú: Un mapeo y análisis preliminar.* Proyecto Industrias Extractivas, Conflictos Sociales e Innovaciones Institucionales en la Región Andino-Amazónica, Working Document 3, August. http://innovaciones institucionales.files.wordpress.com/2013/08/dt-3-la-sociedad-civil-y-las -industrias-extractivas.pdf.

Bebbington, Anthony, and Mark Williams. 2008. "Water and Mining Conflicts in Peru." *Mountain Research and Development* 28, no. 3/4:190–95.

Beck, Ulrich. 1992. *Risk Society: Towards a New Modernity.* London: Sage.

Bendell, Jeremy. 2004. *Barricades and Boardrooms: A Contemporary History of the Corporate Accountability Movement.* Technology, Business and Society Programme Paper 13. Geneva: UNRISD.

Bennett, Jane. 2010. *Vibrant Matter: A Political Ecology of Things.* Durham, NC: Duke University Press.

Blacksmith Institute. 2006. *The World's Worst Polluted Places.* New York: Blacksmith Institute.

Blaser, Mario. 2010. *Storytelling Globalization from the Chaco and Beyond.* Durham, NC: Duke University Press.

———. 2009. "The Threat of the Yrmo: The Political Ontology of a Sustainable Hunting Program." *American Anthropologist* 111, no. 1:10–20.

Bonilla, Heraclio. 1974. *El minero de los Andes.* Lima: Instituto de Estudios Peruanos.

Bordewich, Fergus M. 1997. *Killing the White Man's Indian: Reinventing Native Americans at the End of the Twentieth Century.* New York: Anchor Books.

Boyd, Stephanie. 1998. "Moving Mountains." *New Internationalist,* no. 299.

Braun, Bruce, and Sarah Whatmore, eds. 2010. *Political Matter: Technoscience, Democracy, and Public Life.* Minneapolis: University of Minnesota Press.

Bridge, Gavin. 2004a. "Contested Terrain: Mining and the Environment." *Annual Review of Environment and Resources* 29:205–59.

———. 2004b. "Mapping the Bonanza: Geographies of Mining Investment in an Era of Neoliberal Reform." *Professional Geographer* 56, no. 3:406–21.

Brosius, Peter. 2006. "What Counts as Local Knowledge in Global Environmental Assessments and Conventions?" In *Bridging Scales and Knowledge Systems: Concepts and Applications in Ecosystems Assessment,* ed. Walter Reid, Fikret Berkes, Thomas Wilbanks, and Doris Capistrano, 129–44. Washington, DC: Island Press.

Bryant, Raymond L., and Sinéad Bailey. 1997. *Third World Political Ecology.* London: Routledge.

Budds, Jessica. 2009. "Contested H_2O: Science, Policy and Politics in Water Resources Management in Chile." *Geoforum* 40, no. 3:418–30.

Budds, Jessica, and Leonith Hinojosa-Valencia. 2012. "Restructuring and Rescaling Water Governance in Mining Contexts: The Co-Production of Waterscapes in Peru." *Water Alternatives* 5, no. 1:119–37.

Bunker, Stephen G. 1985. *Underdeveloping the Amazon: Extraction, Unequal Exchange, and the Failure of the Modern State.* Urbana: University of Illinois Press.

Bury, Jeff. 2005. "Mining Mountains: Neoliberalism, Land Tenure, Livelihoods, and the New Peruvian Mining Industry in Cajamarca." *Environment and Planning A* 37, no. 2:221–39.

"Cajamarca acata paro provincial." 2004. *El Comercio,* September 8.

Callon, Michel. 1999. "Some Elements of a Sociology of Translation: Domestication of the Scallops and the Fishermen of St. Brieuc Bay." In *The Science Studies Reader,* ed. M. Biagioli, 67–83. New York: Routledge.

CAO (Compliance Advisor Ombudsman). 2013. *2013 Annual Report.* Washington, DC: Office of the Compliance Advisor Ombudsman.

———. 2006. *Notes from the Information Sharing Meeting of Canal Users from COMOCA Sur and COMOCA Este and Representatives of Minera Yanacocha.* Cajamarca, Peru, July 24–25. Washington, DC: Office of the Compliance Advisor Ombudsman. http://www.cao-ombudsman.org/cases/document-links/documents/InfoSharingMeetingNotesFinal.pdf.

———. 2005. *Evaluation of Water Quality in Cajamarca, Peru.* Annual Monitoring Report 2004–2005. Cajamarca, Peru: Mesa de Diálogo y Consenso CAO.

Caso, Teofilo. 2004. "Protests Continue against Gold Prospecting on Sacred Peruvian Mountain." *Associated Press*, September 15.

Cederstav Anna, and Alberto Barandiarán. 2002. *La Oroya Cannot Wait*. Oakland, CA: Inter-American Association for Environmental Defense (AIDA) and Lima: Peruvian Society of Environmental Law (SPDA).

Centers for Disease Control and Prevention (CDC), National Center for Environmental Health, Agency for Toxic Substances and Disease Registry, and Division of Emergency and Environmental Health Services. 2005. *Development of an Integrated Intervention Plan to Reduce Exposure to Lead and Other Contaminants in the Mining Center of La Oroya, Perú*. Report prepared for United States Agency for International Development, Peru Mission. http://www.cdc.gov/nceh /ehs/Docs/la_oroya_report.pdf.

Centromin. 1975. *Informativo Centromin Perú*. No. 42, November 15. Lima: Centromin.

Cerro de Pasco Corporation. 1957. *El Serrano*. Lima: Cerro de Pasco Corporation.

Chauvin, Lucien. 2009. "Heroes of the Environment 2009—Marco Arana." *Time*, September 22.

Choy, Timothy. 2011. *Ecologies of Comparison: An Ethnography of Endangerment in Hong Kong*. Durham, NC: Duke University Press.

Cisneros, Luis Jaime. 2004. "Agua y oro crean discordia entre campesinos y gigante Minera Yanacocha en Perú." *AFP*, September 5.

Coles, Kimberley. 2007. *Democratic Designs: International Intervention and Electoral Practices in Postwar Bosnia-Herzegovina*. Ann Arbor: University of Michigan Press.

CONACAMI (Confederación Nacional de Comunidades Afectadas for la Minería). 2004. *Las 5 "trampas" de la Minería en el Perú*. Lima: CONACAMI.

CONAM. 2007. *Estudio de factibilidad sobre la reubicación de La Oroya Antigua*. Lima: CONAM.

CooperAcción. 2006. *Informe de conflictos mineros: Los casos de Majaz, Las Bambas, Tintaya y La Oroya*. Lima: CooperAcción.

Cruikshank, Julie. 2005. *Do Glaciers Listen? Local Knowledge, Colonial Encounters, and Social Imagination*. Vancouver: University of British Columbia Press.

Cruz y César Romero, Edmundo. 2006. "Evidencias vinculan a empresa Forza con Operación El Diablo." *La República*, December 6.

de Echave, José, and Victor Torres. 2005. *Hacia una estimación de los efectos de la actividad minera en los índices de pobreza en el Peru*. Lima: CooperAcción.

Defensoría del Pueblo. 2005. *Minería, desarrollo sostenible y derechos ciudadanos: Una aproximación desde la Defensoría del Pueblo*. Lima: Defensoría del Pueblo.

de la Cadena, Marisol. 2010. "Indigenous Cosmopolitics in the Andes: Conceptual Reflections beyond Politics." *Cultural Anthropology* 25, no. 2:334–70.

de la Torre, Ana. 1986. *Los dos lados del mundo y del tiempo: Representaciones de la naturaleza en Cajamarca indígena*. Lima: CIED.

Descola, Philippe, and Gisli Palsson, eds. 1996. *Nature and Society: Anthropological Perspectives*. London: Routledge.

DeWind, Josh. 1987. *Peasants Become Miners: The Evolution of Industrial Mining Systems in Peru, 1902–1974*. New York: Garland.

Deza, Nilton. 2002. *Oro, cianuro, y otras crónicas ambientales*. Cajamarca, Peru: Universidad Nacional de Cajamarca.

de Zutter, Pierre. 1992. *Le paysan, l'expert et la nature: Sept fables et récits sur l'écologie et le développement dans les pays andins*. Paris: Éditions Charles Léopold Mayer.

DIGESA. 1999. *Estudio de plomo en sangre en una población seleccionada de La Oroya*. Lima: DIGESA.

Doe Run Peru. 2006. *La Oroya: Report to Our Communities*. Lima, Peru: Doe Run Peru.

———. 2002. *Estudio de niveles de plomo en la sangre de la población en La Oroya 2000–2001*. La Oroya, Peru: Doe Run Peru.

———. 2001. *Form 10-K*. Washington, DC: U.S. Securities and Exchange Commission.

Dore, Elizabeth. 1988. *The Peruvian Mining Industry: Growth, Stagnation, and Crisis*. Boulder, CO: Westview Press.

Earthworks. 2010. "Denver-Based Newmont Mining Co. Fined Millions for Cyanide Spill at Ghanaian Mine." Press Release issued by Earthworks (USA) and WACAM (Ghana), January 21. http://www.earthworksaction.org/.

"En el 2005 se podrían incrementar problemas sociales con la minería." 2005. *El Comercio*, January 15:B1.

"El Cerro Quilish." 1996. *Clarín* (Cajamarca), June 29:2.

EPA (United States Environmental Protection Agency). 2013. *EPA Main Page*. http://www.epa.gov/.

Escobar, Arturo. 2008. *Territories of Difference: Place, Movements, Life, Redes*. Durham, NC: Duke University Press.

Espeland, Wendy Nelson. 1998. *The Struggle for Water: Politics, Rationality and Identity in the American Southwest*. Chicago: University of Chicago Press.

Espeland, Wendy Nelson, and Mitchell Stevens. 1998. "Commensuration as a Social Process." *Annual Review of Sociology* 24:313–43.

Farrell, Hunter. 2007. "Cleaning Up La Oroya: How American and Peruvian Christians Teamed Up When Factory Pollutants Were Poisoning Children." *Christianity Today* 51, no. 4:70.

Ferguson, James. 2006. *Global Shadows: Africa in the Neoliberal Order*. Durham, NC: Duke University Press.

———. 1994. *The Anti-Politics Machine: "Development," Depoliticization, and Bureaucratic Power in Lesotho*. Minneapolis: University of Minnesota Press.

Ferry, Elizabeth Emma. 2005. *Not Ours Alone: Patrimony, Value, and Collectivity in Contemporary Mexico*. New York: Columbia University Press.

Ferry, Elizabeth Emma, and Mandana E. Limbert, eds. 2008. *Timely Assets: The Politics of Resources and Their Temporalities.* Santa Fe, NM: School for Advanced Research Press.

Fitzpatrick, Patricia, and John Sinclair. 2003. "Learning through Public Involvement in Environmental Assessment Hearings." *Journal of Environmental Management* 67, no. 2:161–74.

Flores Galindo, Alberto. 1974. *Los mineros de Cerro de Pasco, 1900–1930: Un intento de caracterización social.* Lima: Universidad Católica del Perú.

Fortun, Kim. 2001. *Advocacy after Bhopal: Environmentalism, Disaster, New Global Orders.* Chicago: University of Chicago Press.

Frynas, Jedrzej George. 2005. "The False Developmental Promise of Corporate Social Responsibility: Evidence from Multinational Oil Companies." *International Affairs* 81, no. 3:581–98.

García, Alan. 2007. "El Perro del Hortelano." *El Comercio,* October 27.

García, María Elena. 2005. *Making Indigenous Citizens: Identities, Education, and Multicultural Development in Peru.* Palo Alto, CA: Stanford University Press.

Gedicks, Al. 1994. *The New Resource Wars: Native and Environmental Struggles against Multinational Corporations.* Boston: South End Press.

Gelles, Paul. 2000. *Water and Power in Highland Peru: The Cultural Politics of Irrigation and Development.* New Brunswick, NJ: Rutgers University Press.

Gil, Vladimir. 2009. *Aterrizaje minero: Cultura, conflictos, negociaciones y lecciones.* Lima, Peru: IEP.

Godoy, Ricardo. 1985. "Mining: Anthropological Perspectives." *Annual Review of Anthropology* 14:199–217.

Goldman, Michael. 2005. *Imperial Nature: The World Bank and Struggles for Social Justice in the Age of Globalization.* New Haven, CT: Yale University Press.

Gorriti, Gustavo. 2011. "De Lagunas a Desmontes." *IDL Reporteros,* November 25. http://idl-reporteros.pe/2011/11/25/de-lagunas-a-desmontes/.

Graeber, David. 2001. *Toward an Anthropological Theory of Value: The False Coin of Our Own Dreams.* New York: Palgrave.

Grieco, Kyra, and Carmen Salazar-Soler. 2013. "Les enjeux techniques et politiques dans la gestion et le contrôle de l'eau: Le cas du projet Minas Conga au nord du Pérou." *Autrepart,* no. 65:151–68.

GRUFIDES. 2006. *Estudio descriptivo sobre las evaluaciones ambientales de los proyectos de exploración: Yanacocha Zona Este (PEYZE) y Yanacocha Zona Oeste (PEYZO).* Report prepared for the Municipality of Baños del Inca. Cajamarca, Peru: GRUFIDES.

Gutierrez, Zulema, and Gerben Gerbrandy. 1999. "Distribución de agua, organización social y equidad en el pensamiento andino." In *Buscando la equidad: Concepciones sobre justicia y equidad en el riego campesino,* ed. Rutgerd Boelens and Gloria Dávila, 259–68. Assen, Netherlands: Royal Van Gorcum.

Guyer, Jane. 2004. *Marginal Gains: Monetary Transactions in Atlantic Africa.* Chicago: University of Chicago Press.

Guyer, Jane, Naveeda Khan, and Juan Obarrio et al. 2010. "Introduction: Number as Inventive Frontier." Special Section. *Anthropological Theory* 10:36–61.

Halperin, Rhoda. 1994. *Cultural Economies Past and Present.* Austin: University of Texas Press.

Haraway, Donna. 1997. *Modest_Witness@Second_Millennium.FemaleMan©_Meets_Oncomouse™: Feminism and Technoscience.* New York: Routledge.

Hetherington, Kregg. 2011. *Guerrilla Auditors: The Politics of Transparency in Neoliberal Paraguay.* Durham, NC: Duke University Press.

Hilson, Gavin, and A. J. Monhemius. 2006. "Alternatives to Cyanide in the Gold Mining Industry: What Prospects for the Future?" *Journal of Cleaner Production* 14:1158–67.

Himley, Matthew. 2013. "Regularizing Extraction in Andean Peru: Mining and Social Mobilization in an Age of Corporate Social Responsibility." *Antipode* 45, no. 2:394–416.

———. 2010. "Global Mining and the Uneasy Neoliberalization of Sustainable Development." *Sustainability* 2, no. 10:3270–90.

Holt-Himenez, Eric. 2008. *Territorial Restructuring and the Grounding of Agrarian Reform: Indigenous Communities, Gold Mining and the World Bank.* Amsterdam: Transnational Institute and 11.11.11 (Coalition of the North-South Movements).

Horowitz, Leah S. 2010. "'Twenty Years Is Yesterday': Science, Multinational Mining, and the Political Ecology of Trust in New Caledonia." *Geoforum* 41, no. 4:617–26.

Hull, Matthew. 2012. "Documents and Bureaucracy." *Annual Review of Anthropology* 41:251–67.

———. 2003. "The File: Agency, Authority, and Autography in an Islamabad Bureaucracy." *Language and Communication* 23:287–314.

IAIA (International Association for Impact Assessment). 1999. *Principles of Environmental Assessment Best Practice.* Fargo, ND: IAIA. http://www.iaia.org/publicdocuments/special-publications/Principles%20of%20IA_web.pdf.

Ilizarbe, Carmen. 2011. *El abrazo a la laguna: Conga en el imaginario político.* Por las ramas (blog). http://carmenilizarbe.lamula.pe/.

Ingold, Tim. 2000. *The Perception of the Environment: Essays on Livelihood, Dwelling and Skill.* London: Routledge.

Jenkens, Heledd. 2004. "Corporate Social Responsibility and the Mining Industry: Conflicts and Constructs." *Corporate Social Responsibility and Environmental Management* 11, no. 1:23–34.

Johnson, Bob. 2013. *Gold Production History.* GOLDSHEET Mining Directory. http://www.goldsheetlinks.com/production.htm, accessed December 30, 2013.

Kamphuis, Charis. 2011. "Foreign Investment and the Privatization of Coercion: A

Case Study of the Forza Security Company in Peru." *Brooklyn Journal of International Law* 37, no. 2:529–78.

Kinchy, Abby. 2012. *Seeds, Science and Struggle: The Global Politics of Transgenic Crops*. Cambridge, MA: MIT Press.

Kirsch, Stuart. 2010. "Sustainable Mining." *Dialectical Anthropology* 34, no. 1:87–93.

————. 2006. *Reverse Anthropology: Indigenous Analysis of Social and Environmental Relations in New Guinea*. Palo Alto, CA: Stanford University Press.

Kosek, Jake. 2006. *Understories: The Political Life of Forests in Northern New Mexico*. Durham, NC: Duke University Press.

Kruijt, Dirk, and Menno Vellinga. 1979. *Labor Relations and Multinational Corporations: The Cerro de Pasco Corporation in Peru (1902–1974)*. Assen, Netherlands: Van Gorcum.

Kuecker, Glen David. 2007. "Fighting for the Forests: Grassroots Resistance to Mining in Northern Ecuador." *Latin American Perspectives* 34, no. 2:94–107.

Laite, Julian. 1981. *Industrial Development and Migrant Labour*. Manchester, UK: Manchester University Press.

Lakoff, Andrew. 2005. "Diagnostic Liquidity: Mental Illness and the Global Trade in DNA." *Theory and Society* 34:63–92.

Lanegra, Iván. 2008. *El (ausente) Estado Ambiental*. Lima, Peru: Realidades.

Latour, Bruno. 2008. *What Is the Style of Matters of Concern?* Amsterdam: Van Gorcum.

————. 2005. "From Realpolitik to Dingpolitik or How to Make Things Public." In *Making Things Public: Atmospheres of Democracy*, ed. B. Latour and P. Weibel, 14–41. Cambridge, MA: MIT Press.

————. 2004. *Politics of Nature: How to Bring the Sciences into Democracy*. Cambridge, MA: Harvard University Press.

————. 1999. *Pandora's Hope: Essays on the Reality of Science*. Cambridge, MA: Harvard University Press.

————. 1993. *We Have Never Been Modern*. Cambridge, MA: Harvard University Press.

————. 1988. *Science in Action: How to Follow Scientists and Engineers through Society*. Cambridge, MA: Harvard University Press.

Law, John. 2004. *After Method: Mess in Social Science Research*. New York: Routledge.

Leyva Valera, Ana, and Javier Jahncke Benavente. 2002. *Crónica de la presencia de la Minera Yanacocha en Cajamarca*. Lima: Fedepaz.

Long, Norman, and Bryan R. Roberts. 1984. *Miners, Peasants, and Entrepreneurs: Regional Development in the Central Highlands of Peru*. Cambridge: Cambridge University Press.

Lowe, Celia. 2006. *Wild Profusion: Biodiversity Conservation in an Indonesian Archipelago*. Princeton, NJ: Princeton University Press.

Lynch, Barbara. 1991. "Women and Irrigation in Highland Peru." *Society and Natural Resources* 4, no. 1:37–52.

Mallon, Florencia. 1983. *The Defense of Community in Peru's Central Highlands*. Princeton, NJ: Princeton University Press.

Martinez-Alier, J. 1991. "Ecology and the Poor: A Neglected Dimension of Latin American History." *Journal of Latin American Studies* 23:621–39.

Matta Colunche, Segundo. 2012. *Crónica de una visita anunciada: Sacerdotes en Conga*. Cajamarca Regional Government website, posted July 18. http://www .regioncajamarca.gob.pe/noticias/.

Maurer, Bill. 2006. "The Anthropology of Money." *Annual Review of Anthropology* 35:15–36.

McKay, Ramah. 2012. "Documentary Disorders: Managing Medical Multiplicity in Maputo, Mozambique." *American Ethnologist* 39, no. 3:545–61.

Mellado, Tania. 2005. *Peru Mine Town Residents Stone Scientists for Probe*. August 16. http://www.RedOrbit.com/.

Miller, Daniel. 2008. "The Uses of Value." *Geoforum* 39, no. 3:1122–32.

Mineral Policy Center. 2000. *Cyanide Leach Mining Packet*. Washington, DC: MPC.

Minera Yanacocha. 2007. *La gestión del agua en Yanacocha: Cuidados, controles, y generación de activos ambientales*. Lima: Minera Yanacocha SRL.

———. 2006. *Yanacocha: Balance social y ambiental*. Lima: Minera Yanacocha SRL.

———. 2004. *Yanacocha: Responsabilidad social y ambiental*. Lima: Minera Yanacocha SRL.

———. 2002. *Yanacocha: Responsabilidad social*. Lima: Minera Yanacocha SRL.

———. n.d. *Cantidad del agua*. Minera Yanacocha website. http://www.yanacocha .com.pe/cantidad-del-agua/.

Ministerio de Energía y Minas (MEM). 1973. *Decree Law No. 20493*.

MINSA-Doe Run. 2006. *Trabajamos por la Salud de la población Oroína: Convenio de Cooperación MINSA–Doe Run*. La Oroya, Peru: MINSA–Doe Run.

Mitchell, Timothy. 2002. *Rule of Experts: Egypt, Techno-Politics, Modernity*. Berkeley: University of California Press.

———. 1991. "The Limits of the State: Beyond Statist Approaches and Their Critics." *American Political Science Review* 85, no. 1:77–96.

Mol, Annemarie. 2002. *The Body Multiple: Ontology in Medical Practice*. Durham, NC: Duke University Press.

Moran, Robert. 2012. *El proyecto minero Conga, Perú: Comentarios al Estudio de Impacto Ambiental (EIA) y temas relacionados*. Bozeman, MT: Environmental Defender Law Center.

———. 2001a. *An Alternative Look at a Proposed Mine in Tambogrande, Peru*. Report commissioned by Oxfam America (Washington, DC), Mineral Policy Center (Washington, DC), and the Environmental Mining Council of British Columbia (Vancouver, Canada).

————. 2001b. *More Cyanide Uncertainties: Lessons from the Baia Mare, Romania, Spill—Water Quality and Politics*. MPC Issue Paper 3. Washington, DC: Mineral Policy Center.

Muñiz, Pedro. 1935. *Penetración imperialista: Minería y aprismo*. Santiago, Chile: Ediciones Ercilla.

Murphy, Michelle. 2006. *Sick Building Syndrome and the Problem of Uncertainty: Environmental Politics, Technoscience, and Women Workers*. Durham, NC: Duke University Press.

Murray Li, Tania. 2007. *The Will to Improve: Governmentality, Development, and the Practice of Politics*. Durham, NC: Duke University Press.

MWH (Montgomery Watson Harza). 2009. *Modificación del Estudio de Impacto Ambiental del Proyecto Carachugo Suplementario Yanacocha Este*. Lima, Peru: MWH.

————. 2006a. *Componente social del EIA del Proyecto Suplementario Yanacocha Oeste*. Prepared for Minera Yanacocha. Lima, Peru: MWH.

————. 2006b. *Componente técnico ambiental del EIA del Proyecto Suplementario Yanacocha Oeste*. Prepared for Minera Yanacocha. Lima, Peru: MWH.

Nash, June. 1993. *We Eat the Mines and the Mines Eat Us: Dependency and Exploitation in Bolivian Tin Mines*. New York: Columbia University Press.

Obarrio, Juan. 2010. "Beyond Equivalence: The Gift of Justice (Mozambique, 1976, 2004)." *Anthropological Theory* 20, nos. 1–2:163–70.

Observatorio de Conflictos Mineros. 2007. *Primer Informe del Observatorio de Conflictos Mineros*. Lima: Fedepaz, CooperAcción, GRUFIDES.

Orlove, Ben, Ellen Wiegandt, and Brian H. Luckman, eds. 2008. *Darkening Peaks: Glacial Retreat in Scientific and Social Context*. Berkeley: University of California Press.

Paley, Julia, ed. 2008. *Democracy: Anthropological Approaches*. Santa Fe, NM: SAR Press.

————. 2001. *Marketing Democracy: Power and Social Movements in Post-Dictatorship Chile*. Berkeley: University of California Press.

Pascó-Font, Alberto, Alejandro Diez Hurtado, Gerardo Damonte, Ricardo Fort, and Guillermo Salas Carreño. 2001. "Peru: Learning by Doing." In *Large Mines and the Community: Socioeconomic and Environmental Effects in Latin America, Canada, and Spain*, ed. Gary McMahon and Felix Remy, 143–97. Washington, DC: World Bank Publications.

Patriau, Enrique. 2007. "El Perú seguirá siendo un país minero" (Interview of Antonio Brack). *La República*, September 23.

Peet, Richard, and Michael Watts, eds. 1996. *Liberation Ecologies: Environment, Development, Social Movements*. New York: Routledge.

Peluso, Nancy Lee. 1992. *Rich Forests, Poor People Resource Control and Resistance in Java*. Berkeley: University of California Press.

Perlez, Jane. 2005. "Cause of Mystery Ills Splits Indonesian Fishing Village." *New York Times*, March 27.

Perreault, Thomas. 2008. "Popular Protest and Unpopular Policies: State Restructuring, Resource Conflict and Social Justice in Bolivia." In *Environmental Justice in Latin America*, ed. David Carruthers, 239–62. Cambridge MA: MIT Press.

Peru Support Group. 2007. *Mining and Development in Peru*. London: Peru Support Group.

Petryna, Adriana. 2002. *Life Exposed: Biological Citizenship after Chernobyl*. Princeton, NJ: Princeton University Press.

Povinelli, Elizabeth. 2001. "Radical Worlds: The Anthropology of Incommensurability and Inconceivability." *Annual Review of Anthropology* 30:319–34.

Power, Michael. 1994. *The Audit Explosion*. London: DEMOS.

Raffles, Hugh. 2002. *In Amazonia: A Natural History*. Princeton, NJ: Princeton University Press.

Rajak, Dinah. 2011. *In Good Company: An Anatomy of Corporate Social Responsibility*. Palo Alto, CA: Stanford University Press.

Raman, Ravi, and Ronnie D. Lipschutz, eds. 2010. *Corporate Social Responsibility: Comparative Critiques*. Basingstoke, UK: Palgrave Macmillan.

Richardson, Tanya, and Gisa Weszkalnys. 2014. "Introduction: Resource Materialities." *Anthropological Quarterly* 87, no. 1:5–30.

Riles, Annelise. 2006. *Documents: Artifacts of Modern Knowledge*. Ann Arbor: University of Michigan Press.

Sachs, Jeffrey D., and Andrew M. Warner. 2001. "The Curse of Natural Resources." *European Economic Review* 45:827–38.

Sadler, Barry. 1996. *Environmental Assessment in a Changing World: Evaluating Practice to Improve Performance*. Final Report, International Study of the Effectiveness of Environmental Assessment. Ottawa: Minister of Supply and Services Canada.

Salas Carreño, Guillermo. 2008. *Dinámica social y minería: Familias pastoras de puna y la presencia del proyecto Antamina*. Lima: IEP.

Sandoval, Wilfredo. 2004. "Quilish: Ícono sagrado de los Cajamarquinos." *El Comercio*, September 10.

Sawyer, Suzana. 2004. *Crude Chronicles: Indigenous Politics, Multinational Oil, and Neoliberalism in Ecuador*. Durham, NC: Duke University Press.

Sawyer, Suzana, and Edmund Terence Gomez. 2008. *Transnational Governmentality and Resource Extraction: Indigenous Peoples, Multinational Corporations, Multilateral Institutions and the State*. UNRISD Identities, Conflict and Cohesion Paper 13. Geneva: United Nations Research Institute for Social Development (UNRISD).

Scurrah, Martin. 2008. *Defendiendo derechos y promoviendo cambios: El estado, las empresas extractivas y las comunidades locales en el Perú*. Lima: Oxfam/IEP/IBC.

Seifert, Reinhart. 2003. *Yanacocha: El sueño dorado?* Cajamarca, Peru: ECOVIDA.

Sherbondy, Jeanette. 1998. "Andean Irrigation in History." In *Buscando la equidad: Concepciones sobre justicia y equidad en el riego campesino*, ed. Rutgerd Boelens and Gloria Dávila, 210–15. Assen, Netherlands: Royal Van Gorcum.

Shipley, Sara, and Marina Walker. 2006. "Lead Astray." *Mother Jones*, November/December. http://www.motherjones.com/politics/2006/10/lead-astray.

Shnayerson, Michael. 2003. "Devastating Luxury." *Vanity Fair*, July, no. 515.

Sinclair, A. J., and Alan Diduck. 2009. "Public Participation in Canadian Environmental Assessment: Enduring Challenges and Future Directions." In *Environmental Impact Assessment Processes and Practices in Canada*, ed. K. S. Hanna, 56–82. Toronto: Oxford University Press.

Star, Susan Leigh, and James R. Griesemer. 1989. "Institutional Ecology, 'Translations' and Boundary Objects: Amateurs and Professionals in Berkeley's Museum of Vertebrate Zoology, 1907–39." *Social Studies of Science* 19, no. 3:387–420.

Starn, Orin. 1999. *Nightwatch: The Politics of Protest in the Andes.* Durham, NC: Duke University Press.

Strathern, Marilyn, ed. 2000a. *Audit Cultures: Anthropological Studies in Accountability, Ethics, and the Academy.* London: Routledge.

———. 2000b. "The Tyranny of Transparency." *British Educational Research Journal* 26, no. 3:309–21.

———. 1996. "Cutting the Network." *Journal of the Royal Anthropological Institute* 2, no. 3:517–35.

Stratus Consulting. 2003. *Report on the Independent Assessment of Water Quantity and Quality near the Yanacocha Mining District, Cajamarca, Peru.* Boulder, CO: Stratus Consulting.

Szablowski, David. 2007. *Transnational Law and Local Struggles: Mining, Communities, and the World Bank.* Oxford: Hart.

Taussig, Michael T. 1980. *The Devil and Commodity Fetishism in South America.* Chapel Hill: University of North Carolina Press.

Truth and Reconciliation Commission (TRC). 2003. *Final Report.* Lima: TRC.

Tsing, Anna. 2005. *Friction: An Ethnography of Global Connection.* Princeton, NJ: Princeton University Press.

Turnbull, David. 2000. *Masons, Tricksters and Cartographers: Comparative Studies in the Sociology of Scientific and Indigenous Knowledge.* London: Harwood Academic Publishers.

UNEP-UNICEF. 1997. *Childhood Lead Poisoning: Information for Advocacy and Action.* Nairobi: UNEP and UNICEF.

Velásquez, Teresa A. 2012. "The Science of Corporate Social Responsibility (CSR): Contamination and Conflict in a Mining Project in the Southern Ecuadorian Andes." *Resources Policy* 37, no. 2:233–40.

Verran, Helen. 2001. *Science and an African Logic.* Chicago: University of Chicago Press.

Viveiros de Castro, Eduardo. 1998. "Cosmological Deixis and Amerindian Perspectivism." *Journal of the Royal Anthropological Institute* 4:469–88.

Walker Guevara, Marina. 2005. "Los niños del plomo." *Gatopardo*, August, no. 60: 58–69.

Welker, Marina. 2009. "Corporate Security Begins in the Community: Mining, the Corporate Social Responsibility Industry, and Environmental Advocacy in Indonesia." *Cultural Anthropology* 24, no. 1:143–79.

West, Harry G., and Todd Sanders. 2003. *Transparency and Conspiracy: Ethnographies of Suspicion in the New World Order*. Durham, NC: Duke University Press.

Wynne, Brian. 1992. "Misunderstood Misunderstanding: Social Identities and Public Uptake of Science." *Public Understanding of Science* 1, no. 3:281–304.

Yanacocha Cajamarca. 2008. *Yanacocha: Agua hay en Cajamarca*. YouTube. http://www.youtube.com/watch?v=uILSGrSEnlk/.

Zàjec, Lenka. 2005. "Conflictos mineros son por ausencia del Estado" (Interview of José de Echave). *La República*, August 7.

Zelizer, Viviana. 1989. "The Social Meaning of Money: 'Special Moneys.'" *American Journal of Sociology* 95, no. 2:342–77.

INDEX

accountability: conflict resolution and, 23, 31; corporate, 10, 12, 69, 186–88, 193, 198; EIA as a tool of, 32, 186–88, 191, 199, 202–3, 211, 225; of La Oroya smelter, 68; of NGOs, 58; practices, 11, 186; responsibility and, 186–87, 213; science and, 207; of Yanacocha mine, 98

acidic water, 87–88, 101, 143

activism: in Cajamarca, 1–2, 75, 104, 112–17, 185, 188, 215–16; Catholic Church's role in, 53–54; collaboration and, 6; EIAS and, 204, 212, 224–26; in La Oroya, 8, 36, 75; outcomes and limitations of, 233; Peru's history of, 2–3; at public hearings, 188–91, 207–11; science and, 206–7; significance of lagoons in, 218–20; solidarity, 217; surveillance of, 231; in Tambogrande, 8. *See also* protests/protestors; unions

Administración Técnica del Distrito de Riego (ATDR), 145–46, 167, 174, 240n8

Adventism, 125, 126

agriculture: in Cochapampa, 127; effects of toxic smoke on, 42–43, 45; irrigation water, 161, 177; mining work and, 82–83; open-pit mining and, 74;

pastureland, 128, 163; in Tual, 159; near Yanacocha mine, 80–81. *See also* dairy farming

air quality: in La Oroya, 20, 38–39, 42–43, 48–49; trace mineral levels, 28

Andean culture, 126; cosmology, 125, 134, 136

animal deaths, 154–55, 164

Antamina project, 16

anthropology, 24, 241n4

Apu (sacred mountain): Cerro Quilish as, 31, 109–10, 116, 121–23, 133–35, 219; prominence of, 120; term usage, 141–42

aquifers. *See under* Cerro Quilish

Arana, Father Marco, 99, 137, 231; anti-mining activism, 53, 97, 116, 217; critique of EIA process, 201–2; reflections on Cerro Quilish, 117, 120–23, 134–35; role in GRUFIDES, 114–15; rural priesthood, 119–20; Tierra y Libertad activities, 222–23; training and awards, 118–19

Arcuyo Canal, 171

Asociación de Promotoras de Salud, 39, 56–57

assistance programs, 127

Association for Environmental Education and Defense (ADEA), 101
Atahualpa, 71
audits, 11, 20, 225
Aural Gold Plant, 87

Barreto, Archbishop Pedro, 53
Barrick Gold, 18
Barry, Andrew, 230
baseline studies, 188, 191–93, 201, 207, 209
Basso, Keith, 84
Bebbington, Anthony and Denise, 232, 236n12
Beck, Ulrich, 197, 204
belief and politics, 229
Blacksmith Institute, 35, 56
Blaser, Mario, 110
Bonilla, Heraclio, 42
Bordewich, Fergus, 122
boundary object, 111
Brack, Antonio, 1, 7, 236n6

Cajamarca: communities, 90; map, 5; mining activity, 72, 74; political climate, 222; protests and activists, 1–2, 75, 104, 112–17, 185, 188, 215–16; proximity to Yanacocha mine, 77–79; public hearings, 188–90, 200, 207–9; water conflicts, 20, 75, 92–93, 97–98; water forums, 137–38; water sources, 115–16, 138
campesinos (peasant farmers): canal construction, 158–59; community leadership, 152–55; as *empresarios*, 180; Father Arana and, 119–20; identity, 152, 155; land sales, 80–82; livelihoods, 74, 90; manipulation of, 99; mobilization, 2, 113, 155–56, 157, 218–19, 222; pasturelands, 128; in Porcón, 116, 119, 128; relationship with Cerro Quilish, 121–22, 135; science and, 207; testimonies, 155; water concerns, 97, 98, 103, 104, 195–98. *See also* canal users (*usuarios*)

Canadian government, 101
canals: *limpieza* (cleaning), 160, 177; people's relationship with, 31, 156, 176–78, 180–81; security, 169; Tual construction, 157–61; water flows, 3, 90–91, 102–3, 136, 138; water quality and quantity, 90, 94, 96, 102–3, 143–44, 146, 163–68. *See also* Tupac Amaru Canal
canal users (*usuarios*): associations (*juntas de usuarios*), 113–14, 162, 164–65, 169, 240n8; compensation agreements, 27, 143–44, 160, 164–65, 167–68; eligibility for compensation, 149; negotiations with Minera Yanacocha, 168–71, 174–75, 179–80; participation in inspections, 144–46, 148, 179; protests, 157; registry (*padrón*), 149, 174–78, 180; water distribution among, 159–60, 176–78
Casaracra Day Care (*Cuna Jardín Casaracra*), 63, 65–67, 239n15
Catholic Church, 53, 118–19, 121, 130; Cerro Quilish and, 123, 135
Centers for Disease Control and Prevention (CDC), U.S., 63, 65–66
Central Highlands: depictions of, 70; extractive activity, 3–4, 14, 74; map, 5; mineral exploration, 40; subsistence agriculture, 82; water scarcity, 145, 227
Centromin: concern for workers, 47–48; enterprises, 18; social programs, 60
Cerro de Pasco: map, 5; mineral exploration, 40; polluted reputation, 70
Cerro de Pasco Corporation (CPC), 18, 48, 90; hacienda land purchase, 44–45; Industrial Hygiene Division, 46–47; La Oroya smelter construction, 4, 40–42; lawsuits, 43–44; social programs, 60, 73
Cerro Quilish (Mount Quilish): antimining campaigns, 31, 107, 108–9, 111–17, 124–25, 136–38, 142; *Apu*-aquifer identity, 107–10, 115–16, 121–23, 133–

35, 219; ecological view of, 117; offerings made to, 108, 120; *orqo* identity, 141; political actors and, 111; relations to other mountains, 130; stories and spirits, 129–34

chemical mining. *See* open-pit chemical mining

children, 35, 36, 62–68, 75, 239nn14–15

Choropampa, 90–91, 92

Choy, Timothy, 28

cleaning campaigns, 62–63, 65

Cobriza copper mine, 237n3

Cochapampa, 126–28, 129–30, 141

collaboration: CAO's efforts in, 104; corporate, 57; in EIA process, 32, 187, 203–4, 213; networks, 115; of *peritaje*, 225; social relations of, 25; Anna Tsing on, 6

colonialism, 13, 71–72, 77, 120

Combayo, 139–40

Comisión Multisectorial de Prevención de Conflictos, 9, 236n7

commodity exchange, 25

communal land, 44, 161, 163

community leadership, 152–55, 162, 176

comparison: equivalence and, 28–29; international indexes of, 66; mechanisms of, 25–26

compensation agreements: for canal users, 27, 143–44, 151–52; family tension over, 176–77; for land sales, 82; negotiations, 28, 103, 169–71, 174–76, 179–80; proliferation of, 171, 240n7; value and, 26; water distribution and, 176–78

Compliance Advisor Ombudsman (CAO): canal users' workshop, 102–3; criticisms, 99–100; purpose of, 92; studies and monitoring program, 92–97, 101, 104, 201

CONAM (National Environmental Council), 55

Concepción, 54

concessions, mining, 8; maps, 17, 79

conflictos mineros (mining conflicts): corporate practice and, 12, 186; as an ongoing practice, 142; politics of, 155–56; proliferation of, 9, 185, 232; publications on, 236n9; resolution and classification of, 9–11; over sacred mountains, 109, 110; term usage, 8, 10; over water quality and quantity, 75, 92–98. *See also* Conga mining project

conflict resolution: accountability and, 23, 31; equivalence and, 26, 149; public participation and, 211; technical solutions to, 227, 230

Conga mining project: arguments for and against, 218, 225, 227; EIA, 2, 217, 223–28; lagoons, 218–20, 227–29; politics, 222–23; protests and activists, 1–4, 32, 215–17, 231–32

consumption, 195–96

contaminación, term usage, 235n4

Convenio, 62–67, 68

CooperAcción, 48–49

corporate practices: accountability and, 23, 186–87, 198–99, 213; activism and, 38; establishing alliances, 210–11; health monitoring, 37; modern mining and, 7, 30; public participation and, 199; public relations campaigns, 68

corporate security, 74, 218, 231–32

Corporate Social Responsibility (CSR), 10, 23, 27, 186, 238n11, 240n7; of Doe Run, 59–62; of Minera Yanacocha, 77

countryside, the (*el campo*), 125, 222

Cruikshank, Julie, 84, 131

cyanide leaching process, 4, 198, 239n5; at Yanacocha mine, 81, 86–87

cyanide spills, 12, 87

dairy farming: in Cajamarca, 80–81, 83; in Tual, 159, 161, 163, 165–66, 177

Dammert, Bishop José, 119

"defense of life" movement, 3, 53, 75, 109

Goldman, Michael, 192
gold production, 18, 72, 81, 112, 239n1; cyanide usage in, 86–87. *See also* Yanacocha mine
governance, 11, 186, 199, 233, 241n4
Granja Porcón (Porcón Farm), 83, 93; trout deaths, 85
grassroots movements: groups, 49, 57–58, 70, 100, 102, 232; health promotion, 238n12; organization and mobilization, 7, 16, 49, 62, 222, 232, 233
groundwater, 88, 93, 194–96, 228
GRUFIDES, 29, 197, 222–23, 231; Cerro Quilish advocacy, 115; EA evaluations, 204–6; founding and operations, 101, 118; role in Conga conflict, 225, 227; role of women in, 241n6
Guadalupe, Parish of, 118, 222

hacendados (hacienda owners), 43, 45
hacienda system, 80, 128
Halperin, Rhoda, 24
health studies, 37, 53–54, 55–56
heap leach process, 86–87
Herculaneum smelter, 51
Hualgayoc mines, 72, 73, 77, 82
Huancayo Archdiocese, 53–54, 56
Humala, Ollanta, 216, 223, 226, 231
human and nonhuman actors, 45, 48, 68, 231; earth-beings, 74, 110, 121, 123; other-than-human beings, 23, 219. See also *Apu*; "things," concept of
hygiene programs, 61, 62–63, 65–68, 239n14

ichu (bunchgrass), 145, 227
impact, concept of, 193–94, 202–3
Incas, 124
indigeneity, 117
Ingold, Tim, 240n1
inspección ocular, term usage, 145
International Finance Corporation (IFC), 92, 98, 101, 241n7

inventory, 192–93, 198, 212
irrigation water: for agriculture, 161, 177; competition for, 162; contamination, 163–64; distribution of hours for, 159–60, 174, 176–77; standards, 148; technology, 138. *See also* canals; canal users (*usuarios*)

jalca, 80, 239n3
juntas de usuarios (canal users' associations), 113–14, 162, 164–65, 169, 240n8

Kinchy, Abby, 75
Kirsch, Stuart, 175, 240n7
knowledge: *campesino*, 150–51, 154, 159; divergent, 134; encounters, 131, 220; of environment, 240n1; expert, 23, 28, 76, 154, 207, 225–26, 229; participatory, 210; production of, 102; traditional or local, 134, 140, 220–21
knowledge practices: of Doe Run, 56, 57; economic reform and, 186; EIA, 187; equivalence and, 25, 237n19
Kunguna, Mount, 130, 132, 141

labor: division of, 162–63; law, 16, 73; lead levels in workers, 61; local *vs.* foreign, 239n4; recruitment, 41–42; short-term or contract, 19, 73, 82, 163, 169; working conditions, 46–48, 60
lagoons (*lagunas*): Cerro Quilish, 131–33; Conga, 2, 218–21, 224, 227–28; as isolated entities, 228–29
land resources, 127–29
landscapes: *campesinos* and, 151, 154, 178–79; knowledge encounters and, 131; people's relationship with, 23, 31, 111, 117, 123, 219–21; as sentient, 134, 140, 237n16; transformation of, 74, 83, 84, 110
La Oroya: air quality, 20, 38–39, 42–43, 48–49; commercial activity, 41; health advocacy, 51; lead levels, 53–55, 61,

transnational companies, 13, 14, 68, 69, 72

transparency: conflict resolution and, 23; integrity and, 11; knowledge practices and, 186; of MESA, 97; Minera Yanacocha efforts, 138–39, 169, 198, 202; of NGOs, 58; trust and, 202–3. *See also* accountability

transportistas, 112

trust: in government, 226; transparency and, 169, 202–3

Tsing, Anna, 6, 52

Tual: animal deaths, 154; canal construction, 157–61; dairy production, 159, 161, 163, 165–66; development projects, 170–71; location, 79, 152–53; protests, 157

Tupac Amaru Canal: canal association, 180; construction, 154; division of water turns, 176–77; inspection, 144–46, 150–52; source of origin, 146–47; user compensation, 143–44, 164–65, 167–68; water quality and quantity, 144, 146, 148, 166–68, 173

underground mining, 14, 90, 221

unions: mine workers, 47, 73; neoliberal reforms and, 16; organizing, 1, 3; teachers, 112, 222

universalism, 52

urban development, 44–45

usuarios. *See* canal users (*usuarios*)

Valdés, Oscar, 215, 217

value: commensuration and, 26–27, 122; concepts of, 24–25; of water, 177, 179

Vanity Fair, 51

Velasco Alvarado, Juan, 47, 72

water cycle, 197

water quality and quantity: in Cajamarca, 20, 75, 92–93, 97–98; in canals, 90, 94, 96, 102–3, 143–44, 146, 163–68; effects of mining on, 2, 85, 139; legal standards, 24, 27–28, 95–96, 98, 148–49,

166; studies and monitoring programs, 93–97, 104, 201–2; treatment process, 87–90, 144, 148, 167–68

water rights, 159–60, 176, 180, 240n8

water scarcity, 137, 145, 157, 197

water springs (*manantiales*): disappearance of, 3, 90, 198, 221, 227–28; spirits, 129–30, 132; Tupac Amaru, 146, 148

water table, 227, 228; lowering of, 85–86, 136, 195. *See also* groundwater

women: division of labor and, 162–63; lead levels, 62, 68; participation in social programs, 57, 61, 67; role in NGOs, 200, 241n6

workers. *See* labor

World Bank, 15, 18; EIAS, 16, 191; International Finance Corporation, 1

World Health Organization (WHO), 55; recommended blood lead levels, 36, 53, 61, 66; water quality standards, 95–96, 98

Wynne, Brian, 226

Yanacocha, Lake, 84

Yanacocha East and Yanacocha West Exploration Projects (PEYZE and PEYZO), 205–6

Yanacocha mine: *campesino* communities near, 78, 80; employment, 82, 239n4; gold extraction process, 85–87; joint venture partnership, 1, 18; location and expanse, 77–80, 83–84; mercury spill, 90–91; "modern" reputation, 70; protests, 30, 75, 185; Rejo River dike, 85; tours of, 76–77, 85, 87, 88, 90; water controversy, 75, 92–98, 143; water treatment, 87–90, 165, 167–68

Yanacocha Mining Company. *See* Minera Yanacocha

Yanacocha West Supplementary Project (PSYO), 186; EIA, 194, 200, 205, 211

Zelizer, Viviana, 25